English legal terminology

English legal terminology

Legal concepts in language

Helen Gubby M.A., Barrister

Boom Juridische uitgevers
Den Haag
2004

For Richard and my parents Harry and Mary Gubby

ISBN 90 5454 499 6
NUR 820
www.bju.nl

Acknowledgments

As this book is intended as a short, practical handbook on English legal terminology, I did not want to use footnotes. This does not mean, however, that I have not relied heavily on the works of others. I have used a range of books: from standard textbooks mainly on English law, legal dictionaries through to student revision books. They were all useful. The textbooks gave me a sound description of the law, the legal dictionaries helped me out in trying to develop some of the definitions, and the student revision books were an excellent way of isolating the most important terms associated with a particular area of law. The main sources are listed in the bibliography.

I would also like to thank several individuals for the help they offered me with this book. I am, once again, grateful to my old friend Alison Hampton for taking time out of her busy schedule as a judge, this time to check through the English law sections of chapters 1 and 2. My thanks are also due to Dr. Flora Goudappel, lecturer in European law at the Erasmus University Rotterdam who generously gave of her time to read through chapter 3. Sandra Dixon, who now works in the Netherlands as a legal editor and translator but once worked as an attorney in the USA, was kind enough to study the parts on American law in chapters 1 and 2 and to answer specific questions on American law in some of the other chapters. Finally, a word of thanks to another old friend, Vanessa James, who looked at chapter 6, not as a lawyer but through the eyes of an experienced company director.

I have taken great care with the contents of this book. Nonetheless, as an ordinary human being, I am not infallible: it is always possible that inaccuracies creep in. I would, therefore, be very grateful to the readers of this book if they would let me know, via the publisher, of any such inaccuracies. The e-mail address is: info@bju.nl.

Helen Gubby
Capelle aan den IJssel, the Netherlands

June, 2004

Contents

Introduction

It used to be Latin. Now it is English. English has taken over not only as the language of international academia but also of trade and commerce. It is, therefore, not surprising that the international language of the legal transaction is English too. Unfortunately, legal English and ordinary English are not identical languages. A non-native speaker could be very proficient in ordinary English and still be lost for words in a legal discussion. Even a native English speaker may find legal English quite inaccessible if he has no legal training. This is because legal English is a professional language and uses certain words and expressions that are totally outside the experience of a layperson. Some words are only found in legal English, for example the word 'rescission'. Sometimes the word is the same as an ordinary English word but with a quite different, specific legal meaning, for example the word 'consideration'.

For students who have studied law, but have not done so in English, this legal terminology is not familiar. However, ignorance of legal English can hold students back if they are studying law in English. Having to read, write and discuss legal matters entirely in English is often a daunting task for international students.

Legal English may also pose problems for legal practitioners who have not studied law in English, even though their command of ordinary English may be very good. Law firms, with an international clientele, correspond with their clients in English. A Dutch lawyer, for example, may find himself having to write a letter in English to an American client explaining the legal position according to Dutch law. It is also quite possible that neither party is a native English speaker: a letter giving legal advice in English could just as easily be between a German lawyer and a Polish client. In these cases, English law itself is not relevant. Nonetheless, English legal terminology has to be used to explain another country's law. Getting the legal terminology wrong could be a costly mistake.

When I began teaching legal English in the Netherlands, I found that I had to develop my own course material. There were many excellent English legal dictionaries available, ditto textbooks on English law. However, there were no books aimed at teaching English legal terminology itself. English law textbooks are, of course, geared up to teaching the intricacies of English law. Legal dictionaries are helpful, but they are organised according to the traditional framework for dictionaries, i.e. alphabetically. Essentially this means that words are presented to the reader in isolation. Yet English legal terminology can only be understood properly in context. The terminology arises from the common law and must always be viewed against this background. There is a need for law students who have not studied in

English to have a primer that would explain legal terminology while not getting them bogged down in the complexities of English law. This book is based on my experience of teaching legal English to undergraduates, post-graduates and legal professionals at the Erasmus University, Rotterdam and elsewhere. It is aimed in particular at law students and young practitioners, although it will also be of use to legal translators.

How to use this book

The legal subjects selected in the book are the type of core subjects most law students will study at some point in their education. Each chapter is devoted to one of these areas of law. Each chapter also follows the same general pattern.

Vocabulary

The first item in the chapter is a **vocabulary**. The vocabulary is ordered alphabetically but, unlike legal dictionaries, it contains a set of words associated with that particular subject-matter. In this way, the relevant terminology is grouped together. There are, of course, words that are not exclusive to one branch of law but will arise in various contexts, for example the word 'claimant'. In order to prevent the needless repetition of terms that may be found in the vocabulary of an earlier chapter, the reader will be directed to the vocabulary of the chapter in which the terms have already appeared. Sometimes, however, a term will appear in the vocabulary of more than one chapter, for example 'damages' which appears in the vocabulary of civil procedure, tort and contract. In the vocabulary of civil procedure a basic definition is given of damages, then in the tort vocabulary a definition in the context of tort damages and finally one in the context of contract law damages.

Text: terminology in context

The second item is the **terminology in context.** The words from the vocabulary are highlighted in this text so that the reader can see how the terminology fits into the structure of the law. It gives a brief outline of the relevant English law. The word English is used rather than British, as the legal system in Scotland is not identical to the English system. 'English' is also used here as a shortened description of the law applicable to England and Wales.

    The legal terminology derived from English law forms the basis for all other common law jurisdictions. However, the law in other common law jurisdictions has not developed in exactly the same way as in England. This means that while there is still much shared terminology, there may also be terminology that will be found in some but not all of the common law jurisdictions. For example, American criminal law terminology includes the terms 'first degree murder' and 'second degree murder'. This is a distinction unknown in English law, as this approach to grading offences in degrees is not used in England. As mentioned above, the outline given in the text is based on English law. It is beyond the scope of this book to give all possible variations in other common law jurisdictions. Nonetheless, given the prevalence of American legal textbooks in many university libraries throughout the world, reference will be made to American terminology where differences in terminology could cause confusion. For example, the term 'company' has a very specific meaning in English company law. It is an incorporated body and a separate legal person. In American terminology, the word company is used loosely to refer to various sorts of business organisations. When American law is talking about an incorporated body, which is a separate legal person, it uses the word 'corporation'. It is therefore of use to the student to be aware of this difference in word use between English and American lawyers.

The text particularly tries to take into account that many of the readers of this book will be students from civil law systems. Just as common law jurisdictions are not identical in their practice of the law, neither is it possible to speak of one civil law system. What binds all common law and all civil law systems is a shared heritage. Where English common law has a different approach to a legal issue from the more traditional civil law approach, a note will be given in the text. The standard example of a civil law system used in this book is that of the Netherlands.

The section on terminology in context is not meant to teach the reader English law. There are many standard textbooks for that purpose. The aim of the text is simply to give the reader sufficient background knowledge in order to understand how the terms should be used. For this reason, few references are made to cases or statutes. However, a case will be named if it has become so associated with a legal concept that it has become a part of the terminology. For example, in the English law of tort the rule governing a defendant's liability for the escape of a dangerous thing from his property is simply known by the case in which that rule was laid down: the rule in Rylands v Fletcher. Similarly, references to section numbers in statutes are generally avoided as such references are relevant to English law, but not to English legal terminology.

Case discussions

Following on from the text is the item **case discussions** (with the exception of the chapter on the legal system, which has general discussion questions). These cases are either actual cases or cases concocted to include certain legal issues. The case discussions serve as a practical exercise. For the self-study reader, the aim is that he should be able to see what the case is about and then answer the questions using the correct legal terminology. The terminology needed to do this is contained in the vocabulary and explained in the text. If the book is used as a course-work book, these cases form the basis for group discussion. Students, working together in small groups, are asked to analyse the case as a team and then present their findings in class. In this way, students become familiar with using the legal terminology.

Knowledge questions

The final item comprises the **knowledge-based questions**. This too is a practical exercise. It acts as a test for the reader, allowing the reader to check whether he has understood the terminology. If the book is used as a course-work book, these questions can be used as a basis for homework assignments.

Finally, it must be pointed out that the use of the word 'he' in the texts is not meant to be discriminatory to women. It is simply the use of a long-established, stylistic device and its purpose here is to make the text more easily readable than where he/she, h/she or other well meant alternatives appear in a text.

Chapter 1   Legal system terminology

Legal system vocabulary

Act: a specific piece of legislation passed by a legislative body, such as Parliament or Congress. An **Act of Parliament** is divided into **parts**, **sections**, **sub-sections**, **paragraphs** and at the end are the **schedules**.

ADR: these initials stand for alternative dispute resolution. This includes **mediation**, **conciliation** and **arbitration**.

Arbitration: a form of alternative dispute resolution where a third party, acting as an arbitrator, delivers an opinion that is binding on the parties.

Attorney-at-law: usually referred to simply as an attorney. An attorney is a legal professional in the United States with the right to practice law in the state for which he has been admitted to the bar.

Attorney-General: in England he is a legal adviser to the Crown. The Attorney-General has political duties which include advising government departments. In the USA there is also an Attorney-General. He is the head of legal affairs in a state or in the federal government.

Barrister: a legal professional in the English legal system with a right of audience before all courts. As well as acting as an advocate, a barrister may also be a specialist in a certain area of law.

Beneficiary: one who benefits from a **trust** and who has an **equitable interest** in the trust property.

Bill: an Act of Parliament is called a bill before it has been formally approved.

Binding: if a decision is binding, it must be followed. For example, precedents set by a higher court must be followed by lower courts.

Brief: in the English system this refers to the written instructions sent by a solicitor to a barrister briefing him about a case.

Canon law: also referred to as **ecclesiastical law**. This is the law of the church.

Case law: refers to the decisions made by judges applying legal principles from **legislation** and **binding precedent** (see **doctrine of binding precedent**) to the circumstances of the particular disputes before them.

Certiorari: this order usually transfers a case from an appeal court, and in certain special cases from a trial court, to the US Supreme Court for judicial review.

Challenge: potential members of a jury can be challenged, either for a reason that is stated before the court or for no reason. This is a way of excluding potential jurors from a jury.

Chambers: accommodation for a group of barristers. Barristers in chambers are self-employed and group together only to share facilities and staff. It would therefore be wrong to refer to a firm of barristers.

Civil law: this term has two meanings. It can be used in the sense of the law concerned with private rights rather than public law. The term may also be used to describe a legal system. Unlike the common law system, a civil law system has its roots in Roman law and is a codified system.

Clerk: the English legal system knows various types of legal clerks, for example, lay magistrates are assisted by a magistrate's clerk. The clerk in barristers' chambers, often now referred to as the **practice manager**, acts as a business manager for the barristers of that chamber.

Coded systems: systems where the codification of the law has taken place, i.e. the laws of the land have been compiled to form a systematic, formal legal code.

Common law: a system of law which originated in medieval England and was later applied in former British colonies, including the United States. Common law is based on judicial precedent arising from cases rather than law based on codes or other forms of legislative enactments.

Competence: a court has the competence to hear a case if it has **jurisdiction** over the person or property at issue in that case.

Conciliation: alternative form of dispute resolution where a third party, acting as a conciliator, offers the parties a non-binding opinion.

Concur: verb used to indicate that judges in a case agree with the majority conclusion. The reasons for reaching that conclusion may, however, vary.

Congress: the federal legislative body of the United States. It consists of two houses, the Senate and the House of Representatives.

Conveyancing: drawing up legal documents to transfer the ownership of property from seller to buyer; in general the law and procedure with respect to the purchase and sale of property.

Coroner's Court: holds an inquest where death appears to be violent, unnatural or sudden and the cause is unknown.

Counsel: when representing a party in court, a barrister is referred to as counsel and an attorney as counsel or counsellor.

County Court: in the English system it hears civil cases in its local area of jurisdiction. The name county court may also be found in the court systems of several states in the United States, where it has a limited jurisdiction in civil and criminal cases.

Court of Appeal: this is an appellate court to be found in many common law jurisdictions hearing appeals from lower courts.

Court of first instance: this term can be used to describe a court in which proceedings are initiated.

Crown Court: this is a court in the English court system that hears primarily criminal cases.

Custom: this is unwritten law that is legally valid if a practice can be shown to have been continuously in operation since time immemorial.

Discretionary: where a remedy is not available as of right but depends upon the consideration of the court.

Dissent: where a judge disagrees with the majority opinion in a case. A **dissenting judgment** is classed as **obiter dicta**.

Distinguish: if a case is distinguished, a judge finds a precedent laid down in a previous case not binding on the case before him because the **material/key facts** in the present case differ from those of the previous case.

District courts: these are the trial courts of the American federal court system.

Doctrine of binding precedent: the precedent laid down in a prior case of a similar nature must be followed. The Latin term for the doctrine of binding precedent is **stare decisis**.

Doctrine of parliamentary sovereignty: all legislative power in England is vested in Parliament or is derived from the authority of Parliament, Parliament being the House of Commons, the House of Lords and the Crown. Parliament has the right to make any laws it wishes to make, although these laws must now be in keeping with European Union law.

Draft: when a legal document, such as a contract, is being drawn up, the preliminary version (or versions) of the document is referred to as a draft. The draft may be subject to amendments before it is accepted as the final version.

Employment Tribunal: tribunal in the English system with the jurisdiction to hear almost all individual disputes based on statutory employment law claims and common law contract claims up to a set maximum.

Equitable title: under the principles of law developed by the court of equity, one piece of property could be subject to two sorts of interest: a legal interest and an **equitable interest**. The legal owner of the property holds the **legal title**, which was protected by the common law. The one with the equitable interests holds an equitable title, which was protected by the chancellor in the court of equity. The person holding the equitable title is the one intended to benefit from the property, even though that person is not the legal owner. An equitable title is still protected in law against all but the bona fide purchaser without notice.

Equity: historically, equity developed as a separate system of law in England as the common law was too rigid. The court of equity developed its own principles of fairness and its own legal remedies. Now all courts may apply **principles of equity** alongside those of the common law.

European Court of Justice: is the highest court for all those countries that are members of the European Union. It has the competence to make decisions regarding European Union law (see chapter 3).

Federal courts: the courts of the United States as distinguished from the courts of the individual states. Federal courts hear cases that involve disputes or issues governed by federal law or the US Constitution or disputes involving citizens from differing states.

Forum shopping: where more than one court has the competence to hear a case and parties wish to select the forum which would be most favourable for their case.

High Court: a superior court in the English court system.

House of Lords: the House of Lords as a court should be distinguished from its function as the upper house of Parliament. Only those members of the upper house who are Law Lords may hear appeals. The court hears appeals for both civil and criminal cases where the matter is of public importance. As of 2004 it is still the highest appeal court at a national level. However, the British government wishes to reform the court system and one possible reform is that the House of Lords as an appeal court will be replaced by a so-called 'Supreme Court' similar to that of the USA.

Inferior: an adjective used to describe a lower court. It does not mean that the quality of the court is poor. It simply means a court of lower jurisdiction.

Judicial review: an examination by judges of a higher court. This examination may either be of a decision made in an inferior court or of decisions made by public authorities that affect the rights of individuals. In the US Supreme Court, judges may reject any legislation, whether state or federal, that is not in keeping with the US Constitution. Judges in the English system were never allowed to reject parliamentary legislation, as only Parliament could revoke one of its own acts. However, since becoming a member of the European Union, English judges are allowed to review whether parliamentary legislation is in keeping with European Union law.

Jurisdiction: the legal power to hear and decide a case. If the court does not have the jurisdiction to hear a case, its decision will be void.

Jurisprudence: the study or philosophy of law. In the USA it is also used in the sense of case law rather than statute law.

Juror: a member of a jury.

Jury: a cross-section of the public called upon to hear a case. In England and in the US federal system a trial jury consists of twelve persons (**petit jury**), and in some states in the USA of six persons. Some states in the USA also have a **grand jury** of up to twenty-three persons to see whether the accusations should result in an indictment (the indictment sets out the charges against the accused) being filed.

Jury vetting: procedure by which members of the public are selected in court for jury service in England. In the USA, the counsels for the defence/prosecution have far more opportunities to challenge potential members of the jury than in England. This procedure is commonly termed **voir dire** in the USA.

Legal certainty: to protect the expectations of individuals by ensuring that laws are applied consistently and predictably.

Legal remedy: means provided by the law to redress the harm suffered by one party because another party has acted contrary to the rules of law.

Legislation: written laws passed by a legislative body, for example, the Parliament in England and the Congress in the United States.

Litigation: where a party, known as a litigant, brings an action (a lawsuit).

Magistrate: term given to an inferior judicial officer both in England and the United States. In the English court system, magistrates are often lay people.

Magistrates' Court: in the English court system this is an inferior court that hears both civil and criminal cases. However, it should be borne in mind that the Magistrates' Courts handle most of the cases brought to court.

Material: used generally to denote something of importance in a case, for example, material fact or a material witness. The word **key** may also be used in this context.

Mediation: alternative form of dispute resolution where a third party, acting as a mediator, helps the parties to a dispute to reach an agreement.

Obiter dicta: plural of obiter dictum, meaning passing or incidental statements in a judicial opinion that do not form part of the **ratio decidendi** or binding element in a case.

Overrule: a court reaches the decision that a precedent laid down in a different case no longer has precedential value.

Persuasive: if the authority is persuasive rather than binding, the judge is not obliged to follow it, but it should be of importance in reaching a judgment.

Pre-emption: where one system of law takes precedence over another. In the United States, federal legislation is superior to state legislation and will pre-empt state legislation where there is a conflict. In Europe, the law of the European Union is said to override that of the national law of the Member States on matters within its competence.

Probate: legal acceptance that a document usually associated with the administration of estates, such as a will, is valid.

Ratio decidendi: the reason for the decision. This is the part of the judgment in which legal principles are applied to the facts of the particular case before the court. It is this part of the judgment which forms the precedent. In the USA this may also be referred to as a **holding**.

Reverse: when a higher court hearing a case on appeal from a lower court reaches the opposite judgment to that of the lower court.

Revoke: to cancel or annul, for example to annul previous legislation.

Right of audience: the right to appear and conduct proceedings in a court.

Settlor: also referred to as a trustor or donor. This is the person who settles his property on someone, in particular to set up a trust.

Solicitor: is a legal professional within the English system. A solicitor has four main areas of competence: conveyancing, probate, drafting company and commercial contracts and the preparation of litigation. Unless he has an advocacy certificate, his right to be heard in court is in general limited to the lower courts.

State courts: this is the term given to the courts in the individual states of the United States as opposed to the courts in the federal system.

Statute: a form of written law, such as an Act of Parliament, passed by a legislative body.

Statutory instrument: subordinate legislation, usually made by a minister, under the authority granted by an Act of Parliament.

Superior: this adjective is applied to courts to indicate courts of higher jurisdiction. Precedents set in the superior courts must be followed by the lower courts.

Trust: property, either real or personal, that is held by one party for the benefit of another party. Property held in trust comprises two interests: a legal interest and an equitable interest. The legal interest is held by the **trustee** and the equitable interest is held by the **beneficiary**.

Trustee: person who holds the legal title to property which is administered for the benefit of someone else.

US Bankruptcy Court: only the federal courts may hear bankruptcy cases.

US Claims Court: a federal court hearing claims against the United States.

US Court of International Trade: specialised in cases involving international trade.

US Supreme Court: this is the top court in the federal court system of the United States.

US Tax Court: a federal court hearing tax cases.

Voir dire: see jury vetting.

Legal system terminology in context

1   INTRODUCTION

For both the law student and the young practitioner who have not studied law in English, the time may nonetheless come when it is necessary to deal with English legal terminology relating to the operation of a legal system. This necessity may arise in various guises. The law student may find, for instance, that he has to study English or American cases as part of his course work. Reading these law reports requires not just an understanding of the legal issue dealt with in the case, but also of the operation of case law in common law jurisdictions. For example, the student needs to be able to distinguish what part of the case report sets out the **binding precedent** and what parts are **obiter dicta**. It may also seem strange to some students that the opinion of a judge who does not agree with the majority decision is still reported. With respect to the young practitioner, he will often find himself in the position of having to explain the operation of his own legal system in English to a foreign client. Translating the workings of a civil law system into English (common law) terminology can be extremely difficult, as all those who have ever attempted it will know. The reason for the complexity is simple; translating from one system to another system is far from straightforward. When, for example, a Dutch lawyer has to explain his legal system to a common law lawyer, it is not simply a matter of replacing Dutch words with English words. The Dutch system is not a carbon copy of the English system, which means that there will not always be equivalent English terminology at hand for translation purposes. In order to use English legal terminology correctly and effectively, the practitioner must not only be familiar with his own legal system but also have a basic grasp of the structure of the common law system.

The English legal system is a **common law** system. The common law developed, in essence, as a system of case law; authoritative decisions were laid down by judges in court. Over the course of time, the **doctrine of binding precedent** developed which meant that decisions made by judges in the past should be upheld by judges in new cases if these new cases showed marked similarities to those that had gone before. When the English set about establishing colonies, this common law system was often implemented in the colonial regime. Although there is no longer a British empire, the common law system has remained in force in various former colonies, for example, the United States, Canada and Australia.

The common law system should be distinguished from the **civil law** system. Civil law systems are **coded systems**, the laws being laid down in written form. Civil law has been heavily influenced by Roman law. Although it would be incorrect to assert that Roman law has had no effect on the common law, its impact has been considerably less and more indirect. The code drafted under Napoleon in 1804, the 'Code Napoleon', must also be acknowledged as a source and example for many civil law systems in Europe and beyond. The common law and the civil law are often treated as two entirely different approaches to the practice of law. However, these two systems are not as worlds apart as some lawyers maintain. Codes will always have to be interpreted and that will necessarily generate case law. And anyone who thinks a common law system derives its law only from the courts would be very wide of the mark. As can be seen below, **legislation** plays a vital role in all common law systems today.

As explained in the introduction, the basis for all terminology will be English law, as all other common law jurisdictions have grown from English roots. However, these common law jurisdictions have developed in their own way over the years and, although there is still a substantial body of shared terminology, variations in development have led to certain terminology being relevant to some but not necessarily all common law jurisdictions. To give the reader an indication of how terminology may vary, the United States has been selected for comparison.

In this chapter, attention will be paid to the terminology of three elements associated with the legal system. These three elements are:

• the administration of justice via the court structure;
• the legal profession;
• the operation of a common law system.

2 THE COURT STRUCTURE

Trying to find a good English translation for the name of a court in a different law system can sometimes be quite difficult. For this reason, the following sections describe the courts and their **competence** in the English and American court systems. It is common to find the names of the US federal court system used for translation purposes. In general, the highest court in a land is usually translated by the term **Supreme Court**, the appellate court level by **Court of Appeal** and the trial initialisation level by **District Court**. However, court systems vary from land to land and sometimes there is simply no equivalent in the Anglo/American system for a particular court in another system.

2.1 England

The English court structure is not a particularly coherent system as it has been modified from time to time to fit the needs of the day. Although there are courts specialised in criminal cases or civil cases, most courts actually hear both. One generalisation that can be made is the division of English courts into **superior** and **inferior** courts. The **jurisdiction** of the superior courts is not limited to a specific geographical area or to the value of the claim being brought. The jurisdiction of the inferior courts is limited in this way. The superior courts are the House of Lords, the Court of Appeal, the High Court, the Crown Court (and the Restrictive Practices Court and the Employment Appeal Tribunal, which have specialised jurisdictions). The most important of the inferior courts are the County Courts and Magistrates' Courts. The distinction between superior and inferior is important with respect to the **doctrine of binding precedent** (see below).

- **House of Lords**: decisions made by the House of Lords are binding on all the courts below it in the court hierarchy, although the House of Lords itself is not bound by its own previous decisions.
- **Court of Appeal**: is bound by the decisions of the House of Lords and both civil and criminal divisions of the Court of Appeal are bound by their own previous decisions unless certain exceptions apply.
- **High Court**: is bound by the House of Lords and the Court of Appeal but not by itself.
- **Crown Court**: the position of the Crown Court in the hierarchy, in relation to the doctrine of precedent, has not been authoritatively determined. It may depend upon whether a High Court judge is presiding or a lower judge, such as a circuit judge or recorder (a recorder is a part-time judge).
- **County Court**: the jurisdiction of these courts has increased considerably in recent years and their decisions are sometimes reported.
- **Magistrates' Court**: these decisions are not binding on any court.

Note 1: a number of other courts and tribunals exist in addition to this mainstream structure. For example, the **Coroner's Court** and the **Employment Tribunal**.

Note 2: the United Kingdom is a member of the European Union. Although not a national court, the court at the apex of the English court structure for all matters concerning the law of the European Union is the **European Court of Justice**. Its role is to ensure the legal enforcement of European Union obligations and the uniform interpretation of European law throughout the Member States of the European Union.

Note 3: in June 2003 plans were announced by the British government to reform the legal system. One such possible reform would be the abolition of the House of Lords as the final (national) appeal court, to be replaced by a court on similar lines to the US Supreme Court.

Note 4: there is no parallel separate system of administrative courts, such matters being mainly dealt with by High Court judges.

2.2 USA

The distinction between federal and state competence means there are both federal courts and state courts. The **federal courts** may be seen as the creation of the US Constitution. The jurisdiction of the federal courts is set out in the US Constitution and the federal courts have only the powers expressly conferred on them by that Constitution. **State courts**, unlike the federal courts, have a far more general competence. They have the competence to hear most legal controversies, either state or federal, within the geographical area of their jurisdiction, unless federal legislation explicitly states otherwise.

There may be concurrent jurisdiction between federal and state courts. For example, if in a car theft, the car has been driven from one state to another, the case could be tried either in a federal court or in the state court of one of the states involved. Federal courts are typically used where the parties to a dispute are citizens of different states or are US citizens and aliens. The overlapping of competence has given rise to so-called **forum shopping**, where parties select the court they believe to be most favourable to their claim.

2.2.1 Federal court structure

- **US Supreme Court**: the court is composed of a Chief Justice and eight Associate Justices. There is no absolute right to be heard by the US Supreme Court; it hears only a limited number of cases that it is asked to decide. Those cases may begin either in federal or state courts and usually involve important questions concerning constitutional or federal law. An application to be heard has to be made by **certiorari**. The judges of the US Supreme Court have extensive powers of judicial review; they have the power to throw out any legislation, whether state or federal, not in keeping with the US Constitution.
- **US Courts of Appeal**: the ninety-four US judicial districts are organised into twelve regional circuits, each of which has a US Court of Appeal. It hears appeals from the district courts located within its circuit, except in the few cases where there is a direct appeal to the Supreme Court. It also reviews decisions made by federal administrative agencies. The Courts of Appeal also have a nationwide jurisdiction to hear appeals from specialised courts, such as patent laws and cases decided by the Court of International Trade and the US Court of Claims.
- **District Courts**: the district courts are the trial courts of the federal court system for all matters of federal law. There is at least one district court in each state. Within the limits set by the Congress and the US Constitution, they have the jurisdiction to hear nearly all categories of federal cases both criminal and civil. Cases may be heard either by a single judge or a judge and jury.
- **US Bankruptcy Courts**: the federal court system has the exclusive jurisdiction over bankruptcy cases. This means that bankruptcy cases cannot be filed in a state court.

- **US Tax Court**: is a tax cases court.
- **US Claims Court**: this court hears claims against the United States. It has a nation-wide jurisdiction.
- **Court of International Trade**: specialises in cases that involve international trade. It has a nation-wide jurisdiction.

2.2.2 State courts structure

Each state has its own court system. This means that each court system is unique as there are significant differences in the ways in which each state organises its judicial institutions. Some state court systems have many different courts whereas others may only have three courts: a supreme court, a court of appeal and a district court. Names of courts also vary widely. There are fifty state court systems plus the District of Columbia and Puerto Rico. State courts deal with the vast majority of all court cases in the United States.

2.3 Translation note

Sometimes it is not possible to use English or American court names as a translation. For example, the common law system has traditionally not used separate courts to deal with public law matters. This means that where a specific public law court must be given an English name, the best translation may be a simple description of the function of the court, such as the 'Constitutional Court of Spain'. In other cases, the best approach may be to use general terms to describe the position of the court in the court hierarchy. In this way, someone unfamiliar with that court system will be able to gather what kind of status of court is being referred to.

Important courts can be referred to by the terms: high/superior/senior/ courts of higher jurisdiction.

Courts of lesser status can be referred to by the terms: low/inferior/ courts of lower jurisdiction. The term **court of first instance** can be used to describe a court in which proceedings are initiated.

It is recommended that the English translation of the name of the court should always be accompanied by the actual name of the court in the original language (put in brackets after the English translation).

2.4 Alternatives to the courts

Outside the mainstream court systems in both countries there are agencies, tribunals hearing specialised cases, and alternative dispute resolution (**ADR**). The idea behind ADR was that it would be less formal, quicker than the mainstream courts and less expensive. There are three types of ADR: **mediation**, **conciliation** and **arbitration**.

3   THE LEGAL PROFESSION

Many civil law lawyers, when trying to draft an English translation for their business cards, have been forced to conclude that translating their legal qualifications and position in their legal profession into English is not as straightforward as might be expected. For example, in the Netherlands there are two main strands in the legal profession: notaries (notarissen) and advocates (advocaten). As the English legal profession is also split into two main strands, solicitors and barristers, it would seem the translation is ready-made. Unfortunately, that is not the case as the competence of solicitors and barristers is divided in a different way from that of the Dutch notaries and advocates.

A Dutch notary does indeed do the type of work that would be typical of some of the work of an English solicitor, but a Dutch notary would not prepare work for litigation whereas an English solicitor would and an English solicitor may also act as an advocate in the lower courts. On the other hand, a Dutch advocate may have the type of practice which resembles that of an English solicitor far more than it does that of an English barrister. In an international context, Dutch law firms tend to use anglicised versions of their professional functions: notaries and advocates. However, it should be pointed out that the term 'notary' does not denote a separate strand of the legal profession in the USA or England. A 'notary public' has authority to witness and draw up certain documents, and so make them official. In England this is usually done by a solicitor. In the USA, this can be done by an attorney but it can also be done by a private individual who has applied to act as a notary, for example, a real estate agent or clerks in a shop. Those Dutch law firms that are aware of this tend to use the expression 'civil law notaries'. This has the advantage of making their common law colleagues take note that some sort of unfamiliar function is involved here, but the term is not one that will be self-evident to them. Just to add to the complexity of translation, there are even differences in the way the legal profession is organised between England and the USA.

With respect to translating university degree titles, this too may pose unexpected problems. The duration of a university law degree course may vary between countries, as often will the letters used to indicate a degree title. For example, Dutch law graduates have the right to put the letters 'mr' in front of their name (this is easily misunderstood by English and American lawyers who suppose the 'mr' is the English abbreviation for 'mister', as in Mr. Smith. This is particularly confusing if the 'mr' in question turns out to be a woman!). Finding an abbreviation that will be recognisable to the English and Americans will at least soon be simple for those graduating from the universities of the Member States of the European Union. With the introduction of a bachelor/master system of accreditation in the European Union, law degrees will in the future generally be indicated by the letters LL.B for a bachelor's degree and LL.M for a master's degree.

Translating the role and qualifications of legal professionals of a different system into English is not the only problem area. As mentioned above, the functions of legal professionals may be different from that of legal professionals in another land.

Ignorance of this may cause irritation. The Dutch lawyer unfamiliar with the organisation of the English legal profession may have no idea why for certain cases he needs two sets of lawyers, a solicitor and a barrister. In order to assist both in translating and in understanding the competence of the legal professional, the following sections give an overview of the English legal profession and that of the USA.

3.1   England

In the English legal system, a practicing lawyer must have one of two professional qualifications: he must either have been admitted to practice as a solicitor or have been called to the bar as a barrister. An English lawyer may not act both as a solicitor and as a barrister. This traditional split in functions was, however, affected by the Courts and Legal Services Act 1990. Solicitors lost their monopoly on conveyancing, probate and the conduct of litigation. Barristers lost their monopoly over the **right of audience** in the higher courts. A solicitor, if granted an advocacy certificate, would have the same rights of audience as a barrister. And a barrister could perform tasks normally the preserve of solicitors. However, there seems to be at present little momentum from English lawyers to give up the division of the legal duties and fuse to become a unitary profession. As yet there has been no rush by solicitors for an advocacy certificate to take over barristers' tasks, or solicitors going out of business due to the loss of old monopolies.

3.1.1 Solicitor

A **solicitor** holds a university degree and has completed a period of professional training. He then enters a firm of solicitors as a trainee. After passing his examinations and finishing his traineeship, he can apply to the Law Society to be admitted. He is then formally a solicitor of the Supreme Court. Solicitors' offices are usually partnerships, and senior solicitors act as partners in the firm. The solicitor's professional body is the Law Society. Misconduct on the part of the solicitor may lead to the Law Society striking his name off the list.

A solicitor may be described as a general legal adviser. His usual areas of work are **conveyancing** (law and procedure with respect to the purchase and sale of property), **probate** (procedure to verify a document, often a will, and the winding up and distribution of a deceased person's estate), the negotiation and **drafting** of company and commercial contracts and the preparation of **litigation** (court cases), although in the larger firms of solicitors some solicitors have specialised. As mentioned above, they may work as advocates but, without an advocacy certificate, they have only a limited right of audience in the courts.

3.1.2 Barrister

A **barrister** holds a university degree and will go on to complete a period of vocational training. A barrister must belong to one of the four Inns of Court. Having passed his bar examination and eaten a set number of dinners in his Inn of Court, he will be called to the bar by his Inn and must then follow a period of practical training (called pupillage) of one year under an experienced barrister. The professional governing body of the bar is the Bar Council.

Barristers are self-employed but group together for administrative convenience in **chambers** where they share the accommodation, secretariat and the services of the clerk. It is incorrect therefore to refer to a firm of barristers, even though the chambers are often referred to by the name or names of the senior barristers in those chambers. Possibly the most important person in chambers is the **clerk**. He acts as a business manager and is now often referred to as the **practice manager**: he attracts the work, arranges the **briefs** (written instructions from a solicitor to a barrister giving him a case) for individual barristers and negotiates the fee with the solicitors, as a barrister's fee is not paid directly by his client but through the solicitor.

The work of many barristers is that of an advocate, arguing a client's case in court. Barristers have a right of audience in all courts. All practicing barristers are called junior counsel. However, a barrister who has been in practice for ten years can apply to become a Queen's Counsel (QC), which is called taking silk. A QC only appears in the most important cases. He is also known as a leader or leading counsel because he is often accompanied in a court case by one or two junior counsels. When representing a party in court, the barrister is referred to as **counsel** (for the client or in criminal cases for the defence or prosecution). Barristers are often specialists in certain legal domains. Some specialist barristers, for example chancery barristers, will spend most of their time producing written opinions on cases rather than speaking in court.

To summarise, the difference between solicitors and barristers is often compared to that between the family doctor and the hospital specialist. For most legal matters, members of the public will visit a solicitor. The solicitor will call in the aid of a barrister if he needs expert advice and/or the client's case will become a court case and the expertise of a barrister is required.

3.2 USA

The USA broke with the tradition of distinguishing between solicitors and barristers. A practicing lawyer in the USA is an **attorney**. In the USA, an attorney performs either the functions of a solicitor or a barrister or both functions. The terms 'lawyer' and 'attorney' may thus be used interchangeably.

In order to become an attorney, it is first necessary to gain a bachelor's degree, which takes four years, and then go to Law School for a period of three years. The degree from the law school is called Juris Doctor and the graduate may add the letters 'JD' after his name. However, graduation from an approved law school does not give the right to practice law. To do so, he must become an **attorney-at-law**, which means passing the bar examination and being admitted to the bar of one of the states. Only then will a license to practice law be issued. A period of apprenticeship is not necessary. Lawyers who work for companies in their legal departments or for a government agency must also be members of the bar: they are referred to as in-house counsel or staff attorneys.

An attorney may only practice law in the state for which he has been admitted to the bar. This means that a lawyer only has the right to be heard in the state courts of the jurisdiction for which he has been admitted. Separate admission to practice in the federal courts must be obtained.

Note: in the USA, the word 'esquire' (esq) used after the name denotes that that person has been admitted to practice law. However, the word esquire does not have that meaning in England, where it is sometimes used as an alternative to putting Mr. before the name of a man.

3.3 Judges in the common law system

The role of the judge in the common law system is somewhat different from that in many civil law systems. The judge is neither adviser nor investigator. In general, the judge must rely upon the advocates to present legal and factual argument, although if a vital precedent has been ignored, he can ask for counsel's arguments on it. The judge acts as an impartial referee in an adversarial judicial process. He must find upon the evidence presented to the court, apply the existing rules of law to those facts and then reach a decision.

One of the functions of judges is to carry out **judicial review**. The term judicial review covers two situations: that where a higher court examines a case first dealt with by an inferior court or tribunal or where the decisions made by a public body affect the rights of individuals. In England, public law challenges or administration of justice disputes are usually heard by High Court judges. English courts may now also query Acts of Parliament if these do not conform to European Union legislation. In the USA, federal judges may review whether state or federal action is in keeping with the United States Constitution.

In England, senior judges are still mainly appointed from the ranks of practicing barristers with at least ten to fifteen years experience before the courts, although opportunities for solicitors to become judges have increased more recently. In the USA judges are also mainly chosen from outstanding members of the bar. Federal judges are appointed by the President and the Senate for life. As for state judges, the method of appointment depends on the state. Judges may be chosen from outstanding members of the bar by the governor, or by the mayor for lower courts, or elected by the public, or a combination of both methods. This system of appointment stands in stark contrast to some civil law jurisdictions, for example the Netherlands, where law graduates can train specifically to become a judge and where a judge is a civil servant.

In England, for many centuries the most senior judge was the Lord Chancellor. He was not only the most senior judge but also a member of government with a seat in the cabinet. He headed the Lord Chancellor's Department; there is no Ministry of Justice in England. However, one of the legal reforms proposed by the Labour government in June 2003 was the abolition of the position of Lord Chancellor. His tasks would become the responsibility of the Department for Constitutional Affairs. In 2004, it is still unclear whether the office of Lord Chancellor will disappear, but the Lord Chancellor's department has been renamed the Department for Constitutional Affairs.

At present, the Lords of Appeal in Ordinary sit in the House of Lords and the Lord Justices of Appeal in the Court of Appeal. In the High Court are the High Court or puisne judges, who may also sit in the Crown Court, and in the lower courts circuit judges and district judges. At the bottom of the judicial hierarchy in England are the **magistrates**. Many of these justices, who sit in the Magistrates' Courts, are lay people. They are responsible and respected people in their community, sitting on average one day per fortnight. Magistrates are not paid, but only receive expenses. They are advised by magistrates' clerks, who are usually law graduates, or have a special clerk's diploma. In addition to these lay magistrates there are also many salaried, legally qualified magistrates who do not need to sit with a clerk. These judges were formerly known as stipendiary magistrates. Legally qualified judges in the Magistrates' Courts are often district judges.

In the USA, as mentioned above, the state courts have many different names and the types of judges are also various, for example, there may be municipal justices and police magistrates. There is, however, no system of lay justices parallel to the system of lay magistrates in England. At the federal level, the US Supreme Court has at its head a Chief Justice assisted by Associate Justices. At the trial level there are district judges assisted by magistrate judges.

Finally, in this overview mention should be made of the Law Officers. In the English system, one of the most important is the **Attorney-General** (and his deputy, the Solicitor-General). He is a legal adviser to the Crown. The Attorney-General has political duties which include advising government departments. His permission is also necessary to bring certain criminal proceedings and he appears on behalf of a section of the public where public nuisance is involved. Similarly, in the USA there is also an Attorney-General. He is the head of legal affairs in a state or in the federal government. If he is in the federal government, he is in charge of the Department of Justice. The USA also has a district attorney. This is an officer of a governmental body, such as a state, county or municipality with the duty to prosecute all those charged with crimes. District attorneys working for the federal government are called US attorneys.

Note: the common law is often described as a case law system, as being judge-made law. Yet it has long been argued in the theory of the common law that judges do not create law but only interpret the law. They apply existing principles of law to the facts before them in individual cases. Some judges are adamant that any far-reaching changes to the law should be left to the legislature and should not be achieved by the judge in court. However, whether judicial decision-making never creates new law is a moot point; some judicial decisions could be interpreted as doing exactly that. This discussion, as to whether judges simply apply the law or actually create law, is not one that is confined to countries with a common law system. For example in the Netherlands, Paul Scholten argued that finding the law was not a matter of applying the text of a law to a case in a servile way, but rather a creative process. It demanded the construction of a just solution by taking into account unwritten general principles of law within the existing law.

3.3.1 The jury

A mistake that is often made by law students from civil law systems without a jury is to equate a jury system with a common law system. Juries are, however, not confined to common law jurisdictions. For example, in Spain and Belgium juries hear certain types of cases. What can be said, however, is that in both the courts of England and the USA court room proceedings are geared up to the presence of a jury, whether one is actually in sitting or not.

In England, the appearance of a jury in civil cases is now rare. There is no right to jury trial for most civil cases, although certain lawsuits, such as defamation, can still be heard before a jury. In criminal cases, only very serious criminal offences, those on indictment, are heard before a jury. The vast majority of criminal cases are heard by magistrates on summary trial or triable either way offences (offences that may be tried either as summary offences or as indictable offences) where the accused has opted for summary trial.

A jury consists of twelve **jurors** who are laymen and who are supposed to represent a cross-section of the community. In civil cases, the jury decides upon liability and sometimes assesses the damages under the guidance of the judge. In criminal cases, the jurors listen to the facts of the case and, after the judge's summing up of the prosecution and defences cases, they have to reach a verdict: guilty or not guilty. The jury has no part to play on questions dealing with law or legal procedure or on sentencing in criminal cases.

In the USA, the right to jury trial is guaranteed by the US Constitution. Many civil trials are before juries, but if both parties agree to do away with the jury, as this is cheaper and quicker, the case will be resolved by the judge. With respect to criminal cases, the Sixth Amendment of the Constitution guarantees a defendant the right to trial by jury. However, as in England, petty crimes are not heard by juries. In the US a crime must first be punishable by six months or more in prison. Some states, for example Washington, have a **grand jury** of up to twenty-three jurors to see if there is a case to answer; in other words, whether the accusations warrant an indictment. A **petit jury** is the ordinary trial jury, traditionally composed of twelve jurors. Federal courts have twelve jurors as do most state courts, but state court juries may consist of six jurors.

In both England and the USA there are proceedings for the selection of jurors, although this procedure is far more extensive in the USA than in England. In the United States, the French term **voir dire** usually refers to the examination by the court or by the attorneys of prospective jurors. In England it is more commonly referred to as **jury vetting**. Jurors can be **challenged** either by the defence or by the prosecution. They can be challenged 'for cause' (for a reason) or 'without cause' (reason not stated). Another term for a challenge without cause is peremptory challenge.

4   OPERATION OF A COMMON LAW SYSTEM

Today a common law system is based on three major sources of law: **common law**, **equity** and **legislation**. At one time, common law courts could not administer equity as this was the province of the separate court of equity. That was swept away in the latter part of the nineteenth century in England and now all law courts (also in the USA) administer common law and the principles of equity in their courts. Equity developed its own principles, and therefore its own terminology. As this distinction between common law and equity is a characteristic of the common law system, and one unfamiliar to those schooled in the civil law, attention is paid to the development of equity and its terminology in section 4.2 below. The third major source, legislation, has long played an important role in common law systems. Written law has certainly become a significant part of the law of any common law jurisdiction today.

Other sources of law that have played a role in the development of the common law system include **canon law**, or **ecclesiastical law**, certain textbooks and custom. Canon law is the law of the church. It affected the common law with respect to criminal law and matrimonial law. It also influenced the development of equity because of its strong moral content. With respect to textbooks, there are only nine ancient textbooks which are treated as sources of law, the last one being published in 1765. Modern textbooks are not sources of authority although they may well be referred to in the courts. Counsel may adopt their arguments and these arguments are **persuasive** (i.e. should be taken into account, but are not binding). Finally, certain **customs** have survived, for example, in the form of a right of way or rights with respect to the village green.

4.1   Legislation

Even though the English and American legal systems are common law systems, **legislation** plays an important role in law-making. **Statutes** have been in use for centuries, but the momentum for written laws stemming from legislative bodies increased considerably in both England and the United States in the nineteenth century. As commerce and industry progressed, so did governmental regulation.

In England today, legislation rather than the judge in court is more usually responsible for wholly new principles of law. It is also increasingly common for whole areas of law to be put into statute form, for example tax law. Many statutes are a form of codification of certain areas of law, for example the law on theft is now in the form of an Act. The old common law usually forms the basis for the statute, but the legislature takes the opportunity to amend and update the old law.

The same development can be seen in the USA. Federal legislation is published in the 'US Statutes at large' and a 'US Code' which is a compilation of laws dealing with a specific subject. Each state has its own set of statutes and most jurisdictions have now codified a substantial part of their laws. Uniform laws are also of significance. As each state has its own law, the idea behind the development of uniform laws was to cut down the differences in law between all the various states of America. The most successful uniform law is the Uniform Commercial Code (UCC).

Statutes often adopt the old common law terminology, which means that they are very difficult to understand for those with no knowledge of the common law. The judicial interpretation of statutes is, furthermore, in accordance with the common law tradition. The interpretation of statutes by the courts has in turn led to a considerable body of authoritative case law being built up alongside statutory law.

4.1.1 The English system

In England the legislative body is the Parliament, composed of the House of Commons and the House of Lords, the laws being approved by the Crown. The **doctrine of parliamentary sovereignty** means that supreme power is invested in Parliament. Until recently, this doctrine stated that only Parliament could make or **revoke** any law by statute, although it could not bind future parliaments. The English courts could only interpret legislation but not modify or revoke it. Whatever law Parliament has passed in the form of an act must be put into effect by the courts and the courts cannot overrule legislation once passed.

However, this doctrine has had to undergo a certain modification because of England's membership of the European Union (EU). The concept of the supremacy of EU law above that of national law (see chapter 3) means that the national courts of Member States are required to override national legislation where it conflicts with EU law. This has extended the rights of English courts with respect to **judicial review**, as the court may, for example, hold that certain provisions of an **Act of Parliament** are inoperative because they are in breach of EU obligations.

Some terminology is specifically relevant to the legislation itself. A **statute** is a piece of written law, in particular an Act of Parliament. An Act of Parliament is called a **bill** before it has been formally approved. An Act comes into effect from when the royal assent is given unless it contains its own starting date. Every Act is given a chapter number. An Act of Parliament is divided up as follows:
- a heading setting out the aim of the Act;
- the Act is divided into **parts**, each with a number and a title;
- each part is divided into **sections**;
- each section is divided into **subsections** and **paragraphs**;
- at the end of the Act come the **schedules**.

For an example showing how this terminology is used, see the extract from the Unfair Contract Terms Act 1977 in the Appendix.

Note 1: in English national legislation and in the legislation of some of the states of the USA, reference is made to 'sections' of a statute rather than to 'articles'. However, in American federal legislation and in the treaties and directives of the European Union reference is made to 'articles' rather than to sections.

Note 2: there is also delegated legislation meaning that the Parliament gives subordinate authorities the power to make laws. The most important form of delegated legislation is the **statutory instrument**, i.e. ministers are given the power to make laws for specified purposes.

4.1.2 The system in the USA

In the USA, legislation takes place at two levels, the federal and the state. Just as EU law is superior to national legislation, federal legislation is superior to state legislation in its areas of competence. It is said to **pre-empt** state legislation where there is a conflict. It should also be noted that the US Supreme Court has the power to throw out any legislation not in keeping with the US Constitution.

The federal legislature has at its head the President, with the duty to make sure that the laws are faithfully executed and the power to make treaties and veto laws. The federal legislative body is the **Congress**, consisting of the House of Representatives and the Senate, having the power to make 'necessary laws'. Regulations are also developed by federal agencies and departments. Any state legislation which conflicts with the federal laws is void.

States, headed by a governor, have their own legislatures (consisting of two houses except in Nebraska). States have jurisdiction over all matters not reserved to the federal competence.

4.2 Equity

To understand the terminology of equity, it is necessary to look, if only briefly, at the historical development of the common law. Whereas civil law systems developed many of their legal principles from a Roman law basis, the English legal system remained comparatively uninfluenced by this source. The common law developed in the Middle Ages and was the law administered in the king's courts. As the law of the king's courts, it was superior to local customary law. The various local customs were either assimilated or abandoned and gradually the common law of the king's courts became the uniform law of England and Wales.

However, as a form of procedure called the writ system became integral to the common law, the common law became rather rigid and inflexible. If a writ could not be issued, a person had no **legal remedy**. For example, someone who had bought the right to use land but did not own that land, could not obtain a writ to enforce his right of use as the common law only recognised a legal title to land. Those who had no redress at common law turned to the king's chancellor for help. A court of equity developed, where principles of fairness referred to as **principles of equity** prevailed.

Equity supplemented and remedied the deficiencies in the common law. Equity and common law long remained administered in separate courts. Today, all courts can apply rules from the common law and principles of equity.

The development of the principles of equity has had a profound and lasting effect, particularly with respect to property law. A **legal title** to property was recognised at common law, but the courts of equity also recognised an **equitable title**. In the common law system, a legal title and an equitable title can co-exist in the same property. The person with the legal title may be holding the property for the benefit of an individual with an **equitable interest**, for example, where there is a **trust**. To set up a trust, a **settlor** (also called a donor or in the USA a trustor) gives person A property with the intention that he will hold it for the benefit of a specified third person, B. A would have the legal title, and would be the **trustee**, B, the **beneficiary**, would have the equitable title. An equitable title is well protected by the law. However, the legal title usually prevails where there is a conflict between legal and equitable interests if the legal title is sold to a purchaser and bought in good faith, such a purchaser being described as a 'bona fide purchaser without notice'. In common law jurisdictions today, trusts are often set up for a variety of purposes: for individuals, charities, clubs, unit trust schemes and as security for a particular loan.

The equity court also provided remedies that were not available in common law courts. The main remedy at common law is **damages**. Equity offered remedies other than damages, such as the **injunction** and **specific performance** (these terms are dealt with in chapters 2, 4 and 5). The merger of common law and equity courts meant that equitable remedies were no longer the prerogative of one type of court. Nonetheless, they cannot be claimed as a right: equitable remedies have remained **discretionary**.

Note 1: the word 'equity' will be found used in a variety of ways, not just in the sense of a parallel system of law to the common law. For example, equity is also used to refer to the value of property minus incumberances, equity capital is the amount of a company's capital owned by shareholders and equities are ordinary shares.

Note 2: trusts make use of splitting the same property into two interests, legal and equitable. Some jurisdictions do not allow this use of split interests, for example the Netherlands, although foreign trusts may be recognised.

Note 3: US antitrust laws do not refer to trusts as outlined above. The term 'antitrust laws' refers in particular to two statutes which deal with agreements or cooperative attempts to undermine free competition in the marketplace.

4.3   The common law: case law

Despite the increasing growth of legislation in common law jurisdictions, case law is still extremely important. **Case law** refers to the decisions made by judges applying legal principles to the circumstances of the particular disputes before them.

Common law lawyers must be familiar with past cases because the rules of law laid down in these cases remain the law unless they have been overruled.

Note: the English term **jurisprudence** does not mean case law. The section on 'Jurisprudence' in an English library will direct you to books on the study or philosophy of law. In the USA the term jurisprudence can be found used in the English sense as a science of law but also in the sense of case law rather than statute law. This dual use of the term is now creeping into English texts due to the influence of American English and the European Court decisions.

4.3.1 Binding precedent

When a judge comes to try a case he must always look back to see how previous judges have dealt with earlier cases involving similar facts in that area of law. These decisions set a precedent and a judge will be expected to make a decision consistent with the precedents set already. This doctrine is called the **doctrine of binding precedent**. It is also known by the Latin term **stare decisis**. Precedents set by the senior courts are always binding on all lower courts.

It is argued that binding precedent ensures flexibility while giving **legal certainty**. No code or statute, no matter how carefully drafted, can anticipate all the legal problems which can arise from variations of facts. While the judge in a civil law system must generally decide cases on the basis of broad principles, the common law judge will look to see if the legal problem has been raised before in a case and adopt that solution.

Must a precedent always be followed? The answer to that is no, not if a case can be **distinguished**. Cases can only be distinguished on their facts. The facts or a fact in the new case must in some important way be different from the facts or a fact of the case that came before. The court regards as material any fact that was not common to the case which came before. The word **material** is used in general to indicate that something is important or vital, hence material facts, material evidence, material witness. The Americans often use the term **key** in this context.

4.3.2 Case reports

Obviously, in a system where case law is so important there must be a sophisticated system of law reports. Law reports can be traced back to the seventeenth century. In England and the USA, precedents are almost always contained in law reports, and these reports are now of a fairly standardised nature. In England cases are reported in various series, for example:
*   Law Reports, four series: Appeal Cases (A.C.), Queen's Bench (Q.B.), Chancery (Ch) and Family (Fam.);
*   Weekly Law Reports (W.L.R.);
*   All England Law Reports (All E.R.);

- all decisions of the Crown Court, High Court and above are stored on legal databases.

In the USA, there are various possibilities for tracking down case law. Federal or state court decisions are published by the court (official report) or by specialised private companies (unofficial report), such as the 'National Reporter System' and 'American law reports'. Case law may also be found by using the digest system, such as that of West Publishing Co. The digest system makes it possible to track down case law on any area. Citations, in particular those of Shepard, contain texts which give the researcher the history of cases, statutes and other material. Other sources include two major encyclopaedias, 'American Jurisprudence' and 'Corpus Juris Secundum', and so-called Restatements, which are attempts to clarify the status of the law in certain areas (published by the American Law Institute). As in England, cases may be accessed in digital form via data banks.

Each case is given a reference. The form of this reference will depend upon whether the case is a criminal case or a civil case. The reference is followed by the year the case was heard and (an abbreviation of) the name of the series in which the case is reported.

English criminal cases are given the following type of reference:

R v Smith

The 'R' stand for the Latin word Rex or Regina, in other words, the criminal prosecution is brought in the name of the Crown. A different type of annotation may also be found in English criminal cases:

DPP v Smith

Here DPP stands for the Director of Public Prosecutions, who is the head of the Crown Prosecution Service. This is a national service for public prosecutions independent of the police. Criminal proceedings may be taken over by the director where the case is very important or very difficult.

In the USA, the type of reference in criminal cases depends on whether the criminal prosecution is brought by a state or at a federal level. The prosecutor in state cases is then the state itself, for example:

Commonwealth of Massachusetts v Smith

And where the prosecuting authority is federal, the reference would be:

United States v Smith

In civil cases, the names of both parties are used as the reference. For example,

Miliangos v George Frank (Textiles) Ltd

Miliangos is then the plaintiff or claimant, the one bringing the claim, and George Frank is the defendant.

Note 1: in some civil law countries, for example the Netherlands, it is common for textbooks to refer to cases by key words, such as 'the case of the gassed onions'. English and American textbooks typically refer to cases by the names of the participants.

Note 2: the 'v' in the case citations stands for 'versus'. The Americans, rather logically, pronounce the v as versus but in England this is not done. Versus is said as 'and': Miliangos and Frank. Beware, when you hear a reference in this way, as the parties so coupled are not joint parties but opponents.

Every case report sets out:
1   the material facts;
2   the statement of the principle of law applicable to the legal problem disclosed by the facts. This is called the **ratio decidendi**. It is the grounds for the decision. In the USA, the ratio decidendi is referred to more commonly as a **holding**;
3   the judgment based on 1 and 2.

For the parties part 3 is vital. For the purpose of the doctrine of binding precedent part 2 is vital. The judgment itself and the facts are not **binding**, only the ratio decidendi is binding.

Not every statement of law made by a judge in a case is part of the ratio. It may be, for example, that a judge gives his opinion about a hypothetical case while discussing the case at hand. Opinions about a hypothetical case cannot be part of the ratio of the actual case. It is therefore necessary to distinguish what is ratio and what is dictum. Everything outside the ratio decidendi is called **obiter dicta**: things said by the way. The ratio is binding, the obiter dicta are not binding. Obiter dicta are **persuasive** as these comments can be used to help establish legal principles in a future case. When judges agree with each other they are said to **concur**. When a judge disagrees with the majority decision, he is said to **dissent**. A **dissenting judgment** is also published in full but it is classed as obiter dicta.

When the judgment is published in a law report, it begins with a head-note summarising the key facts, the legal principles arising and the decision. This is a convenient short summary and most students read no further than the head-note (an example of a head-note, that of the case of McLoughlin v O'Brian 1982, can be found in the Appendix). In English reports, this head-note is followed by the individual judgment of the judge or judges in that case. Therefore, if five judges have heard the case, five individual opinions will be reported. Consequently, the length of law reports can vary considerably. By reporting each individual judgment, it is possible to see exactly what each judge thought. This approach to law reporting is not universal. Whereas some law systems also publish all the judges' individual opinions, some others only publish an individual opinion if it is a dissenting opinion. There are also civil law systems that opt for the so-called 'secret of the judges' chamber' approach, as in the Netherlands. The result is that only one, amalgamated opinion is published and it is impossible to see what individual judges thought.

4.3.3 Appeal

A decision is **reversed** when a higher court on appeal comes to the opposite conclusion than that of the lower court. An appeal court can either approve or disapprove a precedent. It can **overrule** a principle that has been established in a previous case. This means that the court makes a decision on a point of law that is fundamentally different from that made by a court in a prior case. Once overruled, a decision no longer has any precedential value. Reversing differs from overruling. A decision reversed on appeal directly affects the parties involved in that case. Overruling goes only to the rule of law contained in a decision; it does not affect the parties who were involved in those cases.

Note 1: in the USA, overruling also applies to a court's denial of any motion or point raised in court, for example, 'objection overruled'.

Note 2: a system of cassation courts is not used for appeal cases in England and the USA (see chapter 2).

Legal system discussion questions

1   What are, in your opinion, the advantages and disadvantages of:
    - coded systems of law;
    - traditional common law systems?

2   "The common law was developed by practicing lawyers and judges rather than academics, and that is only too painfully obvious!". Discuss.

3   Where more than one judge has heard a case, should the reasoning of the individual judges be kept secret or does publishing each judge's opinion enhance law reporting?

4   Do you think it is preferable to have a uniform legal profession or a split profession such as in England?

5   Is it better to train law graduates directly as judges or to select judges from those who have worked for years as advocates?

6   Is it useful to have a system of binding precedent?

7   Is jury trial the best way to try cases?

Legal system knowledge questions

1   Some courts are of a higher status than others. Give two general terms which can be used to indicate more important courts.

2   What are magistrates in the English court system?

3   What is meant by the term 'forum shopping'?

4   What alternatives are available for a case to be tried other than in a mainstream court of law?

5   Name the two types of practicing lawyer in the English legal system. In what ways are their functions different?

6   What does the English term 'jurisprudence' mean?

7   Explain the term 'binding precedent'. This term is also known by a Latin term. What is this Latin term?

8   If a judge agrees with the decision reached by the majority of the other judges, he is said to what? What term is used to describe a judge's opinion which does not agree with the majority?

9   What is statute law?

10   What is meant by the term 'equity' in the sense of a system of law?

Chapter 2 Civil procedure terminology

Civil procedure vocabulary

Acknowledgment of service: the defendant should file this document to show he intends to defend. If he does not do this, he has less time in which to serve his defence on the claimant.

Administrative agencies: public bodies to which certain administrative powers have been delegated.

Admissible: evidence is admissible if it is allowed to be brought before the court.

Adversarial proceedings: this is an accusatorial procedure as the opposing parties are responsible for finding and presenting evidence.

Affirmative defence: term used in the USA where the defendant does not deny the allegations but argues that there is some reason why the plaintiff's claim should fail, for example, the claim is barred by the statute of limitations.

American rule: is that the parties pay their own costs, whether they win or lose. There are only a few statutory exceptions.

Answer: document filed in the USA in response to the plaintiff's complaint.

Appeal: the losing party appeals to a higher court for a review of the decision reached by the lower court.

Appellant: the party bringing an appeal is known as the appellant.

Appellate court: an appellate court acts as a court of second instance, hearing the issues afresh, whether of fact, or law or both. It may substitute its decision for that of the court of first instance. Note, however, that although reference is made to the term 'appeal' in the USA, the function of the American appellate courts more often resembles that of the civil law courts of cassation.

Assessment of costs: formerly called taxation of costs in England. There are specific rules for evaluating the costs of an action.

Attachment: in the American sense of the word it is a writ authorising seizure of property, which will be held until the final decision in the case at issue.

Attachment of earnings: English court order requiring an employer to pay the judgment creditor from the earnings of the judgment debtor. In the USA, this is referred to as garnishment, although garnishment can be pre-judgment.

Briefs: term used in the USA for documents that may be drawn up by the plaintiff and defendant for use during a trial: trial briefs. Brief used by the appellant and the appellee for the purposes of an appeal are called appellate briefs. In England, the word brief refers to instructions given by a solicitor to a barrister concerning the details of a client's case.

Burden of proof: in general, it is the claimant who must prove all the elements required for his claim against the defendant. If he cannot do so, then the court must find for the defendant. There are certain circumstances in which the burden of proof may shift to the defendant, for example, where the presumption of res ipsa loquitur arises in negligence claims.

Case management: the judge makes sure that the claim is clear, the issues in dispute have been identified and that all agreements that can be reached between the parties about the issues involved have been reached. At the **case management conference**, the judge gives directions and fixes a date for the trial.

Cassation: a court of cassation is only competent to make a decision upon a point of law. In the English system there are no courts of cassation as the appellate courts have the right to hear issues of fact and law.

Charging order: this order can be granted over the judgment debtor's land, as the writ of fieri facias is only for goods owned by the judgment debtor.

Claim form: the usual way of commencing proceedings in England, replacing the former use of writs in the High Court.

Claimant: the one bringing an action is now referred to as a claimant in English proceedings and the term plaintiff is no longer in use under the new civil procedure rules.

Class action: is used in the USA to bring a lawsuit on behalf of a whole group of individuals who have been affected.

Complainant: term used in the USA for one bringing an action, although the term plaintiff is often used synonymously and is the more usual term.

Complaint: in the USA proceedings are commenced by the plaintiff filing a document called a complaint.

Compulsory counterclaim: term used in the USA for a counterclaim that arises from the plaintiff's original claim against the defendant, in other words, from the same transaction. A **permissive counterclaim** is one that does not arise directly from the present claim. This may have to be re-filed, for example in the appropriate state court.

Conditional fee: the English version of the American contingency fee, which is based on a no win, no fee approach to litigation. The conditional fee agreement usually provides for a 'success fee' in addition to the basic charge.

Contempt of court: this may take various forms, such as failing to pay proper respect to the court or not carrying out a court order.

Contingency fee: American term where the attorney has entered into an agreement with his client that he will only receive his fee if he wins.

Cost-shifting rule: English rule stipulating that whoever loses the case has to pay not only his own costs, but also the costs of the other side.

Counterclaim: a claim brought by a defendant in response to the claimant's claim in the same proceedings.

Cross-claim: document filed in American courts where a claim is brought by one joint party against another joint party.

Cross-examination: questioning of a witness, by a party that has not called the witness, with respect to the witness's testimony during the examination-in-chief.

Damages: financial compensation awarded to a claimant by the court.

Defence: document produced by the defendant in response to the claim form.

Defendant: the one against whom the claim is brought.

De novo: Latin term used in the USA to describe the process by which a case is heard afresh. The findings and judgment of the trial court need not be taken into account by the appeal court as the case is heard as if it has not been heard before.

Deposition: prior to the trial itself, the witness gives evidence before an examiner and he may be cross-examined as if it were the trial itself. The evidence so given is then reduced to writing and put into evidence at the trial. This is called a deposition and the one giving evidence in this way is referred to as the **deponent**. In the USA it is not usually the case that an examiner will be present, just the party being examined and the lawyers.

Disclosure: in English procedural law disclosure is defined as 'stating that a document exists or has existed'. The court can impose a duty on all parties to disclose documents relevant to the issues in dispute. Standard disclosure requires the disclosure of any document that a party intends to make use of at trial; documents that adversely affect the party's own case, another party's case or support another party's case or documents that must be disclosed because of a practice order. Standard disclosure is achieved by making a list of said documents available to the other party. This process was formerly referred to as discovery. There is, in general, a right to inspect a disclosed document.

Discovery: the American term for a pre-trial procedure by which one party gains information held by another party. The term discovery is quite broad as used in federal civil procedure and covers varying sorts of material such as facts, deeds and documents.

Document: defined in English proceedings as anything in which information of any description is recorded.

Endorse: where the particulars of claim are written on the claim form itself, rather than served as a separate legal document, the claim form is said to be endorsed.

Equitable receivership: will only be ordered if the other methods of enforcement are not possible or are unsuitable. The receiver has the right to demand payment from rent due to the judgment debtor from his tenants, income from a trust fund, a legacy or payment from the sale of land.

Evidence: there are four main types of evidence: **oral evidence** given by witnesses during the trial; **real evidence** of a physical nature; **documentary evidence** and **circumstantial evidence**, which is evidence that can be inferred from the facts.

Evidence-in-chief: the evidence given by a witness for the party who called him.

Examination-in-chief: is the term given to direct examination, where counsel calls a witness to support his client's version of events.

Expert opinion: evidence given by a witness who is a specialist in a certain subject.

Fast track: this is the track used for claims for a value above that for small claims but less than that for multi-track claims. It will usually be heard in the County Court.

Fieri facias: Latin term for an English writ authorising the sheriff to seize the goods of the debtor and to sell them to satisfy the judgment debt.

File: a document is filed if it is delivered, by post or otherwise, to the court office. It may have to be **re-filed** if it was not submitted to the appropriate court.

Freezing injunction: order of an English court to stop a party removing or disposing assets before trial.

Garnishment: term still used in the USA where a writ of garnishment allows the judgment creditor to seize the property of the judgment debtor which is in the possession of a third party. In certain cases there may be pre-judgment garnishment.

Group action: term used in England for group litigation, usually where there are many claimants, but there may also be a multitude of defendants. On the grant of a Group Litigation Order, the court takes control of the proceedings. In England this form of action seems to be preferred to the representative or class action form.

Hearsay: hearsay evidence covers statements made by persons who are not themselves witnesses but their evidence is brought to the fore either by someone who is a witness or through a document. There are rules as to its admissibility.

Improperly obtained evidence: is evidence that has been acquired unlawfully.

Inadmissible: certain types of evidence may not be brought before the court. For example, traditionally hearsay evidence was inadmissible unless it was covered by either a common law or statutory exception. The rules on inadmissibility have been relaxed in civil cases in England because most are no longer heard by a jury.

Indemnity costs: indemnity costs, rather than standard costs, will be awarded only in certain situations.

Injunction: court order which is either mandatory, requiring a person to do something, or prohibitory, requiring a person not to do something.

Interim injunctions: an interim injunction is a temporary court order, either mandatory or prohibitory.

Interim payment: this is a payment made before the trial to a person claiming a money judgment.

Interim remedies: are discretionary and may be ordered any time after the court has issued a claim form. Interim remedies include interim payments, a freezing injunction, a search order and interim injunctions in general.

Interrogatory: term used in the USA for a written request to the other party to answer certain questions under oath.

Joinder of parties: uniting parties in a single action, whether as claimants or defendants.

Judgment creditor: is the name given to the party who has been awarded a money judgment by the court.

Judgment debtor: the one against whom a money judgment has been ordered.

Judgment in default: where the defendant has failed to serve a defence within the required time.

Judicial review: one of the tasks of the courts is to review whether public bodies have breached the principles of public law, for example, whether a public body has abused its administrative powers.

Letter of request (also called a **letter rogatory**): may be issued to compel a witness outside the English courts' jurisdiction to give evidence in an English court. This evidence is usually in the form of a deposition.

Lien: a charge on the property of another as security.

Mandatory order: English court order (formerly called mandamus) that orders a public body to carry out a legal duty.

Motion: an application made to the court with a request for an order or ruling in favour of the applicant. In the USA, use is made of various types of motions, for example a **motion to dismiss** where the plaintiff has not been able to show a claim recognised in law.

Multi-track: this track is for claims for a value higher than that specified for the fast track. A multi-track case will be heard either by the County Court or the High Court.

Notice pleadings: the term given in the USA for a form of pleadings that is simple, short and not detailed.

Part 20 claim: this refers to Part 20 of the new English Civil Procedure Rules. It covers a counterclaim and an application for indemnity or contribution.

Part 36 payment: this refers to Part 36 of the new English Civil Procedure Rules, which allows for payments to be made into court.

Particulars of claim: may be on the claim form itself or served as a separate document. The particulars must contain certain information about the nature of the claim and the remedy required by the claimant.

Paying party/receiving party: in England, the one ordered to pay the costs of the proceedings is now referred to as the **paying party**, the one receiving payment is the **receiving party**.

Perjury: telling lies in court while under oath.

Permission: here used in English legal terminology to indicate that permission must be given before a civil case can be appealed. This is in contrast to the USA where there is usually a right to appeal once.

Petition: means of commencing certain specialist proceedings in the High Court, such as an action to wind up a company.

Petitioner: the one submitting a petition.

Plaintiff: the term still in use in the USA to indicate the one bringing an action.

Pleadings: this word refers to all the documents exchanged between the parties setting out their claims and defences.

Pre-trial review: a review of matters prior to the trial in order to manage the action and prepare for trial.

Prima facie: Latin term meaning 'on the face of it' or 'at first sight'. A prima facie case is one where a party has sufficient evidence to show there is a case to answer.

Privilege: the right of a party to refuse to produce documents or answer questions on the ground of some special interest recognised by law.

Prohibitory order: English court order (formerly called prohibition) that stops a public body from acting in excess of its authority.

Public interest immunity: this allows a party not to disclose matters on the grounds that disclosure would be injurious to the public interest, for example with respect to matters of national security.

Quashing order: English court order (formerly called certiorari) to quash a decision either by a public body or an inferior court.

Reply: a document in which the claimant replies to the claims made by the defendant.

Representative action: this term is used in England where the claimant is representing not only his individual interests but also those who have been similarly affected. However, in England damages are not usually awarded in representative actions.

Request for further information: term now used in England, instead of the word interrogatory, where a party requests more information or clarification.

Requests for production: requesting the other party to produce documentary or other forms of evidence relevant to the claim.

Respondent: when a case is appealed, the appealing party is called the appellant and the other party is called the respondent. A respondent is also known as an **appellee** in the USA.

Responsive pleadings: used in the USA to indicate the defendant has responded to the complaint by admitting or denying the allegations, or by stating that he has insufficient information either to admit or deny.

Search order: authorises the representatives of the applicant to enter the defendant's premises for the purpose of searching and seizing evidence where there is a risk that it will be concealed or destroyed.

Security for costs: this court order is discretionary and may be available to a defendant or respondent against a claimant, an appellant or a defendant bringing a counterclaim. The protection usually takes the form of an order for payment into court by the claimant.

Seizure of goods: the court issues a writ authorising the sheriff to seize the goods of the debtor and to sell them to satisfy the judgment debt.

Service: documents used in court proceedings must be brought to the attention of the other party. The delivery, or service, of documents can take various forms, for example personal service on the defendant/claimant or via the post.

Set off: the defendant claims he is owed money by the claimant which he intends to set off against the claimant's claim.

Settlement: parties avoid going to trial by reaching agreement on the claim.

Similar fact evidence: is admissible in English courts if it is used to prove a fact in issue, for example, that the defendant has made a habit of doing something.

Skeleton argument: both parties have to set down in a written document a summary of the submissions to be put forward during the trial.

Small claims: claims of under a certain specified, relatively low value are allocated to the small claims track. It will be heard in the County Court.

Standard costs: this award means that the receiving party will be paid for legal costs reasonably incurred. The costs should be proportionate.

Standard of proof: this is less stringent in civil cases than in criminal cases. Whereas in criminal trials the prosecution must prove the guilt of an accused beyond a reasonable doubt, in civil cases the English standard is on the **balance of probabilities** and in American the usual formulation is **a preponderance of evidence**.

Standing (also known by the Latin term **locus standi**): the potential claimant must be able to show that he has standing, i.e. that he has a sufficient interest in the matter to entitle him to commence proceedings.

Statement of truth: a statement of truth is added to statements of case or a witness statement to verify that the contents of the statement are accurate and honest.

Statements of case: under the English Civil Procedure Rules this is the collective term for the claim form, particulars of claim, a defence, any reply to the defence, requests for further information and the so-called Part 20 claim.

Stop order: English court order that can be obtained to prohibit the judgment debtor from dealing with his securities.

Strike out: to delete a claim, or cancel an action, for example, because the claim reveals no grounds for bringing an action.

Subpoena: court order requiring a witness to appear in court. In England this term is no longer used and has been replaced by the term 'witness summons'.

Summary judgment: it enables a claimant or a defendant to obtain judgment on the whole claim or on a particular issue without going to full trial when it is clear that either the claimant or the defendant has no real chance of success at trial.

Summons: this term is no longer used in England as a means of commencing an action in the County Court. It has, however, not disappeared from English legal terminology entirely, for example a witness summons. In the USA it is still used in the sense of a legally binding notice from the court ordering the defendant to appear and defend, failing which the plaintiff may be entitled to judgment on the basis of the allegations in the complaint.

Supreme Court: in the English court system, this is formed bij the Court of Appeal and the High Court.

Third party debt order: new English term for a **garnishee order**. It enables the judgment creditor to divert money that would normally have been paid by a third party to the judgment debtor.

Third party proceedings: where a person other than the original claimant and defendant becomes an additional party to the proceedings. For example, where the defendant brings a claim against a person for a contribution or indemnification. In the US federal courts this is known as impleader.

Trial: hearing of the issues in contention tried either by a judge alone or by a judge and jury. Common law trials are a mixture of oral and written submissions. Juries in civil trials are now rare in England but usual in the USA.

Wage garnishment: American term indicating that a certain proportion of the judgment debtor's earnings is subject to garnishment. Wage garnishment may in certain circumstances be available pre-judgment.

Wasted costs order: can be obtained to impose liability on lawyers whose conduct has been improper, unreasonable or negligent.

Without prejudice: negotiations with a view to settlement are usually without prejudice, meaning that only in certain exceptional circumstances may the content of those negotiations be revealed to the court.

Witness: person who gives evidence to the court either as to facts or in the form of an expert opinion.

Witness statements: whether as to facts or in the form of expert opinions these statements are prepared in a written form. The statement must be signed, include a statement of truth and be served on the other party prior to the hearing.

Witness summons: witnesses can be compelled to attend a trial. This is the term now used in England but before the new Civil Procedure Rules, this summons was referred to by the Latin term subpoena.

Writ of execution: directed to the sheriff of the county. Writs of execution in the USA can be obtained against all types of property belonging to the judgment debtor, both real and personal, although some property is exempt.

Civil procedure terminology in context

1   INTRODUCTION

There are a number of major differences between the usual form of civil procedure in common law jurisdictions and that in many civil law systems. Traditionally, common law civil procedure has reflected an **adversarial** approach to litigation. The two parties enter the legal arena as protagonists ready to fight out the issue. Some civil law lawyers are quite amazed at the cut and thrust they have witnessed in English trials. This adversarial approach is based on the presumption that the issue will be fought out in open court and addressed to a jury. In England, civil procedure is still geared up to having a jury present, even though juries are now rare in civil cases. In the USA, litigants have retained a general right to jury trial for civil actions. The tradition of a jury presence in common law jurisdictions has dictated the form of civil proceedings in various ways, for example, the culmination of the procedure is a trial that takes place within a specific, concentrated period of time and certain rules of evidence, such as hearsay, have been developed with a jury in mind.

It should also be noted that there has been a reorganisation of the civil justice system in England. Important changes were made to English civil procedure by a statutory instrument of April 1999 (these changes are relevant to England and Wales but not to Scotland or Northern Ireland which have their own rules and procedures). A new set of rules was developed, which was intended not only to simplify civil procedure but also to make proceedings less adversarial and more efficient. These civil procedure rules have had a considerable impact upon the terminology of English civil procedure. Since 1999, certain archaic terminology has been done away with. This was not simply the accidental result of a reorganisation, but a purposeful attempt to make the terminology of the civil courts more accessible to the ordinary man. Students should, therefore, be aware that some of the terminology used in English textbooks written before 1999 will no longer be current. Another consequence of the reorganisation in England is that more discrepancies in terminology now exist between England and the USA than before.

2   CIVIL PROCEDURE IN ENGLAND

Depending on the nature, complexity and the sums of money involved, civil proceedings in England begin in the Magistrates' Court, the County Court or the High Court. The courts will allocate cases to one of three so-called tracks:

1   **Small claims** track for cases under £5,000;
2   **Fast track** for most cases less than £15,000;
3   **Multi-track** for most cases over £15,000 and cases where the remedy sought is other than damages, for example an injunction. Most commercial actions will follow the multi-track.

2.1   The civil courts in England

An outline is given below of the competence of the various civil courts in England. In conjunction with the descriptions given in chapter 1, it is hoped that this will further help civil law lawyers to describe the nature and competence of their own civil courts. The names of these English civil courts have already been noted in the vocabulary belonging to chapter 1. The internal divisions of the courts are dealt with in the text of this chapter but, in order to keep the civil procedure vocabulary as general as possible, they are not noted in the vocabulary.

2.1.1 Magistrates' Court

Magistrates' Courts have a low level but nonetheless substantial civil jurisdiction. They enforce the community charge (tax per person), rates (local taxes) and VAT (value added tax). These proceedings are of a quasi-criminal nature as the magistrates may impose prison sentences where there has been serious default. They are also competent concerning many family proceedings. Their domestic proceedings courts have been renamed family proceedings courts and specially trained magistrates sit in these courts. They can make and enforce financial provisions following a family breakdown, as well as make orders relating to children, for example care and supervision orders, contact and residence orders (formerly known as access and custody orders).

2.1.2 County Court

There has been a redistribution of work between the High Court and the County Court. The result is an increase in the competence of the County Court. Much of the work of the County Court is concentrated on debt collection and personal injury claims. It also deals with tort, contract, race relations, bankruptcy (this term applies to individuals), insolvency (this term applies to companies), many property disputes and it can deal with the more complex cases in relation to children.

2.1.3 The High Court

Together with the Court of Appeal, the High Court is part of the **Supreme Court** of Judicature. This often surprises those less familiar with the, sometimes rather idiosyncratic, English legal system as the House of Lords is the supreme appeal court. The reason why it is the Court of Appeal and the High Court that form the Supreme Court is historical: at the time the intention was to abolish the House of Lords.

The High Court is divided into three divisions, each dealing with different types of cases: the Queen's Bench Division, the Family Division and the Chancery Division.

Queen's Bench Division

This division has a general contract and tort competence. More specifically, it is divided into three courts: the Commercial Court, the Admiralty Court and the Technology and Construction Court.

*   **Commercial Court**: is staffed by judges with special commercial experience hearing cases of a commercial nature, such as insurance, banking, and the interpretation of mercantile documents.
*   **Admiralty Court**: deals with shipping and aircraft, and such particulars as collisions and cargo.
*   **Technology and Construction Court**: deals with disputes of a highly technical nature, for example cases dealing with information technology issues.

The Chancery Division

This division is the modern descendant of the old equity court. The sale of land, mortgages, trusts, estates of deceased people, bankruptcy, the dissolution of partnerships and intellectual property matters are typically legal actions that will be heard in the Chancery Division. It also contains two special courts, the Patents Court and the Companies Court.

*   **Companies Court**: deals with the constitution and liquidation of companies. Its divisional court hears appeals from County Courts in bankruptcy and land registration. It also hears copyright cases in the Copyright Tribunal.
*   **Patents Court**: this court acts both as a court of first instance and on appeal.

The Family Division

This division deals with matrimonial issues, in particular the more complex cases, such as defended or complex divorce cases and applications relating to children. Its divisional court hears appeals from the Magistrates and County Courts concerning family law matters.

2.1.4 The Appeal Courts

The **Court of Appeal** hears most appeals in civil cases. It hears appeals from both the County Court and the High Court. Nearly all civil appeals now require **permission** (the old term 'leave' is no longer in use in England). The final national court of appeal is the **House of Lords**, which tends to hear appeals of general public interest.

It should be noted that in some court systems there is a difference between **appeal** and **cassation** courts. An appellate court acts as a court of second instance, hearing the issues afresh, whether of fact or law or both. It may substitute its decision for that of the court of first instance. Cassation deals with the legality of the decision and a court of cassation can only affirm or annul the decision. In this system, a court of cassation is only competent to make a decision upon a point of law. It may disagree with a decision made in a lower court but it may not substitute its own decision for that of the lower court. In general, it must send the case back to the same or a different lower court, which will re-examine the decision bearing in mind the decision on the point of law made in the court of cassation. The traditional model for this type of system was developed in France and this system has influenced a number of civil law systems. For example, in the Netherlands there is a system of appeal and cassation, the supreme court of the Netherlands being a court of cassation.

In England, there is no court of cassation. Neither the Court of Appeal nor the House of Lords is restricted to questions of law, although in practice the small number of appeal cases dealt with by the House of Lords involve questions of law. It is also unusual for an appeal court to overturn a finding of facts made by the judge at first instance.

2.1.5 Other civil courts

There are various other civil courts in the English system:
- **ecclesiastical courts**: these courts deal with matters concerning the Church of England.
- **Court of Protection**: administers the estate of a person of unsound mind.
- **Restrictive Practices Court**: as its name suggests, it deals with restrictive trade practices related to the supply of goods or services.
- **Employment Appeal Tribunal**: hears appeals from employment tribunals relating to such matters as unfair dismissal, equal pay and redundancy. Appeals on points of law go to the Court of Appeal.
- **Immigration Appeal Tribunal**.

2.2 Civil procedure reforms in England

Before April 1999, the language of civil procedure was rather obscure. This was in part caused by the use of antiquated terms and Latin words, but also because the procedural rules varied from court to court. This in turn produced differing sets of procedural terminology. For example, if a claim was **filed** in the High Court, the document issued was called a writ whereas if it was filed in the County Court it was called a summons. There were also procedural variations between the divisions of the High Court itself.

One of the aims of the new Civil Procedure Rules (CPR) was the simplification of civil procedure. Now all High Court actions governed by the CPR are commenced by a **claim form**. However, the former diversity remains discernable with respect to certain specialist proceedings in the High Court, such as insolvency proceedings and family proceedings. These specialist proceedings still have their own specific set of rules although the CPR may be partially applicable. This is why when an action to wind up a company is commenced, the document filed is not a claim form but a **petition**.

Translation note: one unfortunate aspect of the new CPR terminology is that in certain instances it lends itself less readily for translation purposes. These instances are where reference is made to specific parts of the CPR. For example, English lawyers now use the terms **Part 20 claim** and **Part 36 payment**. A Part 20 claim covers a counterclaim and third party proceedings for an indemnity or contribution. A Part 36 payment is the old payment into court. Using references to parts of the CPR is clear to all English lawyers, but not to those outside the system. It is also not a useful form of terminology for a legal translator. Unless the translation is being made for a specifically English audience, references to parts should be avoided and the translation should keep to more generally accessible terminology.

2.3   Commencing proceedings in the High Court

Described below is the procedure for bringing an action in the High Court. The County Court is not dealt with here as its area of competence is less relevant to foreign students and practitioners. The County Court is not a senior court and therefore its precedents are not binding on the higher courts (and so its decisions rarely appear in textbooks). Furthermore, cases involving foreign lawyers tend not to be heard by the County Court, as this is essentially a local court dealing with cases in its geographical area, those cases being neither too challenging nor involving sums of money over a certain value.

2.3.1 The claimant

The one bringing an action used to be referred to as a **plaintiff** until April 1999. The word plaintiff has now disappeared from English legal terminology and has been replaced by the term **claimant**. Where the claimant claims a remedy to which two or more persons are entitled, there may be a **joinder of parties**. The claimant may also bring the action in a representative capacity. In a **representative action**, the claimant is representing not only his individual interests but also the interests of those who have been similarly affected. However, damages are usually not awarded in representative actions unless the total loss can be ascertained at the time of judgment or the damages can be paid to a collective body rather than individually. This difficulty has made **group actions** based on a group litigation order more popular than class actions based on representation.

Note: the English group action is not quite the same as the American **class action**. The American class action is a well-developed, if not entirely non-controversial, means of bringing a lawsuit on behalf of a whole group of individuals that has been affected. It is based on a representative model.

2.3.2 Bringing an action

Before the CPR, the usual way of commencing proceedings in the High Court was by writ. The term 'writ' has now disappeared from CPR terminology. Most proceedings in the High Court are now commenced by a claimant filling out a **claim form**. **Particulars of claim** may be **endorsed** on the claim form itself or served as a separate document within fourteen days of the claim form. The particulars must contain certain information about the nature of the claim and the remedy required by the claimant. It must also give details about the basis of the claim against the defendant, including a concise statement of the facts upon which the claimant intends to rely. The claimant or his counsel must sign a **statement of truth**, verifying that the claim is a truthful one. Proceedings begin once the claim form has been issued by the court. It must be **served** on the other party. Various modes of service are permissible, for example personal service on the defendant or via the post.

2.3.3 Defending an action

The one against whom the claim is made is still referred to as the **defendant**. If the defendant intends to defend, he should file a document with the court called an **acknowledgment of service**. If he does not file an acknowledgment of service, he has less time in which to file a defence. The defendant must serve a **defence** within a certain time. If he fails to do so, there will be **judgment in default**. The defence should give details, as a defence which simply denies all the claims made in the claim form is no longer acceptable. The claimant can file a **reply** to the defence. However, according to the new Civil Procedure Rules, parties may not file any other statements after a reply. The idea is to get rid of the practice of filing various statements in response to those made by the other party. Prior to the new rules, it was possible for the defendant to file a rejoinder, the plaintiff to file a surrejoinder, then the defendant could file a rebutter and the plaintiff a surrebutter. These documents have now disappeared from English civil proceedings.

The defendant may have a defence of **set-off**. The defendant claims he is owed money by the claimant, which he intends to set off against the claimant's claim. This may be a defence to the whole claim or part of the claim as, depending on the value of the set-off, the monetary claim can either be reduced or wiped out altogether. Under the so-called Part 20 claim proceedings, the defendant can also bring a counterclaim. A **counterclaim** is a cross-action which is not a defence but the defendant's own particulars of claim. The claimant in turn will have to file a defence to the counterclaim and serve it on all parties concerned. If the defendant wishes to claim against a person other than the original claimant, he must apply to the court for permission. A defendant may also bring a claim for a contribution or indemnity from a co-defendant under Part 20 proceedings. The introduction of third parties to a claim is in general referred to as **third party proceedings**.

2.3.4 Further information

The court may order a party to clarify or give further information concerning a matter at issue. A party wishing for further information must first have served a written **request (for further information or clarification)** upon the other party. These requests were formerly referred to as 'requests for further and better particulars and interrogatories'. The response to the request must also be in writing and a **statement of truth** must appear at the bottom.

2.3.5 Statements of case

Under the CPR, the term **statements of case** covers the claim form, particulars of claim, a defence, any reply to the defence, requests for further information and the so-called Part 20 claim (which covers a counterclaim and third party proceedings). Prior to the CPR, all these documents were referred to by the collective term **pleadings**. In practice, it would appear that the term pleadings is still in use and has not yet been totally superseded by the CPR term statements of case.

The court has the power to **strike out** a statement of case either in whole or in part. There are three reasons for doing so: there are no grounds for bringing or defending the case; it is an abuse of the court process; or there has been a failure to comply with a rule, practice direction or court order.

2.4 Summary judgment

In England, either a claimant or a defendant can apply for a **summary judgment**. This procedure is relatively quick. It enables a claimant or a defendant to obtain judgment on the whole claim or on a particular issue without going to full trial. Relevant here is **striking out**, which is a procedure to dispose of claims, defences and counterclaims. Summary judgment enables courts to dispose of weak cases without wasting time when it is clear that either the claimant or the defendant has no real chance of success at trial.

2.5 Settlement

Courts are very much geared up to promoting **settlement**. In a settlement, parties avoid going to trial by reaching agreement on the claim. Either the claimant or the defendant may make a payment into court or an offer to settle at any time after the commencement of proceedings. The system of payments into court where a money claim is at issue is now called a Part 36 payment. Offers to settle are now called Part 36 offers. These Part 36 offers are not necessarily monetary, for example, the remedy sought could be an injunction. Both payments and offers are covered by **without**

prejudice privilege. That means that whatever passed between the parties during settlement negotiations is confidential and will not be disclosed during trial.

If the other party rejects a settlement offer, and he later loses the case, he can incur a costs penalty. The vast majority of cases do not come to trial, as most are settled before the hearing.

2.6   Case management

The new rules in England have meant that the onus is now on the courts to manage a case rather than to leave it to the parties themselves. Once the claim form and the defence have been filed, the parties must fill out an Allocation Questionnaire. The case will then be allocated to a track: small claims track, fast track or multi-track. The High Court will only hear multi-track cases.

If the case has been allocated to the multi-track, a **case management conference** will be set up. This case management conference gives the judge an opportunity to make sure that the claim is clear, the issues in dispute have been identified and that all agreements that can be reached between the parties about the issues involved have been reached. The judge gives directions and fixes a date for the trial. He may direct that the trial should be heard within a certain period, usually up to three weeks. This is referred to as the trial window. In many cases, where the trial is expected to last more than ten days, there may be a **pre-trial review**. This pre-trial review is to offer the parties an opportunity to settle before the costs of a full trial are incurred. If the attempt at settlement is unsuccessful, then the agenda for the trial is set down.

2.6.1 Order for disclosure of documents

In English proceedings, there is a duty on all parties to disclose documents relevant to the issues in dispute. A **document** is defined as anything in which information of any description is recorded. This covers information in an electronic format. Any document that a party intends to make use of at trial must be made available to the other party. This process is now termed **disclosure** (it was formerly called discovery).

Disclosure requires each party to produce a list of all relevant documents with a disclosure statement made by the party disclosing the documents. This list must be served on the other party. Each party then has the right to inspect and ask for copies of all the opponent's documents that are not subject to **privilege**. That privilege may, for example, be in the form of confidential communication between legal counsel and client or where documents are covered by **public interest immunity**. In this way, each party can determine before the trial the basis on which the other will argue his case. The disclosure obligation does not end once the list has been drawn up. If after the list has been served other relevant documents appear, these too must be disclosed.

2.6.2 *Interim remedies*

Interim remedies are discretionary and may be ordered any time after the court has issued a claim form. Interim remedies include interim payments, the freezing injunction, the search order and general interim injunctions.

- **Interim payment**: this is a payment made before the trial to a person claiming a money judgment. In this way, it is possible to prevent prolonged economic hardship to a claimant, as the length of time between commencing proceedings and the final judgment can be considerable.
- **Freezing injunction**: formerly known as a Mareva injunction, it stops a party removing or disposing of assets before trial. The court must be satisfied that there is a real risk that the assets will be removed or disposed of before it grants an injunction. A freezing injunction is not limited to assets in England and Wales but can be worldwide.
- **Interim injunctions**: an interim injunction may be either **mandatory** or **prohibitory**, i.e. it may be a court order requiring a person to do something or prohibiting a person from doing something. The test for awarding an interim injunction is open to some debate: should it be awarded on the basis that the applicant can show a **prima facie** case or that the hardship caused by the refusal to grant an interim injunction would outweigh the hardship of inflicting a temporary injunction on the other party? The party applying for the injunction will usually be required to give an undertaking as to damages.
- **Search order**: formerly known as an Anton Piller order, a search order may also be obtained at this stage. It authorises the representatives of the applicant to enter the defendant's premises for the purpose of preserving evidence. The order allows the representative to search for and seize articles and documents relevant to the applicant's claim if there is a real danger that the defendant would otherwise conceal or destroy that evidence.

2.7   Trial

For many centuries, civil cases were heard by juries in England. Now only a very few civil cases are tried by jury in England. Nonetheless, the legacy of a jury is still apparent in trial procedure. Traditionally trial proceedings have always been largely oral. The reason was that some members of the jury might have been illiterate. Today, most trials are heard by judges, but the typical English trial is still a mixture of oral and written submissions. A so-called **skeleton argument** will now normally be required from both parties.

The trial continues to be heard in a concentrated period of time, as it was when a jury had to be called together. The former presence of a jury also accounts for the clear distinction between pre-trial directions and the trial itself. As noted above, documents that a party intends to rely on at trial must be disclosed to the other party and the court before the trial itself. Finally, certain rules of evidence were developed with a jury in mind.

2.7.1 The trial timetable

The following gives an outline of the main sequence of events in the trial:
- opening speech: this is optional;
- although witnesses have already submitted written statements, a personal appearance by witnesses may be required at the trial for clarification and cross-examination purposes. Witnesses may be called by the claimant and the defendant;
- examination of the witnesses called by the claimant. **Examination-in-chief** is the term given to direct examination, where counsel calls a witness to support his client's version of events. The defence counsel may **cross-examine** the claimant's witnesses;
- re-examination of witnesses;
- examination of the defendant's witnesses. Again, there is examination-in-chief by the defence counsel followed by cross-examination by the claimant's counsel;
- re-examination;
- closing speech by the counsel for the defence;
- closing speech by the counsel for the claimant;
- judgment;
- order for costs.

2.7.2 Evidence

There are four main types of evidence:
- **oral evidence**: this evidence is given by witnesses during the trial. These days, evidence may be given to the court via a video link or even a telephone if a video link is not available. A witness must take an oath or make an affirmation that what he says is true. If a witness deliberately gives false evidence, he is guilty of **perjury**;
- **real evidence**: this covers evidence of a physical nature, such as material objects;
- **documentary evidence**: this covers all evidence that falls under the definition of **document**;
- **circumstantial evidence**: evidence that can be inferred from the facts.

Pre-trial, written evidence is the norm. It is usually in the form of a witness statement rather than an affidavit (which is a written, sworn statement of evidence). **Witness statements**, whether as to facts or in the form of **expert opinions**, must be signed, include a statement of truth and be served on the other party prior to the hearing. A witness statement is the equivalent of the oral evidence which that witness would give if called to give evidence. A party may apply for an order for a person to be examined before the hearing takes place. The witness gives evidence before an examiner and he may be cross-examined as if it were the trial itself. The evidence so given is then reduced to writing and put into evidence at the trial. The one who gives evidence in this way is called a **deponent** and the evidence is referred to as a **deposition**.

However, witnesses can be summoned to appear in person in order to clarify a statement and to allow cross-examination during the trial. Witnesses can be compelled to attend a trial. In that case, a **witness summons** is issued. Before the CPR this summons was referred to by the Latin term **subpoena** (ad testificandum or duces tecum).

It may be the case that evidence must be obtained from outside the jurisdiction of the English courts. A **letter of request** (also called a **letter rogatory**) may be issued to compel a witness outside the courts' jurisdiction to give evidence in an English court. This evidence is usually in the form of a deposition. Depositions may also be used as evidence in foreign courts.

The law of evidence has been simplified in England because most civil trials are no longer heard by juries. This is reflected in the rules relating to **hearsay** evidence in civil proceedings. Hearsay covers statements made by persons who are not themselves witnesses, but their evidence is brought to the fore either by someone who is a witness or through a document. Traditionally, this evidence was **inadmissible** unless it was covered by either a common law or statutory exception. Since 1995, the prohibition on hearsay evidence has been abolished. It is now **admissible** evidence if the one who made the statement would be a competent witness. Similarly, the best evidence rule has also been swept away in civil cases. This rule required a party who wished to rely on a document to produce an original of that document.

Improperly obtained evidence is evidence that has been acquired unlawfully. The general position is that it will be admissible in civil cases, as long as the material is relevant. So-called **similar fact evidence** is also admissible if it is used to prove a fact in issue, for example, that the defendant has made a habit of infringing people's copyright.

2.7.3 The burden and standard of proof

In general, the **burden of proof** falls upon the one who brings the claim. If the claimant cannot prove all the elements required for his claim then the court must find for the defendant. There are certain circumstances in which the burden of proof may shift to the defendant, for example in a negligence claim, where a defendant must rebut the presumption of **res ipsa loquitur** (see chapter 4 on tort).

The **standard of proof** in civil cases is less stringent than in criminal cases. Whereas in criminal trials the prosecution must prove the guilt of an accused **beyond a reasonable doubt**, in civil cases the standard is **on the balance of probabilities**.

2.8 Appeal

Since 1999, **permission** must be given by the court to bring an appeal in a civil case. The term permission replaces the old term 'leave'. A court that can hear appeals may be referred to as an **appellate court**. The party bringing an appeal is referred to as the **appellant** and the other party is the **respondent**. An appeal may be based on a perceived error of fact, expert evidence, an exercise of discretion or a point of law. New evidence, in other words, evidence that was not heard by the lower court, will only be admissible in a number of limited circumstances, for example, because the evidence could not be obtained at an earlier stage.

An appeal is normally heard by the next court up in the hierarchy. However, if the appeal raises an important point of principle it may go straight to the **Court of Appeal**. The **House of Lords** is the final (national) appellate court. This court only hears appeals where a question of public interest is concerned. The reference to the House of Lords in this context is not to its function as an upper house of Parliament. Not all those who sit in the House of Lords may hear appeals, but only those members of the House who are the most senior judges of the land. It is possible that in the near future the House of Lords may be replaced as a court of appeal by a new style supreme court.

2.9   Costs

It is a simple fact of life that litigation is expensive. The value of the claim to the claimant can be completely overshadowed by the costs of the action. Costs are awarded at the discretion of the court. However, in most cases they are awarded in accordance with the so-called **cost-shifting rule**: whoever loses the case has to pay not only his own costs, but also the costs of the other side. The one ordered to pay is now referred to as the **paying party**; the one receiving payment is the **receiving party**. Payment of the costs may in total be more than the original claim itself. The costs rise even higher where one of the parties appeals. A grant of **security for costs** is within the court's discretion. This may be available to a defendant or respondent against a claimant, an appellant or a defendant bringing a counterclaim. The protection usually takes the form of an order for payment into court by the claimant. A **wasted costs order** can be obtained to impose liability on lawyers whose conduct has been improper, unreasonable or negligent.

2.9.1 Awards of costs

In multi-track cases, an order for costs is usually awarded on a standard basis to the winning party. A **standard costs** award means that the receiving party will be paid for legal costs reasonably incurred. The costs should be proportionate. An award of standard costs will not necessarily cover the total costs incurred by the receiving party. An award of **indemnity costs**, rather than standard costs, tends to be more favourable to the receiving party. In this case, it is the receiving party rather than the paying party who is given the benefit of the doubt and the concept of proportionality does not apply. Indemnity costs will be awarded only in certain situations: in favour of a trustee, where the parties have agreed that costs will be paid on this basis, where the defendant lost the trial but had earlier refused to accept a settlement offer made by the claimant and as a means for the court to express its disapproval of the way in which the paying party conducted the case. There are specific rules for the **assessment of costs** (the term assessment has taken over from the old term 'taxation of costs').

2.9.2 Legal fees

For those who cannot afford the services of a lawyer, it may be possible for them to call upon the Community Legal Service Fund, which replaced the old system of civil legal aid in 2000. A few years ago, another option also became available. Legislation has now made it possible for English lawyers to enter into **conditional fee** agreements with their clients. Put simply, this is the 'no win, no fee' approach to litigation common in the USA. These conditional fees are the English version of the American **contingency fees**. The conditional fee agreement usually provides for a 'success fee' in addition to the basic charge. What percentage this success fee should be has been the subject of discussion in England. What can be said with certainty is that it cannot exceed 100% of the normal fee, as this is the statutory maximum. Nor is it a percentage of the damages. This means that the conditional fee system is less advantageous to lawyers than the American system of contingency fees.

2.10   Enforcement of judgments

When the new CPR went through in April 1999, the old rules on enforcement remained. However, since 1999, certain amendments to the rules on enforcement have been made and more are probably on the way. A certain simplification of terminology has resulted already, for example, the old term garnishee order has been replaced by the more immediately understandable term **third party debt order**.

2.10.1 Seizure of goods

A **judgment creditor** is the name given to the party who has been awarded a money judgment by the court. This judgment is enforceable against the **judgment debtor**. The High Court makes use of a writ of execution, which is at present still referred to by the Latin term **fieri facias**, that authorises the sheriff to seize the goods of the debtor and to sell them to satisfy the judgment debt. The debtor is, however, allowed to keep certain personal items and other items necessary for his work.

2.10.2 Third party debt orders

This order, formerly called a garnishee order, enables the judgment creditor to divert money that would normally have been paid by a third party to the judgment debtor. For example, the debtor's bank can be ordered to pay the judgment debt out of the debtor's bank account. A similar third party debt order is available in the County Court: **attachment of earnings**. This requires an employer to pay the judgment creditor from the earnings of the judgment debtor.

2.10.3 Charging orders

A **charging order** can be granted over the judgment debtor's land. It operates in a similar way to a mortgage over a house. If the interest involved is not land but securities, then a **stop order** can be obtained to prohibit the judgment debtor from dealing with the securities.

2.10.4 Equitable receivership

Equitable receivership will only be ordered if the other methods of enforcement are not possible or are unsuitable. The receiver has the right to demand payment from rent due to the judgment debtor from his tenants, income from a trust fund, a legacy or payment from the sale of land.

2.10.5 Non-money judgments

A party will be guilty of **contempt of court** if he does not abide by an injunction issued by the court. Committal proceedings are then commenced and, if found guilty, he can be imprisoned or fined. The High Court can also issue writs to order the delivery of goods and for the possession of land.

2.11 Judicial review

One of the tasks of the courts is to review whether public bodies have breached the principles of public law, for example by acting in excess of their administrative authority. The courts' right of **judicial review** only arises where the decision, act or omission is by a body performing a public function. The applicant will not be given permission to proceed with his claim for judicial review if he does not have **standing**, which is also still referred to by the Latin term **locus standi**. Standing means that the potential claimant must be able to show that he has a sufficient interest in the matter to entitle him to commence proceedings. If the claimant may proceed, he must then serve his claim form on the defendant. Judicial review now takes place by a High Court judge sitting alone. The High Court can issue the following orders:
- **mandatory order** (formerly called mandamus): this orders a public body to carry out a legal duty;
- **prohibitory order** (formerly called prohibition): this stops a public body from acting in excess of its authority;
- **quashing order** (formerly called certiorari): to quash a decision by either a public body or an inferior court.

An injunction, declaration and damages may also be awarded.

3   Civil procedure in the USA

There have always been certain differences in civil procedure, and therefore terminology, between the USA and England. Since the new CPR in England, these differences have increased. The CPR changed and simplified civil procedure and its language. One of the effects of this process is that some terms that have been shared by the two nations for centuries are no longer shared, for example, the words plaintiff, discovery, and interrogatory are no longer mutual. An attempt is made below to highlight some of these differences.

3.1   Civil jurisdiction in the USA

Civil proceedings may be heard in federal courts and state courts. Within certain statutory and constitutional limitations, the federal district courts have jurisdiction over nearly all categories of federal cases. It is the federal system that is usually used by foreigners. The state courts have a general jurisdiction over state law and some federal court matters.

3.2   Commencing proceedings in the federal courts

The terminology described below is that of the federal system. Again, it is the federal system of courts that is usually the forum for foreign parties. Furthermore, the federal system stands as a model for a number of state systems. The level of trial initiation for most civil actions is the District Court. The decisions of the District Court can be appealed to the Courts of Appeal, but only a small number of cases will be heard by the US Supreme Court. Federal civil procedure is governed by the Federal Rules of Civil Procedure, which are issued by the US Supreme Court.

3.2.1 *The plaintiff*

The one bringing the action is generally referred to as the **plaintiff**. For practical purposes, the term plaintiff is now synonymous with **petitioner** and **complainant**, although the terms petitioner and complainant are still in use and depend upon the nature of the proceedings and the court.

As in England, there can be **joinder of parties** where more than one individual has a claim against the same defendant. The most common type of multi-party action is the so-called **class action** where one or more named plaintiffs sue on behalf of a larger group who are not formally named as plaintiffs. The class action is a popular means of bringing an action where the group affected is large and without the class action there would be a considerable number of individual hearings, which would take up much of the court's time and cause expense for each individual member of the group. Class actions can be brought either for **damages** or for other forms of relief, such as an **injunction**. Both class actions for damages and injunctive relief cannot be settled by the parties without the approval of the court.

3.2.2 Bringing an action

Proceedings are commenced by the plaintiff filing a **complaint**. The complaint is a simple document and need not contain a detailed statement of the plaintiff's claim. All that is required is that the other party has a general idea of the nature of the plaintiff's claim. This lack of detail means that pleadings in the federal system are so-called **notice pleadings**.

The complaint together with a summons is **served** on the defendant. A **summons** is a legally binding notice from the court which, if not answered, will entitle the plaintiff to judgment based on the allegations in the complaint. Once the defendant has been served with the complaint and the summons he must respond within a fixed period of time (usually twenty days).

3.2.3 Defending an action

Having received the complaint and the summons, the **defendant** has two options open to him. The first option is to file an **answer**. In the answer, the defendant must deal in short and plain terms with the allegations made by the plaintiff. He may admit or deny the allegations, or state that he has insufficient information either to admit or deny. This is referred to as a **responsive pleading**. An **affirmative defence** is where the defendant does not deny the allegations but argues that there is some reason why the plaintiff's claim should fail, for example, the claim is barred by the statute of limitations, which sets fixed periods in which an action must be commenced. The defendant may also file a **counterclaim**, which is the defendant's own cause of action against the plaintiff. In federal proceedings, there are two types of counterclaims:

- **compulsory counterclaim**: this is a counterclaim that arises from the plaintiff's original claim against the defendant, in other words, from the same transaction;
- **permissive counterclaim**: one that does not arise directly from the present claim. This may have to be **re-filed**, for example in the appropriate state court.

Rather than file an answer, the second possible option is for the defendant to ask the court via a document known as a **motion** to have the complaint dismissed. There are various reasons for a motion to dismiss, such as the complaint was filed in the wrong court or the plaintiff has not shown a claim recognised by the law.

3.2.4 Pleadings

In addition to the documents referred to above, a **cross-claim** may be filed. This is a claim brought by one joint party against the other joint party (or one of the other joint parties). In other words, a cross-claim is not brought against the opposing party, as in a counterclaim, but against a co-plaintiff or a co-defendant. There may also be a third party claim. The defendant may serve a summons and a complaint on a person who is not already a party to the action but who may be liable to the defending party. The plaintiff may file a **reply** in answer to a counterclaim, but he can only file a reply to an answer if given permission to do so by the court. All these documents are referred to as the **pleadings**.

3.3 Summary judgment

A motion can be brought for **summary judgment**. This is usually brought by the defendant, but in some cases by the plaintiff. The motion for summary judgment may be to dismiss the whole claim or one of the claims made. An application for summary judgment comes at a later stage than a motion to dismiss. The reason is that the process of summary judgment is used where the one filing a motion for summary judgment asserts that the facts are not in dispute. The dispute here is a question of law.

3.4 Pre-trial

As in England, there are pre-trial activities. Pre-trial conferences take place to facilitate settlement, to manage the action and prepare for trial. In this phase, pleadings may be amended, motions filed and discovery takes place.

Discovery is the term given to a pre-trial procedure by which one party gains information held by another party. The term discovery is quite broad as used in federal civil procedure and covers varying sorts of material such as facts, deeds and documents. All relevant information must be made available unless it is covered by privilege. There are various methods of discovery including:

- **interrogatory**: written request to the other party to answer certain questions under oath;
- **requests for production**: requesting the other party to produce documentary or other forms of evidence relevant to the claim. Broad requests, as a means of trying to find out exactly what evidence the other party intends to rely on, are called 'fishing trips';
- **deposition**: written (or videotape) evidence given by witnesses under oath. The witnesses may be questioned and both sides have the right to be present.

3.5 Trial

Again, as in England, the majority of cases do not come to trial. Most are **settled** or have been disposed of by a **motion to dismiss** or **summary judgment**. Unlike in England, according to federal law, there is a right to jury trial in all civil cases involving damages. Nonetheless, parties may opt to have the case tried by a judge rather than a jury. Trial by a judge tends to be faster than jury trial and certain evidence that would be inadmissible before a jury will be admissible in a trial by a judge. This option is, however, only possible if both parties agree to trial without a jury. The sequence of events in the trial itself is rather similar to that in England. The rules of evidence are, however, more stringent in the USA as most civil trials are still heard by juries.

3.6 Appeal

The American appellate process is designed to review and correct errors of law raised at the trial. Appeal courts do not, in general, review facts. This means that, although the procedure is referred to as appeal in the USA, it is not usually a rehearing of the case. The appeal courts may, however, hear a case **de novo**, in other words, as if the case had not been heard before. Evidence of a factual nature may also be heard, for example where the case has been heard by a judge rather than a jury and a judge's finding of fact is overturned as 'clearly erroneous', or whether as a matter of law there was insufficient evidence for the matter to be decided by a jury.

Due to the importance of jury trial in civil proceedings in the USA, if a court of appeal does conclude there was an error of law, a new trial before a jury will usually be ordered. The court of appeal may substitute its own decision if the case was heard by a judge rather than a jury and the court agrees with the judge's findings of fact but not with the legal conclusion applied to these facts.

In the USA, the losing party usually has the right to one appeal, being an appeal to the next court in the hierarchy. The one bringing an appeal is referred to as the **appellant** and the one defending an appeal is referred to either as the **respondent** or as the **appellee**. A notice of appeal is filed with the appellate court and served on the other party. However, if an appeal is made to the US Supreme Court, any review is at the discretion of the court. The US Supreme Court will only hear appeals if there are special reasons. Appeals are decided on the basis of documents drawn up by the appellant and respondent, known as appellate **briefs**, followed by oral presentations and answers by the clients' lawyers.

3.7 Enforcement of judgments

The enforcement of federal court judgments is largely governed by the state law in which the federal court is located. As in England, reference is made to a **judgment creditor** and a **judgment debtor**. The types of enforcement are similar to those in England, but some of the terminology is different, particularly since the new CPR updated civil procedure in England.

- **Seizure of goods**: is effected by a **writ of execution** directed to the sheriff of the county. Writs of execution can be obtained against all the property of the judgment debtor both real and personal, or any legal or equitable interest, unless the property is exempt by law. This is different in England where a charging order is needed for land and a stop order for securities. The judgment creates a **lien** on the property of the judgment debtor in the county where the federal court sits. The sheriff may then enter, seize and sell real and personal property.

- **Garnishment**: a writ of garnishment allows the judgment creditor to seize the property of the judgment debtor which is in the possession of a third party. The **garnishee** is the one to whom the writ is directed. **Wage garnishment** means that a certain proportion of the judgment debtor's earnings are subject to garnishment.

Note: the term **attachment** refers to a quite different action in American legal terminology than in English. In English civil procedure, attachment is attachment of earnings, the American wage garnishment. The term attachment in American terminology means a writ authorising seizure of property, which will be held until the final decision in the case. This action has more in common with the English freezing injunction.

3.8 Judicial review

The function of the Supreme Court is to interpret the Constitution. If there is a challenge, it determines whether law passed at a federal level by Congress or at a state level is consistent with the US Constitution. It is the Supreme Court that decides upon the constitutionality of these laws and if it finds that the law conflicts with the Constitution, the law is declared illegal. The Court's decision is final.

In the USA, there is a system of **administrative agencies** at both the federal and state level. Often broad powers have been delegated to these agencies. Examples of federal agencies are the Environmental Protection Agency, the Food and Drug Administration, and the Internal Revenue Service, which is a branch of the Treasury Department. Typical agencies at the state level would be the state conservation department, the state employment department, and the state highway department. The actions of these agencies are generally subject to **judicial review** by the courts.

3.9 Costs

In England, the loser pays not only his own costs but also those of the successful party. This is not the case in the USA: the practice known as the **American rule** is that the parties pay their own costs, whether they win or lose. There are only a few statutory exceptions to this rule when the losing party will be ordered to pay the other party's costs as well as his own.

The use of **contingency fees** is well established in the USA. Here the attorney has entered into an agreement with his client that he will only receive his fee if he wins. Particularly in actions brought for personal injuries, this is the usual practice. An average contingent fee is around 30% (one third) of the damages recovered, although the percentage can vary. Some states have taken action to cap the percentage that a lawyer can claim.

Civil procedure discussion questions and case discussion

1   "How ridiculous to have a legally trained judge and then allow a case to be decided by twelve people with no legal training at all!" Discuss this opinion about the merits of the jury system.

2   In what ways is the approach to civil procedure in common law jurisdictions different from that in many civil law systems?

3   Richard Smith wanted to buy a hotel in London. Before entering into the contract, he hired a surveying company to check out the structural integrity of the building. He was told that all was well. On the basis of this report he entered into the contract. A month later the roof of the hotel collapsed causing considerable damage. He decides to bring a civil action against the surveying company. The company in turn states that it has not yet been paid for the surveying report. Explain how that action might proceed.

Civil procedure knowledge questions

1   In the USA the one bringing a civil action is generally called the plaintiff. What name is given to the one bringing a civil action in England?

2   Since the CPR, what is the usual document used to commence an action in the High Court in England?

3   What are statements of case? What term is used in the USA instead of statements of case?

4   Explain the difference between a counterclaim and a set-off.

5   What is a summary judgment?

6   The English term disclosure and the American term discovery refer to what sort of pre-trial procedure?

7   Explain the term freezing injunction.

8   What is meant by the term standard of proof?

9   What is the difference between the American rule and the English cost-shifting rule with respect to costs?

10   What term is given in the USA to fees paid on a 'no win, no pay basis'? How is this referred to in England?

Chapter 3   European Union law terminology

European Union law vocabulary

Abuse (of a dominant position): this term is relevant to EU competition law. It relates to the abuse of a dominant position in the market. The term 'abuse' is not defined in the Treaty but examples of abuse in the shape of exploitative behaviour are given. There is no need to show that the undertaking intended to cause harm.

Advocate General: his task is to review a case and present his opinion to the judges hearing the case. The judges are not bound by his opinion and may accept or reject it.

Agreement: as used in EU competition law it is meant to cover both formal and informal arrangements between undertakings.

Anti-competitive abuses: the EC Treaty does not define abuse as such but lists types of anti-competitive abuse. The following would fall under that heading:
- **unfair prices**: prices that have no reasonable relation to the value of a product, such as **predatory pricing** where the price of goods is set too low in order to drive out competitors. **Discriminatory prices** arise where different customers are charged different prices for the same product;
- **exclusive dealing**: where it is a condition of the sale that the buyer will deal only with that seller;
- **fidelity rebates**: a loyalty discount is a reduction in price granted on condition that a specific proportion of the buyer's requirements are bought from the supplier;
- **tying**: where a condition of entering into a contract is that supplementary obligations are entered into as well. In order to buy one product (the tying product), the buyer must agree to buy a second product (the tied product) from the seller;
- **refusal to supply**: where a dominant undertaking refuses to supply another undertaking, intending to drive it out of business.

Antitrust law: the American term for competition law to encourage competition in the market place.

Assent procedure: for certain matters, the Council may only adopt a measure if it has the express approval of the Parliament.

Associations of undertakings: these are usually trade associations sharing the same interests.

Block exemption: certain categories of agreement will not infringe EU competition law.

Cassis de Dijon principle: otherwise known as the **rule of reason**. Even where a measure does not discriminate against imports from other Member States, it may still be prohibited if it restricts trade. An exception is made if the measure was necessary to satisfy the mandatory requirements of that Member State with regard to fiscal supervision, protection of public health, the fairness of commercial transactions and the defence of the consumer.

Co-decision: a legislative procedure introduced by the Maastricht Treaty by which legislation is adopted jointly by the European Parliament and the Council.

Commissioners: those who have been nominated by the governments of the Member States to sit in the Commission.

Common customs tariff: a common tariff on goods entering the EU from non-Member States. Once third countries have paid the customs duties, which should be the same in all EU countries, their goods will be in **free circulation** in the Member States.

Common market (also referred to as the internal market or the single market): a form of economic integration established by the European Community.

Competition: the EC Treaty does not define competition but it does prohibit certain practices that would restrain trade and obstruct fair competition.

Concentration: here where a merger would create a large market share.

Concerted practice: practical co-operation between undertakings instead of the risks of competition.

Conferral: the principle of conferral states that the Union can only act within its competence as conferred upon it in the new European Constitution.

Consultation procedure: the Commission sends a draft of proposed legislation to Parliament for its consideration and advice.

Co-operation procedure: the Parliament may propose amendments to draft legislation submitted by the Council.

Council: it has the power to take general policy decisions and adopt secondary legislation together with the European Parliament. It approves the EU's budget together with the European Parliament.

Council of Ministers: this is the name for the Council under the new Constitution.

Court of Auditors: the Court is not a judicial court hearing cases, but a financial office which examines the revenue and expenditure of the EU.

Court of First Instance: created to assist the European Court of Justice. Its competence has increased as it now may hear all direct actions brought by private parties, but it does not have the competence to give preliminary rulings.

Court of Justice: under the new Constitution, the Court of Justice will be composed of the European Court of Justice, the High Court and certain specialised courts.

Customs duty: a charge levied on goods because they have crossed the frontier.

Dassonville formula: all trading rules that hinder trade within the EU are considered as measures having an effect equivalent to quantitative restrictions unless they fall within the 'rule of reason'.

Decisions: at present the term means binding on those to whom they are addressed.

Dependent right: this is granted to the family of a person with an independent right of residence. They may lose a dependent right to reside if the one who has the independent right gives up that right or the relationship ends.

Derogation: partial release from a law.

Direct applicability: a provision becomes operative in a Member State immediately without the need for the national legislature to pass implementing legislation to incorporate it into national law.

Direct effect: the EU legal order differs from international law in that it can create rights for citizens that are enforceable before national courts. Where there is **vertical direct effect** there is an obligation on an organ of state, with a corresponding right of individuals. **Horizontal direct effect** means that an individual may call upon an obligation owed by another individual.

Directives: in present EU law these are binding as to the result to be achieved. National authorities are responsible for transposing them into nation law.

Distinctly applicable: measures applicable only to imports.

Dominant position: the power to exclude effective competition. The greater the market share an undertaking has in the relevant market, the greater the likelihood of dominance. A dominant position is not in itself illegal, only the abuse of that position.

Economic and monetary union: this would mean the co-ordination of economic policies within the EU, in accordance with the principle of subsidiarity, and sharing a single monetary policy and a single exchange rate.

Enlargement: term used to describe the growth of the EU through the accession of new Member States.

European Commission: the European Commission initiates policy and proposals for legislation to be adopted by the Council. It implements agreed policies and acts as the guardian of the Treaties.

European Community: now forms an important pillar within the European Union and is governed by the EC Treaty. The European Community is the legal framework for Community policies relating to, amongst others, the common market, international trade, monetary policy, agriculture, the environment and energy. The term European Community will disappear once the Constitution has been accepted.

European Constitution: a European Convention on the future of Europe produced a draft of a Constitution for the European Union in 2003. The Constitution was signed in June 2004. However, it must still be accepted by the Member States. At the time of writing, it was unclear when, and if, that acceptance would take place.

European Council: a meeting of the heads of government of the Member States. It has no formal role in the legislative process but plays a part in deciding the future political direction. Under the new Constitution it will become part of the institutional framework.

European Court of Justice: this Court ensures that EU law is observed. It hears actions and provides preliminary rulings on preliminary references.

European decision: under the new Constitution this now refers to a non-legislative act, binding in its entirety on those to whom it is addressed.

European framework law: under the new Constitution, the old term 'directive' disappears and is replaced by the term European framework law. This is a legislative act binding as to the result to be achieved but allowing the national authorities to choose the form and means of its implementation.

European law: under the European Constitution this is a legislative act of general application, binding in its entirety and directly applicable in all Member States. The term European law replaces the old term 'regulation' used in the sense of a legislative act.

European Parliament: this Parliament is directly elected and participates in the legislative process. It also has several supervisory functions: the Commission is accountable to Parliament and, together with the Council, it exercises budgetary supervision.

European regulation: under the new Constitution this term is used to describe a non-legislative act of general application for the implementation of legislative acts and certain specific provisions.

European Union: the EU contains not only the European Community, but also two other pillars. These other pillars are foreign and security policy and co-operation in judicial and criminal matters. After the adoption of the new Constitution, reference will only be made to the European Union.

Family (of an EU worker): this includes spouse, children plus descendants if under twenty-one years, parents, grandparents and other ascendants if dependent on the worker.

Force majeur: an event outside the control of the parties to an agreement.

Free circulation: see **common customs tariff**.

Free movement of capital and payments: the basic principle is that there must be full freedom of capital movements and payments between Member States and between Member States and third countries.

Free movement of goods: the European Community established a common market, which could only be achieved by taking down any internal barriers to trade within the EC.

Free movement of workers: a worker in one Member State generally has the right to accept work in another Member State.

Freedom of establishment: this freedom is geared up to self-employed people or companies rather than 'workers'. The right of establishment depends upon the recognition of professional qualifications.

Freedom to provide services: the provision of services is often connected to the exercise of a profession and in this respect it is inseparable from the right of establishment.

General principles of EU law: general principles of law, originating inter alia from international law and the national systems of various Member States, are applied uniformly throughout the EU. Examples of such principles are **proportionality, legal certainty, procedural rights**, and the **principle of equality**.

Genuine tax: internal duties are applied to a certain category of products, regardless of the origin of the products.

Goods: ECJ case law has defined a good as being something of monetary value that can constitute the object of commercial transactions.

Harmonisation (or approximation): to bring the laws of the various Member States into line.

High Court: the new name for the Court of First Instance under the European Constitution.

Horizontal agreements: agreements between producers.

Independent right: an independent right of residence in the country in which an EU worker has accepted employment.

Indistinctly applicable: measures applicable to domestic and imported products alike.

Judge rapporteur: is asked to produce a preliminary report on a case. It is this preliminary report together with the views of the Advocate General that help the court to determine which issues have to be addressed.

Legal certainty: a general principle of EU law. Certainty is achieved by **non-retroactivity**: legislation is not expected to be applicable in the period before it became law. Law should also not frustrate the **legitimate expectations** of its citizens.

Merger: means that a company (or more than one) becomes a part of or merges with another company. The former company ceases to exist and the latter acquires all the assets, liabilities, franchises and power of that company. The European Commission may stop a merger if it would significantly impede competition within the EU.

Mutual recognition principle: it is presumed that goods that have been lawfully marketed in one Member State will already comply with the mandatory requirements of other Member States.

Opinions: are non-binding guidelines issued by the EU.

Override: with respect to the EU, the principle of supremacy means that EU law takes precedence over the national law of the Member States in areas covered by EU competence.

Pillar: in the context of the European Union, this term is used to denote the elements that make up the Union at present. The three pillars of the EU are: the EC, foreign and security policy, and co-operation in justice and criminal matters.

Preliminary reference: is a request by a national court of a Member State to the European Court of Justice to give a ruling on a question of interpretation and validity of EU law.

Preliminary ruling: is the answer given by the European Court of Justice concerning a question on the validity or interpretation of EU law.

Primary sources of EU law: consist of the founding treaties and their amendments.

Principle of equality: general principle of EU law that makes various types of discrimination illegal, for example sexual discrimination.

Principle of subsidiarity: the EU has only the right to deal with those matters that fall within the exclusive EU competence. Matters that are not covered by the EU competence remain the prerogative of the individual Member States.

Principle of supremacy: where there is EU competence, EU law cannot be overridden by national legal provisions regardless of whether these provisions were drawn up earlier or later than the EU law.

Procedural rights: principle of EU law. These rights cover the principles of the **right to be heard** and of **due process**.

Proportionality: a general principle of EU law stating that a public authority may not impose obligations on a citizen except to the extent to which they are strictly necessary or proportionate to the aim to be achieved.

Protection of human rights: principle of EU law in accordance with the European Convention on Human Rights.

Qualified majority: a weighted voting procedure where the vote of each Member State reflects the size of the population.

Quantitative restrictions: a national measure that places a physical/non-pecuniary restriction on the amount of goods that may enter or leave a state, for example a **quota**.

Real work: in the context of the free movement of workers it means that the work must be effective work and not work created to rehabilitate someone.

Recommendations: like opinions, recommendations are not binding but are only persuasive guidelines.

Regulations: at present this term refers to laws that are binding in their entirety and directly applicable in all Member States.

Residence permit: gives a person the legal right to live in a country other than the country of which he is a citizen.

Restrictive practices: those that prevent fair competition. Such practices would include any agreements that would prevent or distort competition within the common market.

Revoke: to annul, for example, to repeal a piece of legislation so that it is no longer in force.

Secondary sources of law: the major EC Treaties delegated the power to legislate to certain institutions. The law made by these institutions is classed as **secondary legislation**.

Severable contract: where a contract is treated as having several independent agreements. The failure of one of those agreements, for example because the clause is void, does not render the entire agreement inoperative.

Subsidiary institutions: in addition to the major EU institutions, there are a number of other important organisations, for example, the **European ombudsman**, the **Committee of Permanent Representatives** and the **Economic and Social Committee**.

Subsidies: here a subsidy is a payment by a Member State to producers or distributors. It is intended to reduce the prices paid by consumers in order to stimulate domestic production. This is usually prohibited.

Undertaking: this is a natural or legal person carrying on commercial or economic activity. It includes a company, partnership, sole trader and association.

Vertical agreements: agreements between a producer and distributors.

Worker: a person, who is a citizen of a Member State, in genuine and effective employment and performing services for an employer under his direction and control in return for remuneration.

European Union law terminology in context

1   INTRODUCTION

In all the other chapters of this book, the English legal terminology expresses English legal concepts and English legal institutions. The English terminology used to express European Union (EU) law, is not born of the English legal system. English legal terminology is used here to describe the legal concepts and institutions that have arisen from a supranational legal system: that of the European Union. These concepts and institutions are shared by all the Member States.

As of May 2004, the EU consists of twenty-five Member States. There are almost as many languages spoken within the EU as there are Member States. The number of official languages recognised by the EU has now gone up from eleven to twenty. Over the years, the number of translators working for the institutions of the EU has also grown considerably.

Students or practitioners who come from Member States may well be familiar with EU law as expressed in their own language. Problems may arise, however, if they have not studied EU law in English and circumstances dictate that they need to use English terminology to describe EU law. For example, the Dutch word for directive is 'richtlijn'. It is quite common to see this word wrongly translated into English as 'guideline', as this is the literal translation from the Dutch. An English lawyer would not immediately equate the word 'guideline' with 'directive' and a certain amount of muddle could ensue! This chapter on EU law has, therefore, been included to provide a brief overview of some of the most important English terminology used with respect to the EU. It is suggested that students who are unfamiliar with EU law may find it helpful first to consult a textbook on the subject in their own language, as the aim of this chapter is simply to provide the reader with a number of appropriate English labels.

Finally, it should also be pointed out that once the European Constitution is implemented, the structural changes laid down in that document will necessarily affect terminology. As at the time of writing there was no certainty as to when, or even if, the European Constitution would be accepted by the Member States, the terminology as it is at present has been set down together with an outline of some of the major changes in terminology that would arise upon the implementation of the current draft of the Constitution.

2   HISTORICAL BACKGROUND

The idea behind the setting up of a supranational organisation in post-Second World War Europe was to foster peaceful co-operation through economic activity. In 1952, the first of the so-called **European Communities** was established in the form of the European Coal and Steel Community (ECSC), under the Treaty of Paris 1951. The intention was to create a common market for coal and steel. Then in 1957 the European Atomic Energy Community Treaty came into force creating a specialist market for atomic energy (EURATOM). The European Economic Community (EEC) was created in 1957 by a separate Treaty of Rome (now usually referred to as the EC Treaty). The EEC was meant to achieve economic integration between the original six Member States by creating a **common market**.

The impetus behind the establishment of the EC institutions and law was the desire to regulate the rights and duties of Member States with respect to economic activity. However, the form that the European Economic Community took on was remarkable. The principle behind the Community was not just that Member States should act together, but that the Community would be a distinct legal entity. All Member States would be bound by Community law.

Since its inception, a number of changes have taken place within the European Community. Its membership has increased and so has its sphere of activity. Its name has been altered accordingly. Having begun life as the European Economic Community, the word 'Economic' was dropped and reference is now made simply to the **European Community**. In 1992, the Treaty on European Union (TEU), otherwise known as the Maastricht Treaty, created a **European Union** (EU). The aims of this EU are far wider than those of the original, largely economic, aims set down by the Treaty of Rome. The European Union consists of three main elements, or so-called **pillars**:

1   the European Community (including the ECSC and EURATOM);
2   foreign and security policy and
3   co-operation in judicial and criminal matters.

In 2002, a European Convention on the future of Europe was convened, motivated in part by the prospect of the future **enlargement** of the Union. It produced a draft of a Constitution for the European Union, which was presented to the Council Meeting in June 2003. The Constitution was signed in June 2004. However, at the time of writing, this Constitution has not yet been accepted by the Member States. Once it is accepted, the European Union will then not be formed by the three pillars, but will consist of one integrated Union.

Note 1: since the EU was set up in 1992, some confusion has arisen with respect to terminology. Should it be EC law or EU law? The European Community is only a part of the European Union. Some commentators argue that it is more correct to speak of European Community law rather than European Union law, as at present it is the EC that is legally regulated and the other two pillars are still subject to intergovernmental regulation. Not all commentators share this view and both descriptions can be found. However, once the **European Constitution** has been accepted, this debate will be resolved as the three pillar arrangement referred to above will be obsolete and the term European Community will no longer be used. It will then only be correct to speak of EU law. Looking ahead, reference will be made to EU law in this chapter. For the same reason, reference will also be made to EU institutions rather than EC institutions: in practice the EU already operates through the institutions originally set up for the European Community. The term 'EC' or 'Community' will sometimes be found below used in a historical context.

Note 2: as EU law and legal principles are binding on all Member States, certain concepts that are familiar to civil law jurisdictions, but less familiar to a common law jurisdiction, have crept into English law. For example, the EC Directive on Unfair Terms in Consumer Contracts, implemented into English law via a statutory instrument 'The Unfair Terms in Consumer Contracts Regulations 1994', brought the principle of good faith into the law on consumer contracts. Traditionally, the principle of good faith is not one recognised by the English common law of contract.

3   THE MAIN SOURCES OF EU LAW

3.1   Primary sources of law: the founding treaties

The EU is founded on particular treaties and the major treaties form a **primary** source of EU law. These treaties have been ratified by the national parliaments of the Member States, as have the amendments to the treaties. It is useful to note the following treaties and the amendments to these treaties:

- **ECSC Treaty** (established by the Treaty of Paris 1951): to create a common market for coal and steel products;
- **EURATOM Treaty** (established by the Treaty of Rome 1957): to create a specialist market for atomic energy;
- **EC Treaty** (established by a separate Treaty of Rome 1957): to set up the European Economic Community and create a common market;
- **Merger Treaty** (1965): all three communities now have the same institutions;
- **Single European Act** (1986): the first major amendment to the EC Treaty. It included the creation of an internal market programme, greater powers for the European Parliament and the creation of the Court of First Instance;
- **Treaty on European Union** (TEU, also known as the Treaty of Maastricht 1992): another amendment to the EC Treaty, creating a European Union with three pillars: the European Community (containing the three communities of ECSC, EURATOM and EC), common foreign and security policy, and co-operation in justice and criminal matters;
- **Treaty of Amsterdam** (1997): amended the TEU.

The main foundations of EU law are to be found in the Treaty of Rome 1957, as amended by the Single European Act 1986, and the Treaty of European Union 1992. In practice, these founding treaties take priority over subsidiary treaties and any secondary legislation.

3.2   Secondary sources: secondary legislation

The creation of the EC demanded a certain transfer of sovereignty or powers from the Member States to the institutions of the Community. The major EC Treaties gave these institutions the power to legislate in certain areas. Today, areas within the competence of EU lawgiving include company law, consumer protection, data protection, environmental protection, intellectual property rights and employment law. This type of legislation is made under the authority of the treaties and is therefore to be regarded as **secondary legislation**.

However, the EU institutions only have the power to legislate on matters within EU competence, although what falls within that competence has increased considerably over the years. Where the EU does have the competence to legislate, the legality of such legislative measures may not be contended by the courts of the individual Member States. Only the European Court of Justice has the power to declare EU measures invalid, but not the national courts. Certain areas of law remain outside the legal competence of the EU, for example most criminal law, family law and the law of inheritance.

At present, there are three types of legally **binding** acts that may be classed as EU legislation:

1   regulations;
2   directives; and
3   decisions.

There are also two measures that are not classed as legislation because they are not binding, although they do have **persuasive** authority:

1   recommendations; and
2   opinions.

3.2.1 Regulations

Regulations set out general rules that are applicable throughout the EU. They are binding in their entirety and **directly applicable** in all Member States. There is no need for further national legislation for implementation purposes. Individual citizens of the Member States have the right to call upon the rules laid down in regulations in lawsuits brought in their own national courts.

3.2.2 Directives

Directives are binding as to the result to be achieved. A directive lays down an objective and then leaves it to the individual Member State to decide how best to achieve it. The choice of form and the method of transposing the objectives into national law are left to the national authorities. Every directive specifies a time limit by which time the Member States should have achieved the required result. Directives do allow a certain measure of flexibility in the way in which the objectives are formulated. Nonetheless, they are an important means for achieving harmonisation of law between the Member States. For example, as a result of directives, consumer protection will be broadly similar in all Member States.

    With respect to directives, some confusion in terminology has arisen. The very essence of a directive is that the goal still has to be implemented in national legislation. Logically therefore, it can be argued that a directive is not directly applicable (see below).

3.2.3 Decisions

Decisions are binding in their entirety on those to whom they are addressed. Decisions may be addressed to individual Member States, corporations or private individuals. Decisions are commonly used where it has been concluded that an undertaking is acting contrary to EU competition policy.

3.2.4 Non-binding measures

Recommendations and **opinions** are usually addressed to Member States, setting out a view or guidelines on a particular issue. They have no binding force and are of **persuasive authority** only. The European Court of Justice has stated, however, that it expects national judges to take recommendations into account when reaching their decisions.

3.3   General principles of EU law

Again, there is some disagreement as to what is covered by the term **general principles of EU law**. Consensus has been reached, however, that the term does cover principles derived from international law, from the national legal systems of the Member States and from decisions made in the European Court of Justice.

    The European Court of Justice has adopted general principles of EU law both from other treaties, for example the European Convention on Human Rights, and from the national laws of Member States. Principles derived from national systems need not be common to every Member State. For example, the principle of proportionality, which is found in the EC Treaty and German law, is unknown in English law. That principle then becomes a principle of EU law, which is applicable in all Member States. These principles are an important source of EU law, as they provide a useful tool for interpretation. They also allow EU law to be challenged on the basis that it is contrary to a general principle of EU law. Examples of such principles are proportionality, legal certainty, procedural rights, and the principle of equality.

3.3.1 Proportionality

Proportionality is a principle borrowed from German law. A public authority may not impose obligations on a citizen except to the extent to which they are strictly necessary or proportionate to the aim that is to be achieved.

3.3.2 Legal certainty

This principle of **legal certainty** covers two aspects: **retroactivity** and **legitimate expectations**. With respect to retroactivity, legislation is interpreted with the presumption that it is not expected to have a retroactive effect. It may also not be altered once adopted. The idea of legitimate expectations is one common in the civil law tradition. EU measures should not frustrate the valid expectations of those concerned, unless there is a matter of public interest at stake.

3.3.3 Procedural rights

These rights are familiar to many national legal systems and well known in English law. They reflect the principles of the right to be heard and of due process. **Due process** refers to the regular course of the law through the courts, the decision having been derived at honestly after a proper hearing. The **right to be heard** refers to giving the accused person notice of what he is accused and an opportunity to be heard.

3.3.4 Principle of equality

The EC Treaty refers to the **principle of equality**. It prohibits discrimination on the grounds of nationality and between employees on the grounds of sex and other grounds. For instance, it requires that men and women should receive equal pay for equal work.

Directives on sex discrimination have added to the basics laid down in the Treaty. For example, men and women must receive equal treatment in access to employment, vocational training and promotion. There must also be equal treatment in occupational and social security schemes. Member States are under an obligation to provide effective remedies where there has been a breach of the equal treatment principle.

3.3.5 Protection of human rights

Every Member State has signed the European Convention on Human Rights. Furthermore, such rights must be protected and be treated as part of EU law.

3.4 Decisions of the European Court of Justice

Over the years, a comprehensive body of case law has been built up by the **European Court of Justice** (ECJ) which, in addition to EU legislation, forms an important source of EU law. The Court has the right to hear actions brought against Member States and EU institutions. It may also act as an employment tribunal hearing cases between the EU and its employees.

It is the task of the ECJ to interpret and to ensure the proper application of EU law. Where a national court of a Member State is unsure of the correct interpretation or application of EU law, it may draft a **preliminary reference**, which is then reviewed by the ECJ. Having considered the matter, the Court then gives a **preliminary ruling** on the question of interpretation and validity of the EU law at issue. Any 'court or tribunal' may request a preliminary ruling. A preliminary ruling is binding on the national court that referred the question for consideration. They may be cited as precedents in all jurisdictions.

4 THE RELATIONSHIP BETWEEN EU LAW AND NATIONAL LAW

The relationship between EU law and that of the individual states is characterised in part by two principles: the **principle of supremacy** and the **principle of subsidiarity**. The principle of supremacy reflects the primacy of EU law. The principle of subsidiarity recognises that the power to deal with certain matters may be reserved to the individual Member States and is outside the competence of the EU. A parallel can be drawn here between the relationship of the European Union with the Member States and that between the federal and state competence in the USA.

Another important characteristic of the relationship between EU law and national law is that of **direct applicability** and **direct effect**. Usually international treaties are agreements between governments and do not create rights for citizens enforceable before national courts. The EU legal order differs from international law in this respect. If an EU provision is directly applicable and clearly gives rights to individuals or it is considered by the ECJ to have direct effect, that provision may be relied upon by an individual because it creates legally enforceable rights in the Member State.

4.1 Principle of supremacy

Where there is a conflict between EU law and national law, or national constitutions, in an area of law in which the EU has competence, EU law **overrides** national law. EU law may not be overridden by domestic legal provisions, regardless of whether those provisions came earlier or later than the EU law. Nor may Member States plead **force majeure** – that they tried to implement EU law but were prevented from doing so by the legislature. EU law overrides statutes and judicial precedent. Conflicting national legislation must simply be **revoked**.

4.2   Principle of subsidiarity

The EC Treaty states that the Community will act within the limits of the power conferred on it by the Treaty. In areas which do not fall within its exclusive competence, the Community shall take action, in accordance with the **principle of subsidiarity**, only if the proposed action cannot be achieved by the Member States individually and, therefore, it can better be achieved by the Community. Any action by the Community should not go beyond what is necessary to achieve the objectives of the Treaty.

4.3   Direct applicability

In the case of **direct applicability**, a provision becomes operative in a Member State immediately and there is no need for the national legislature to pass implementing legislation to incorporate it into national law. Directly applicable EU law prevails in any conflict with national measures. Not only the Member States but also individuals may be able to derive rights from the provisions, these rights being enforceable in the national courts of the Member States.

4.4   Direct effect

The two terms, **direct applicability** and **direct effect**, are often confused and even the courts tend to use them interchangeably these days. However, direct effect and direct applicability do not mean exactly the same thing. As seen in section 4.3, direct applicability means that the provisions are incorporated automatically into the law of the Member States. This does not mean, however, that they automatically have direct effect. Whether they have direct effect will depend upon the interpretation of the provisions.

The principle of direct effect was created by the ECJ and follows from the principle of the supremacy of EU law. Provisions in treaties, regulations, directives and decisions may have direct effect. That means that individual rights are created which must be upheld by the national courts of the Member States. For EU law to have direct effect, certain conditions must be satisfied.

4.4.1 Vertical and horizontal direct effect

Vertical direct effect means that an obligation is imposed on national governments, with a corresponding right for individuals. An individual may rely upon this obligation before a national court against the state. In the case of the treaties and regulations there may also be **horizontal direct effect**. This means that a private individual can call upon an obligation arising from a provision of EU law against another private individual before the national court. These obligations may be imposed on individuals in the Member State as well as create rights for individuals in the Member State.

4.4.2 Direct effect of Treaty provisions

The European Court of Justice established in the landmark case of Van Gend en Loos v Nederlandse Administratie der Belastingen (1963) that articles in a treaty, which impose on Member States an obligation to abstain from doing something, have direct effect. In Van Gend en Loos a private firm sought to invoke community law against the Dutch customs authorities in proceedings before a Dutch tribunal. The Dutch government argued that the infringement of a treaty did not give a right to an individual to bring an action. It argued that actions could only be brought against the government of a Member State by another Member State or by the Commission. The ECJ held that a new legal order had been created which created rights for individuals.

However, not all treaty provisions are directly effective. It is a matter for interpretation by the court. There are certain criteria that must now be met if a provision is to have direct effect. The provisions must:

* be clear and unambiguous;
* be unconditional; and
* not require further action by the EU or a national authority.

4.4.3 Direct effect of regulations

A regulation is directly applicable. The enforcement of its provisions is immediate, as no national action is required to bring it into effect. This means that national courts must apply a regulation when it clearly gives rights to individuals or imposes obligations on individuals. The ECJ has stated that, by reason of their nature and function, regulations have direct effect. Nonetheless, if a regulation is considered by the ECJ to be too vague as to give individuals enforceable rights, it may not have direct effect, for example, where it requires further legislation.

4.4.4 Direct effect of directives

In contrast to regulations, directives are not directly applicable as they require national legislation. A directive may have direct effect provided it is sufficiently clear, unconditional and precise. The principle that a state organisation (which would include a public sector organisation, such as a local authority) should not be able to take advantage of the failure of a national government to implement a directive is the reason why a directive can have direct effect where its terms are clear and precise. Case law indicates that a directive only has vertical direct effect but not horizontal direct effect.

4.5 Changes in terminology upon the implementation of the European Constitution

The European Constitution, as signed in 2004, established the Union as a legal personality. In title III the Union competences are laid down. The limits to EU competence are governed by the principles of **conferral**, **subsidiarity** and **proportionality**. The principle of conferral simply states that the Union can only act within its competence as conferred upon it in the Constitution. Competences not conferred upon the Union in the Constitution remain with the Member States. The meaning of the other two principles has been dealt with above.

The terminology with respect to the legal acts of the Union is changed by the Constitution. A **European law** is a legislative act of general application, binding in its entirety and directly applicable in all Member States. The term European law replaces the old term 'regulation' used in the sense of a legislative act. The old term 'directive' disappears and is replaced by **European framework law**, which is a legislative act binding as to the result to be achieved but allowing the national authorities to choose the form and means of its implementation.

Under the European Constitution, several types of non-legislative acts are specified. The term **European regulation** is used to describe a non-legislative act of general application for the implementation of legislative acts and certain specific provisions. It may be binding in its entirety and directly applicable or binding as to the result to be achieved. It is a delegated regulation where the Commission has been given the power to supplement or amend non-essential elements of European law or European framework law. Similarly, the term **European decision** now refers to a non-legislative act, binding in its entirety on those to whom it is addressed. The terms **recommendations** and **opinions** remain and have retained their former meaning as guidelines without binding force.

5 EUROPEAN UNION INSTITUTIONS

These institutions originated as institutions of the European Community. Once the European Constitution is implemented, reference will be made to EU institutions but in practice the EU already operates through these institutions. The main institutions of the EU were created by the EC Treaty. Since their inception, the competence of these institutions has evolved and, in some cases, even their names have changed. For example, the European Parliament was initially called the Assembly. At present there are five major institutions: the European Commission, the Council, the European Parliament, the European Court of Justice and the Court of Auditors. A number of subsidiary institutions now also play a significant role within the EU.

5.1   The European Commission

The **commissioners** who sit in the Commission are nominated by the governments of the Member States. The TEU has made the Commission responsible to the European Parliament and the appointment of the commissioners is subject to the approval of that body. The commissioners must act independently, not taking instructions from their national governments, as the interests of the EU as a whole must always be their first priority.

The Commission has three major functions. It acts as the executive of the EU, as it is responsible for the implementation of the policies decided by the Council and the European Parliament. The Commission also initiates EU legislation, in the form of proposals to the Council. Finally, the Commission acts as the so-called guardian of the treaties, which means it must ensure the compliance of Member States with the obligations laid down in EU law. As the guardian, it also has the power to fine organisations and individuals who act in breach of EU competition law.

5.2   The Council

The Council's membership consists of one member from each of the Member States, although that member may vary depending on the issue being discussed. When general matters are discussed the representative attending is the foreign minister; if the main business of the meeting is specific, for example agriculture, then agricultural ministers will attend. At present, the presidency of the Council also rotates. Although subject to certain important exceptions, voting is usually by **qualified majority** (with larger countries having more votes than smaller ones).

The Council is the main decision-making institution of the EU, being an important legislative body. It largely exercises its legislative power in co-decision with the European Parliament. It may legislate on the basis of a Commission proposal.

Note 1: the Council should not be confused with the Council of Europe. The Council of Europe is not an institution of the European Union. It is an intergovernmental organisation aiming to achieve greater unity between its forty-five Member States with respect, in particular, to human rights.

Note 2: it should also not be confused with the European Council, which is a meeting of the heads of government of the Member States (see section 5.7).

5.3   European Parliament

The members of the European Parliament (MEPs) are directly elected by the citizens of the Member States from national political parties. The members tend to reflect the ideologies of those political parties, for example Socialist or Christian Democrat, rather than forming national blocks. Various measures have increased the powers of the European Parliament. Its competence now includes:

- a supervisory function: the Commission is accountable to the Parliament. Parliament may censure the Commission and even has the right to dismiss the Commission as a whole;
- **consultation procedure**: the Commission sends a draft of proposed legislation to Parliament for its consideration and advice;
- **co-operation procedure**: the Parliament may propose amendments to draft legislation submitted by the Council;
- **co-decision**: this is a joint decision process by the Parliament and the Council. Both Parliament and the Council must accept the legislation in order for it to go through;
- **assent procedure**: for certain matters, usually involving questions of a more constitutional nature, the Council may only adopt a measure if it has the express approval of the Parliament;
- budgetary supervision: Parliament exercises joint control over the budget with the Council, although the Council has the final say on 'compulsory expenditure'.

5.4   Court of Auditors

Although it is referred to as a 'court', the **Court of Auditors** is not a court in the sense of a court of law. The duty of this Court is to examine the revenue and expenditure of the EU. It must draw up an annual report, which is presented to the other EU institutions.

5.5   European Court of Justice

The function of the European Court of Justice (ECJ) is to ensure that EU law is observed. With respect to jurisdiction, the Court can hear actions against Member States and EU institutions. It can give **preliminary rulings** on references from any national court or tribunal that exercises a judicial function concerning questions of interpretation of the treaties and secondary legislation as well as questions concerning the validity of secondary legislation. Its competence also includes enforcement proceedings brought either by the Commission or a Member State concerning a failure to fulfil EU obligations, and it hears appeals from the Court of First Instance on points of law.

5.5.1 Personnel

The ECJ at present consists of twenty-five judges, with each Member State providing one. The judges elect a President of the Court. The Court is also assisted by Advocates General. The post of **Advocate General** is derived from the French legal system and has no equivalent in the English legal system. An Advocate General is not of inferior status to that of the judges themselves. The task of the Advocate General is to give reasoned submissions on cases brought before the Court as to the application of EU law. He hears and reads all the evidence, as a judge would, but he gives his opinion to the court as to what the judgment should be before the judges themselves reach their decision. His opinion is, however, not binding on the judges.

5.5.2 Procedures

The procedures of the ECJ are more in line with those of the civil law system than of the common law system. Whereas oral submissions are still important in a common law hearing, even if no jury is present, in the civil law system the emphasis is on written submissions and that tradition is the one followed in the ECJ. So too is the role of the judge in the ECJ an inquisitorial one rather than the impartial referee known to the common law courts. The four major stages in the procedure of the ECJ reflect its familiarity with civil law system procedures.

1   **Pleadings**: the written proceedings are commenced by the applicant filing an application, with the defendant serving a defence in reply to the application and it is possible for the applicant to serve a reply to the defence.
2   **Preparatory inquiry**: the case is first assigned to one of the judges to act as 'rapporteur'. The **judge rapporteur** must then produce a preliminary report. An Advocate General is also assigned to the case. The preliminary report together with the views of the Advocate General help the Court to determine the issues to be addressed.
3   **Court proceedings**: the oral proceedings are held in open court. The case may be heard by the full court (plenary hearing), which is usual where the case is between Member States or EU institutions. The Advocate General delivers his opinion to the Court. The Advocate General's opinion is not binding on the judges.
4   **Judgment**: unlike senior courts in England, where each judge gives his opinion, even if that opinion is not in agreement with the majority, only one judgment is given in the European Court of Justice. There is no **dissenting judgment** (see chapter 1 for this term). However, where the opinion of the Advocate General has not been followed, it acts as a sort of dissenting judgment.

5.6   Court of First Instance

This Court became operational in 1989 to help the European Court of Justice with its increasing workload. It now has the competence to hear all direct actions brought by private parties against EU institutions and EU personnel cases, but it does not have the competence to hear references for preliminary rulings. Nor may it hear cases brought by Member States or EU institutions. Appeals can be made on points of law only to the ECJ.

5.7 Subsidiary institutions

The above-mentioned institutions are the most important organisations in the EU. There are, however, a number of subsidiary institutions. Worth noting here are the following:

- **European ombudsman**: the ombudsman may hear complaints from any citizen of the Union about EU institutions;
- **Committee of Permanent Representatives**: this committee consists of diplomats who liaise with the various government ministries as a preparation for the Council;
- **Economic and Social Committee**: this is an advisory committee. Its opinions are not binding but are persuasive;
- **European Council**: this council is a meeting of the heads of government of the Member States, and should not be confused with the Council. Although it has no formal role in the legislative process of the EU, it does play a part in deciding the future political direction.

5.8 Institutional changes upon the implementation of the European Constitution

The institutional framework under the European Constitution will comprise:
- the European Parliament;
- the European Council;
- the Council of Ministers;
- the European Commission; and
- the Court of Justice.

The European Parliament will act jointly with the Council of Ministers to enact legislation and supervise the budget, as well as having a general political control function. The European Council continues in its function in defining the Union's political direction and priorities; it remains a body without legislative functions. The **Council of Ministers** (the former Council) is responsible for carrying out policy-making and coordination as well as its legislative function together with the Parliament. The European Commission retains its executive functions and Union legislative acts can, in general, only be adopted on the basis of a Commission proposal. The **Court of Justice** will include the European Court of Justice, the **High Court** (which is the old Court of First Instance) and specialised courts. It will rule on actions brought by Member States, institutions and individuals, give preliminary rulings and ensure respect for the law in the interpretation and application of the Constitution. In this new set-up, the Court of Auditors becomes a subsidiary body.

6   THE COMMON MARKET

The Treaty of Rome laid down the framework for the establishment of a **common market**, also referred to as the internal market or single market. Essential to that common market is the series of freedoms, which form the basis of the Community. These comprise the free movement of goods, the free movement of workers, the freedom of establishment and the freedom to provide services and the free movement of capital. EU competition policy helps to protect the functioning of the common market.

6.1   Free movement of goods

Note: the legal meaning of the word **goods** is open to some interpretation. With respect to EU law, the word was not defined in the EC Treaty. However, the ECJ has defined 'goods' as being anything that can have a monetary value and can constitute the object of commercial transactions.

The primary aim in setting up the EC was to achieve economic integration. That could not be achieved, however, without the **free movement of goods**. All internal barriers to trade within the Community had to be broken down and a common commercial front to the rest of the world had to be maintained. The internal barriers to trade were removed by the abolition of customs duties between Member States, establishing provisions with respect to national taxes and by addressing the problem of quantitative restrictions. The common commercial front resulted from the application of a common customs tariff.

Within the European Union, there must be no discrimination between exports and imports as between the Member States. This required the abolition of customs duties, or charges having an equivalent effect, between Member States. **Customs duties** are charges levied on goods by reason of the fact they have crossed a border. Nor are national taxes allowed if they would in effect act as a customs duty. **Genuine taxes**, nonetheless, fall outside the scope of this prohibition. The distinction between a genuine tax and a charge having an equivalent effect to a customs duty is therefore an important one. A genuine tax is where internal duties are applied systematically to all products falling within a certain category of products, in accordance with objective criteria. The origin of the product is irrelevant. Imports can be subject to internal taxation, established by the Member States, provided the system does not discriminate between imports and domestic products.

The abolition of customs duties and the like does not, in itself, guarantee the free movement of goods within the common market. Free movement would be hindered if the governments of the Member States choose to impose quantitative restrictions. **Quantitative restrictions** have been defined by the ECJ as measures amounting to a total or partial restraint on imports, exports or goods in transit. An example of such a restriction is imposing a **quota**, which places a restraint on the value of goods or the amount of goods that may enter or leave that Member State. Not only does the EC Treaty prohibit quantitative restrictions, it also prohibits **measures equivalent to quantitative restrictions**. A definition of measures that amount to quantitative restrictions was laid down by the ECJ in the Dassonville case 1974. Since then this definition is referred to as the **Dassonville formula**. The Dassonville formula states that:

> "All trading rules enacted by Member States which are capable of hindering, directly or indirectly, actually or potentially, intra Community trade are to be considered as measures having effect equivalent to quantitative restrictions."

Measures that are applicable only to imports are called **distinctly applicable**. (If the measure is distinctly applicable it will normally breach Article 28 of the EC Treaty but it may be justified under Article 30.) Measures that are applicable to domestic and imported products alike are called **indistinctly applicable**. Even if a measure is indistinctly applicable, it may still have the effect of restricting imports. If that is the case, then under the so-called **Cassis de Dijon principle**, also known as the **rule of reason** principle, the measure could be void as contrary to the prohibition laid down in Article 28. The term 'Cassis de Dijon principle' comes from the case brought by the German importers of a liqueur called Cassis de Dijon. German law laid down a minimum alcohol level for cassis. German cassis complied with that minimum level, but French cassis did not. Although the German measure was indistinctly applicable, it effectively banned French cassis from the German market.

The ECJ concluded that certain restrictions on trade, caused by differences in national law between the Member States regarding the marketing of a particular product, must be accepted in so far as those provisions may be regarded as necessary in order to satisfy mandatory requirements relating in particular to fiscal supervision, the protection of public health, the fairness of commercial transactions and the defence of the consumer. In other words, if the government in question could show that the measure fell within the rule of reason. In the Cassis case, the ECJ found German law in breach of Article 28, as the measure was neither necessary for the interests of public health, nor for the fairness of commercial transactions, nor for the defence of the consumer.

The Cassis de Dijon principle has been further refined. There is now also a presumption, which may be rebutted by evidence, that goods that have been lawfully marketed in another Member State will comply with the mandatory requirements of the importing state. This is referred to as the **mutual recognition principle**. It needs to be laid down in all national legislation.

There are exceptions to the principle of free movement. Article 30 EC Treaty lays down the main grounds for **derogation**. Restriction on imports and exports or goods in transit can be justified on the grounds of public morality, policy and security; the protection of public health and the life of humans, animals or plants; the protection of national treasures; and the protection of industrial and commercial property (which includes patents, trademarks and copyright).

Finally, a **common customs tariff** applies to all products imported from outside the European Union. However, once these third countries have paid the customs duties, which should be the same in all EU lands, such goods will be in **free circulation** in the Member States.

6.2 Free movement of workers

The free movement of workers is provided for in the EC Treaty, with the intention of creating a 'common market in manpower'. A worker from one Member State has the right to accept work in another Member State. A right to a **residence permit** is conditional on finding employment, but this right is not lost if the worker is involuntarily unemployed. The right to reside in that state exists for the purposes of employment, but a worker may have his residence permit extended beyond the period of employment. The members of a worker's family also have the right of residence. **Independent rights** are available to the worker; **dependent rights** are granted to the family of a person with an independent right. **Family** is understood to mean the spouse, children plus descendants if under twenty-one years of age, parents, grandparents and other ascendants if dependent on the worker.

The term **worker** is not defined in the Treaty itself. The ECJ has stated that the term worker in EU law must not be given an interpretation that is determined by any definition in the national law of the Member States. From EU legislation and case law, it may be concluded that the term 'worker' in EU law simply means an employed person, irrespective of whether he performs managerial or manual functions. The ECJ has described the essential characteristics of a worker to be that he is performing services for an employer under his direction and control in return for remuneration during a certain period of time. Nonetheless, in order to qualify as a worker, certain conditions apply. A worker must be in effective employment, in other words, doing **real work**, although he may be a trainee. Real work is not a nominal job such as one created for someone's rehabilitation. An example of a nominal job is the 'social employment' created by Dutch legislation, which was not considered to be genuine work as the work was specially created to fit the applicant's capacity, as opposed to him being selected to do a particular job.

There must be no discrimination between workers from different Member States. They are entitled to the same social and tax advantages as a national worker. This applies only to those in employment, not to those who migrate and are looking for work. All workers must have the same access to vocational training and retraining, the same rights with respect to trade union membership and the right to equal treatment concerning housing.

There are certain exceptions to the free movement of workers on the grounds of public policy, public security or public health. There are also public service exemptions, which apply only to the exercise of official authority, such as employees who may be seen to be safeguarding the general interests of the state. It should also be pointed out that most of the older Member States have put limits on the free movement of workers coming from the new Member States that joined in May 2004.

6.3   Freedom of establishment and the freedom to provide services

These freedoms are relevant to carrying out a business or profession in another Member State. The **right of establishment** gives both individuals and **legal persons** (such as companies, see chapter 6) the right to set up a business in a Member State other than their own. The freedom to provide services, and to receive them, similarly gives nationals from a Member State the right to provide services in a different Member State. **Services** means 'services for remuneration, in particular activities of an industrial and commercial character, craftsmanship and exercise of a profession'.

Just as the term 'worker' is not defined, neither is the group of persons entitled to the right of establishment and freedom to provide services. It is clear from the EC Treaty that companies and firms are to be treated in the same way as natural persons. There should also be no restriction on nationals of a Member State setting up agencies, branches or subsidiaries in another Member State. Whereas 'workers' are employees, these freedoms are more geared up to the self-employed.

One idea behind granting this right was to make it easier for a person practicing a profession in one Member State to practice that profession in another Member State. For example, if someone has trained as a solicitor in England and is fully qualified to practice law as a solicitor in that Member State, then he should have the right to practice law in any other Member State.

At present, it cannot be said that all professional qualifications obtained in Member States are recognised throughout the EU. Some Member States have shown a reluctance to accept the professional qualifications of those qualified elsewhere. This has led to the need for a **harmonisation** policy (also known as approximation) to make sure that the national law of a Member State accepts the qualifications obtained for a professional status in a different Member State.

6.4   The free movement of capital

In its original version, the EC Treaty did not impose formal requirements for the liberalisation of capital markets. The Treaty was later amended to introduce new arrangements for capital movements: the basic principle is that there must be full freedom of capital movements and payments between Member States and between Member States and third countries. All restrictions on the movement of capital and payments between Member States are thus prohibited. Certain existing restrictions may be maintained with respect to movements of capital between Member States and third countries. The liberalisation of capital markets and the introduction of a single currency, the euro, are stages in the implementation of an **economic and monetary union**.

Note: not all Member States have switched over to the euro, for example, the United Kingdom still uses the pound sterling.

7   COMPETITION LAW

Note 1: in the USA the term used for competition law is **antitrust law**.

Note 2: EU competition law regulations may well affect **undertakings**, such as companies, outside the European Union. EU competition law will apply to under-takings established outside the Union if their trading activities will affect trade between Member States. Companies outside the Union will also be directly affected if they have a **subsidiary** in the EU and the **parent company** exercises control (for an explanation of this terminology, see chapter 6 on company law).

The aim of the EC Treaty was to create fair competition, efficiency, consumer protection and integration within the European Community. This required the dismantling of various trade barriers. Restrictions on trade between the Member States, such as customs duties, quantitative restrictions and state **subsidies** to protect domestic industries, had to go. However, any such attempt to abolish these trade barriers would be undermined if commercial organisations could replace former governmental trading constraints with restrictions of their own creation. A coherent policy on competition was, therefore, vital not only to ensure fair competition between traders but also to protect consumers against non-competitive trading agreements and monopolies fixing prices.

The EC Treaty itself does not define **competition**. It does, however, refer to certain measures that interfere with fair competition. Measures that would hinder fair competition are, therefore, prohibited, subject to exemptions granted by the Commission. EU law has laid down regulations with respect to certain fundamental aspects of competition policy. Some of the most important of these regulations are laid down in two articles, in particular: Articles 81 and 82. These articles cover **restrictive practices** (Article 81) and the prevention of the **abuse of a dominant position** (Article 82). Specific attention is now also paid to **merger** control (1990 Merger Regulation). Article 81 and Article 82 are both intended to secure fair competition by preventing improper restraints on trade. It is not the intention of these two articles to prevent the creation of economic power positions, but to restrain any abuse of economic power.

7.1   Article 81: restrictive practices

The main purpose of this article is to prohibit agreements, whether **horizontal** or **vertical**, that would restrict, prevent or distort competition within the common market. Such agreements will automatically be void. Article 81 prohibits all agreements between **undertakings**, decisions by **associations of undertakings**, and **concerted practices** that will affect trading between the Member States, where the object or the effect is the distortion of competition within the common market.

The term **agreement** is not defined but its application seems to be a general one, covering even informal arrangements, such as a so-called 'gentleman's agreement'. In particular, those agreements that fix prices, limit production and disadvantage certain trading parties, are prohibited by this article. An **undertaking** is also not defined, but from case law it would seem it is also used in a general sense to mean any legal or natural person involved in commercial activity. **Associations of undertakings** are usually trade associations. **Concerted practices** have been defined by the ECJ as a form of co-operation between undertakings where there is no formal agreement to work together but practical co-operation has replaced the risks of competition.

These agreements and practices must, at least potentially, *affect* trade between the Member States. The ECJ stated that they must have an influence, whether direct or indirect, actual or potential, on the pattern of trade between Member States. It may sometimes be obvious that the object of the agreement or practice was to distort competition, but even where it cannot be shown that that was the object of the agreement, it may still be prohibited if that is the *effect* of the agreement.

Exemptions may be granted where the agreement, decision or concerted practice contributes to improving the production or distribution of goods or promoting technical or economic progress, while not acting unfairly to the detriment of the consumer. **Block exemptions** have also been issued, meaning that certain categories of agreement will be covered by an exemption and will not constitute an infringement. For example, it is permissible to have a clause in a distribution agreement restricting the right of a party to search for business outside that party's own territory.

Case law also indicates that only the clauses in the agreement that are prohibited by Article 81 will be void and not the whole agreement if the prohibited clauses can be **severed** from the remaining terms of the agreement. There is at present no general principle of severance.

7.2 Article 82: abuse of a dominant position

The aim of this article is to prevent an undertaking that has a commanding position in the market from abusing that position. Any such **abuse** will be prohibited as being incompatible with the common market insofar as it may affect trade between Member States. Again, that abuse may result from agreements to fix prices, limit production and disadvantage certain trading parties.

The first requirement is a **dominant position**. This is not defined in the article itself, but the ECJ has on various occasions attempted to define what is meant by a dominant position. It may be concluded from their determinations that the power to prevent or exclude effective competition in the relevant market would be an important criterion in determining whether an undertaking enjoyed a dominant position. Whether there is a dominant position in the relevant market would be a question of fact in each individual case. It should be noted that a dominant position is in itself not prohibited. It is the abuse of that dominant position that is prohibited.

There is, however, no definition of **abuse** set down in Article 82. Only particular instances of abuse are listed. The type of **anti-competitive abuses** that would fall under the article include unfair pricing, limiting production, discrimination in contractual obligations and imposing ancillary obligations.

- The imposition of **unfair pricing**: an unfair price is one that is not related to the economic value of the product. This may be in the form of a too high price or a too low price. A price is excessive where it is much too high to reflect the value of the product. The term **predatory pricing** is often used to describe the practice of pricing goods too low in order to drive out competitors. **Discriminatory prices** arise where different customers are charged different prices for the same product.
- **Limiting production**: the available markets or technical development may be restricted to the detriment of consumers, for example by exclusivity agreements (an exclusive licence grants the right to market a product to only one seller).
- **Unfair contract terms**: for example, the seller will not enter into the contract unless the purchaser agrees to buy the product only from the seller, which is the dominant undertaking, and not from someone else. **Fidelity rebates** is a practice to encourage purchasers to buy all or a very large part of the necessary supplies from the dominant undertaking otherwise they will not receive a discount. **Tying** applies where a condition of entering into a contract is that supplementary obligations are entered into as well.
- **Refusal to supply**: it may also be the case that the dominant undertaking will refuse to supply another undertaking with the intention of driving it out of business.

Note: a **merger** can in itself form an abuse of a dominant position. Merging undertakings may create a **concentration** within the common market that would have a detrimental effect on competition. For this reason, mergers with a potential impact on the EU are subject to the control of the European Commission.

European Union law case discussions

1   Drop BV is a Dutch company specialised in producing salty black liquorice sweets. Drop BV is a well-known brand in the Netherlands with a considerable turnover. It wishes to break into the United Kingdom sweet market and export the salty liquorices to the UK. However, the UK has laid down stringent rules concerning the level of salt in products. These rules were drawn up in response to concerns about the health of its citizens. The UK rules would mean that the salty liquorice would be prohibited in the UK. Drop BV contends that the rules are against EU law because the company is allowed to market the salty liquorices in the Netherlands. Advise Drop BV.

2   Mrs. Duke is 59 and is a nurse working for the London Health Authority. She is told that she has to retire at age 60. Mrs. Duke does not want to retire. She is particularly annoyed that the male nurses working for the London Health Authority do not have to retire until age 65. Her friend, Mrs. Gamble, is also aged 59 and is working as a nurse for a small private company called Health Care Ltd. Just like the London Health Authority, Health Care Ltd has a policy that women have to retire at 60 but that men can stay on to age 65.

- Both ladies invoke EU law to help them gain equality with the men. Will they succeed?
- While Mrs. Duke's case is pending, she accepts the offer of a job as a nurse in a public hospital in Spain. She wants to take her elderly mother with her. Will Mrs. Duke be able to take her mother?

3   Reed manufactures digital cameras. It was one of the first producers of digital cameras in Europe and is a well-known brand name. Copperfield has specialised in producing lenses for digital cameras. It has supplied Reed for a number of years with lenses specifically made for the Reed digital camera. However, Copperfield has come to the conclusion that it could make a better digital camera than Reed's and for a lower price. Copperfield decides that it wants to market its own brand of digital camera. When the supply contract with Reed ends, Copperfield starts producing its own digital camera. Copperfield then refuses to supply lenses to Reed. Advise Reed.

European Union law knowledge questions

1   In the European Court of Justice there are judges and Advocates General. What is the difference between them?

2   What is the purpose of a preliminary ruling?

3   In what way is a Regulation different from a Directive?

4   Explain the operation of the 'principle of supremacy' and the 'principle of subsidiarity'.

5   Explain what is meant by the term 'direct effect'.

6   What is meant by 'co-decision' procedure?

7   Explain the phrase 'abuse by one or more undertakings of a dominant position' in Article 82 EC Treaty.

8   Under the new Constitution the old term Directive disappears. By what term will it be replaced?

9   What is meant by the term 'worker' for the purposes of EU provisions?

10   Explain the difference between 'indistinctly applicable' and 'distinctly applicable'.

Chapter 4 Tort terminology

Tort vocabulary

Action: a claimant is said to **bring an action** in civil law. Alternatively, the claimant could be said to **sue** the defendant.

Aggravated damages: damages given to the claimant in excess of straightforward compensation because the defendant has behaved badly.

Amenity damage: the nuisance does not cause physical damage to the property, but it does interfere with the claimant's enjoyment of his property.

Antitrust law: term given in the USA to competition law, in particular the branch of competition law that bans agreements that undermine free competition.

Assault: the defendant causes the claimant to believe he is going to commit a battery.

Assumption of a duty: although the defendant does not owe a duty of care fixed in law to the claimant, by voluntarily assuming a duty of care he becomes liable in tort to the claimant if he is negligent.

Assumption of the risk: term often used in the USA where the defence to a negligence claim is that the plaintiff had accepted and consented to the risk of injury.

Award: damages are said to be awarded by the court to the claimant.

Balance of probabilities: the standard of proof in civil cases in England. The claimant in a tort action must show, therefore, 'on the balance of probabilities' that the defendant was at fault.

Battery: the defendant interferes with the claimant's person. There must be some form of contact but physical injury is not necessary.

Breach of a duty of care: the party owing a duty of care has failed in the performance of that duty.

Break the chain of causation: where another action intervenes and breaks the chain of causation between the defendant's act and the harm suffered by the claimant.

Burden of proof: obligation to prove facts. This burden is usually on the claimant but the burden can shift to the other party in certain circumstances, for example, where the evidential rule of res ipsa loquitur applies in negligence cases.

But for rule: this is a rule of causation. The claimant must show but for the act of the defendant he would not have suffered his injury.

Causation: there must be a link between the damage suffered by the claimant and the defendant's act or omission.

Chattel: personal property rather than real property.

Chose in action: a personal right that can be enforced as if it were property. It is a thing recoverable by a lawsuit rather than a thing in actual possession.

Comparative negligence: term used in the USA. The negligence of the plaintiff is compared to the negligence of the defendant. The plaintiff's damages will be reduced in proportion to the extent of his negligence.

Compensatory damages: an amount awarded to recompense the claimant for damage suffered due to the tortious conduct of the defendant.

Consumer protection: a consumer is someone not acting in the course of business. Consumer protection under the law of tort is particularly concerned with defective products that have caused damage to a consumer or his property.

Contemptuous damages: an insignificant amount is awarded where the claimant has won his case but the action had little merit.

Contributory negligence: a defence established where it is proved that an injured party failed to take reasonable care of himself, thus contributing to his own injury. In England, the defence of contributory negligence no longer means that the claimant cannot recover damages, but that the amount of damages recoverable will be less. In the USA, contributory negligence will totally defeat a plaintiff's claim.

Conversion: the tort is committed when a person deals with personal property in a way that is inconsistent with another person's right to the possession of that property. That interference goes so far as to amount to a denial of the claimant's right to possess the chattel.

Course of employment: that the employee was doing his job at the time the tort was committed.

Damages: this is an important and common remedy in tort, and many other branches of civil law. It means financial compensation for the claimant for the harm suffered. In tort, damages are usually calculated to restore the claimant to the position he was in before the tort was committed.

Defamation: where the claimant's reputation has been damaged by a published, defamatory statement.

Defamatory statement: a statement which has lowered the claimant's reputation in the eyes of right thinking people.

Defences to defamation: **justification**, **fair comment** upon a matter of public interest, **absolute** or **qualified privilege**, or an **unintentional defamation** made by a publisher.

Defendant: the one accused of committing a tort is often referred to as a **tortfeasor**.

Disclaimer: notice given that legal responsibility will not be accepted.

Discrimination torts: torts laid down in statute regulating sexual, racial and disability discrimination.

Duty of care: a duty binding on one party to avoid acts or omissions, which could reasonably be foreseen as likely to injure the other party.

Duty to mitigate: where a party has been harmed by the tortious behaviour of another, he is nonetheless under a duty to ensure that his losses are no greater than strictly necessary.

Economic torts: this term covers a range of torts where the defendant can be held liable for intentionally inflicting economic loss upon another. It includes the torts of **deceit**, **malicious** or **injurious falsehood**, **passing-off**, **interference with contract**, **intimidation** and **conspiracy**.

Employee: an individual who has entered into or works under a contract of employment. Whether someone is an employee cannot solely be determined by whether he is under an obligation to follow orders. Today various factors are taken into account in determining whether someone is employed or self-employed.

Employer: an employer may be held liable for torts committed by those who work for him according to a contract of employment.

Exemplary or punitive damages: an amount awarded well in excess of straight-forward compensation for the claimant, as the intention is to punish the defendant for his conduct.

False imprisonment: the defendant deprives the claimant of his liberty.

Fraudulent misrepresentation: the maker of the statement either knows the statement is not true or is reckless as to whether it is true.

Goods: personal property but not a chose in action, money (in the sense of currency) or securities.

Immediate aftermath: this term is relevant where a claimant for nervous shock in a negligence case has not directly witnessed the accident, but witnesses the consequences of that accident soon afterwards.

Incorporeal chattels: intangible personal property that is of value but has itself no inherent value, for example a grant of patent.

Independent contractor: does not work under a contract of employment but under a contract for services. As an independent contractor is self-employed, different rules apply to independent contractors than to employees.

Injunction: an order of the court directed at the defendant compelling him to stop doing something or to do something. A **prohibitory injunction** prohibits a person from doing something. A **mandatory injunction** requires the direct performance of a positive act. An **interim injunction** is granted before the outcome of a trial. A **final injunction**, also known as a **perpetual** or **permanent injunction**, may be granted upon the completion of a trial. The term **interlocutory injunction** is still used in the USA, but in England the term interim injunction is now preferred.

Joint and several liability: this refers to the situation where more than one person can be held liable for a tort or each person can be held individually liable.

Law of obligations: this area of law covers contractual obligations, which are voluntary and owed to specific persons, obligations in tort, which are fixed by law and not limited to specific persons, and restitution where the defendant has unjustly enriched himself at the claimant's expense.

Legal person: this is an artificial construct. An abstract entity, for example a registered company, is a separate person in law.

Libel: where the defamatory statements are in a more permanent form, such as in the form of writing.

Limitation period: a claim must be brought within a specified, fixed period of time. This period may vary from tort to tort.

Loss of amenity: damages are awarded in tort not just for the pain and suffering of a victim but also for loss of amenity. For example, the loss of a hand itself imposes a standard tariff, but the loss will be greater for a claimant who loved playing the piano.

Lump sum: damages may be awarded in the form of one, final payment. A **discount rate** applies where a lump sum has been awarded which takes into account future losses and expenses, as that lump sum can earn interest in the meantime.

Menacing: some states in the USA, that have a statutory definition of assault that includes battery, no longer refer to assault but refer instead to menacing.

Natural person: this is a human being rather than an artificial legal construct, such as a company.

Negligence: this is more than mere carelessness. It requires a breach of a duty of care fixed by law, which causes damage to the one to whom the duty was owed.

Negligent act: pure financial loss caused by a negligent act rather than a negligent statement is not actionable.

Negligent misstatement: a false statement made negligently. In certain circumstances, a duty of care is imposed on the maker of a negligent misstatement.

Neighbour principle: in the tort of negligence, this principle helps to determine whether the defendant owed the claimant a duty of care. It states that you must take reasonable care to avoid acts or omissions which you could reasonably foresee would be likely to injure your neighbour, a neighbour being defined as one who would be so closely and directly affected by your act that you should have him in mind.

Nervous shock: where psychiatric harm has been suffered by the claimant. Emotional distress or grief is insufficient to constitute psychiatric harm for this purpose.

Nominal damages: are awarded where the claimant has been successful but has suffered very little damage.

Non-pecuniary loss: loss of enjoyment in life due to the pain and suffering caused by the defendant's tortious conduct.

Novus actus interveniens (nova causa interveniens): an intervening event breaking the chain of causation.

Nuisance: in general, infringement of the claimant's use or enjoyment of his land.

Objective test: the test in negligence for breach of a duty of care is not whether this particular defendant has acted unreasonably but whether a reasonable man would have acted in this way.

Occupier: if a person controls premises, he is deemed to be the occupier and as such owes a duty of care to all visitors. In certain circumstances this duty is owed even to persons who are not invited visitors.

Pecuniary loss: where the loss suffered by the claimant is of an economic or financial nature.

Personal property: property other than real property, such as goods and chattels.

Physical damage: with respect to nuisance, physical damage means that the property itself has been harmed, whereas amenity damage is interference that prevents the claimant from enjoying his land.

Premises: the word premises refers to the land and any buildings or structures on that land.

Preponderance of evidence: in the USA, the usual formulation for the standard of proof in a civil action is 'a preponderance of evidence', although sometimes **clear and convincing evidence** is required.

Private nuisance: where the defendant has interfered in an unreasonable way with an individual's use or enjoyment of his land.

Proximity: is a factor to be taken into account in establishing a duty of care in negligence. There must be a sufficiently close relationship between the claimant and the defendant to show that the claimant would be closely and directly affected by the defendant's conduct. There is no precise formulation as to what constitutes proximity.

Public nuisance: where the harm is to a class of members of the public. To bring an action for public nuisance, an individual must show that he has suffered special damage.

Publish: with respect to the tort of defamation, a defamatory statement must have been published, in other words, brought to the attention of a third party.

Quasi-contractual: although there is no contract between the parties, the relationship resembles a contractual one.

Real chattel: a leasehold is termed a real chattel. The word 'real' in real chattel indicates that a lease is an estate in land, but in the past a lease was not a ground for a so-called real action. This meant that a leasehold could not be classed as real property and for this reason it falls under the category of personal property.

Real property: land and structures attached to the land.

Reasonable care: whether the defendant took reasonable care to prevent harm to the claimant is judged on the facts of the case.

Reasonable foreseeability: in a negligence claim, one factor that must be taken into account in establishing a duty of care is whether the conduct that injured the claimant could be reasonable foreseen by the defendant as having that effect. There is no precise formulation as to what will and what will not be considered to be reasonably foreseeable.

Reasonable man/person: the test for determining whether there has been a breach of a duty of care is objective. The standard is one of **reasonableness**; whether the defendant has acted as a reasonable man would have acted in the situation.

Reckless: a misrepresentation made recklessly is where the maker did not care whether the statement he made was true or not.

Remoteness: the defendant is only liable for damage that is foreseeable. If the damage could not have been reasonably foreseen at the time of the defendant's act or omission, it is said to be too remote.

Res ipsa loquitur: this is an important rule in negligence cases. It means 'the facts speak for themselves'. This rule of evidence applies where it would be hard to explain how the claimant was injured unless the defendant was negligent. The evidential burden of proof is then reversed, as the defendant must now prove that his negligence did not cause the claimant's injury.

Rule in Rylands v Fletcher: a person can be held strictly liable if he has brought onto his land, or keeps there, anything that could cause 'mischief' to a neighbour were it to escape. This thing capable of causing mischief must constitute a non-natural use of the land and the damage must be a natural consequence of the escape.

Slander: usually an oral defamatory statement.

Special damage: in the context of the tort of public nuisance, it means that the claimant must show that he has suffered more than the others who have been affected by the nuisance.

Special relationship: there may be liability for a negligent misstatement if the nature of the relationship between the claimant and the defendant is such that the defendant could expect the claimant to **rely** on the statement.

State of the art defence: this defence may be called upon where the defendant is held responsible for the damage caused by a defective product. Given the state of scientific knowledge at the time, it is argued that the defendant could not possibly have known that the product was defective.

Statute barred: if a claim is not brought within the fixed period available for that particular action, it can no longer be heard by a court.

Statutory duties of care: where a statute imposes a duty of care upon the defendant.

Statutory nuisances: particular forms of common law nuisance are also covered by statute, such as a nuisance that could have a detrimental effect on the environment.

Statutory product liability: English statute law imposes strict liability for **defective** (i.e. not safe) products causing damage to consumers. **Damage** must be in the form of death, personal injury, or damage to other private property. The claimant must still prove that the **product caused** the damage.

Strict liability: the defendant has neither acted negligently nor intentionally. This terminology arises both in civil and criminal law. In tort, an area of strict liability both in the USA and England is that of consumer product liability.

Structured settlement: where the damages awarded to the claimant take the form of a lump sum followed by periodic payments.

Sue: the verb 'to sue' means to initiate legal proceedings with the intention to have the case heard in court.

Tangible property: in simple terms, if property is tangible it can be seen and touched. Intangible property, on the other hand, is an abstract entity, for example a copyright. Tangible property can be either real or personal property.

Thin skull rule: if the claimant could reasonably foresee the type of injury, then he is liable for the full extent of that injury, even though he could not foresee that full extent because he was unaware of some peculiarity of the claimant.

Tort: is a private or civil wrong resulting from a breach of a legal duty. The law of tort is a collection of different causes of action as there is no general principle of liability for unjustifiable harm.

Tortfeasor: this term refers to one accused of tortious conduct and in a tort case it is interchangeable with the term defendant.

Tortious: is the adjective referring to tort, hence 'tortious liability'.

Trademark: any sign which is capable of distinguishing the goods or services of one undertaking from those of another.

Trespass to chattels: intentional interference with a chattel in the possession of the claimant.

Trespass to land: intentional interference with another's peaceful possession of his land.

Trespass to the person: intentional interference with the person.

Unfair competition: is the violation of accepted fair trade practices.

Vicarious liability: the 'master' is held responsible for the acts of the 'servant'. This can arise where an employer is held liable for the torts of an employee committed in the course of the employee's employment.

Volenti non fit injuria: there is no cause of action in negligence for a person who has consented to taking the risk of injury. This defence now has a limited application.

Tort terminology in context

1   Introduction

The law of tort, together with contract law and unjust enrichment, belongs to the **law of obligations**. The term **tort** itself is not an easy one to define; indeed finding an adequate definition has taxed the minds of many legal scholars. A tort is a civil wrong, rather than a criminal wrongdoing. Broadly speaking, the law of tort is concerned with the protection of certain private interests against certain types of wrongful conduct. Liability arises when a duty fixed by law has been breached. This duty is towards persons generally.

Coded systems too have wrestled with the problem of definition. In the Netherlands, for example, the old Civil Code made no attempt to define 'onrecht-matige daad', which may be translated as a civil 'wrongful act'. The new Dutch Civil Code has drafted general principles as to what conduct will be considered to be wrongful. This conduct consists of the following possible elements: where there is an infringement of a right; an act or omission that conflicts with a legal duty; an act or omission that is not in accordance with unwritten law as to proper social interaction; and there are no grounds for justifying such behaviour. The wrongful conduct must be attributable to the actor: it is his fault or he can be held responsible for causing it because of the law or current social concepts.

It can be argued that the generality of these principles leaves the concept of 'wrongful act' still open to interpretation. Nonetheless, the Dutch Code has made an attempt to define what constitutes wrongful behaviour. In the common law there is no general, all-embracing principle of liability for causing unjustifiable harm. The English law of tort is rather a collection of different causes of action, for example, trespass, negligence, deceit, defamation or malicious prosecution. Conduct is **tortious** when a defendant has committed a specific tort. Each tort lays down the circumstances in which a defendant can be held responsible for an act or in some cases an omission. The law of tort could, therefore, be described as being the sum total of these separate, individual torts. The major types of tort will be considered in the sections below.

In English law, there is a certain overlap between tort and several other areas of law. Contractual and tortious liability may arise from the same facts. The major difference between the two is that whereas contract law governs a breach of an agreement made between the parties, in tort the legal duties have not been accepted voluntarily but are imposed by the operation of the law.

There is also a considerable overlap between the law of tort and criminal law, as the same facts could give rise to both tortious and criminal liability. Many crimes are also torts. However, the law of tort and the criminal law serve different purposes: the law of tort exists to give a personal remedy to individuals for any wrong they have suffered, whereas criminal law is primarily concerned with the protection of the public at large and will punish offenders in order to suppress certain forms of socially undesirable behaviour.

Tort is a civil action; if it goes to trial, this is referred to as **to sue** or to **bring an action** (compare 'prosecute' in criminal cases). If an action in tort comes to trial, in England it is not usually heard by a jury. Jury trial is now rare in actions of tort and only available for a limited number of torts, such as defamation (libel and slander). In the USA, the position is somewhat different, as the Constitution guarantees the right to jury trial in civil and criminal cases. However, if both parties agree, a jury may be dispensed with. As for the **burden of proof**, in general it is the claimant who must show fault on the part of the defendant (or someone for whose acts the defendant is responsible in law). The standard of proof, as in all civil cases, is **on the balance of probabilities**. The American formulation for civil actions is **a preponderance of evidence** or in certain cases **clear and convincing evidence**.

2   PARTIES

A defendant in a tort case is also referred to as the **tortfeasor**. The tortfeasor may be either a **natural person** or a **legal person**. An unincorporated body, such as a partnership, has no legal personality distinct from its members. All the partners would then be jointly and severally liable for any wrongful acts or omissions of any of the partners which were done in the ordinary course of business, or with the authority of the partners. **Joint and several liability** describes the situation where more than one person combined to cause harm to the claimant, so that the claimant may sue for damages from all or any one of them for the full amount.

A legal person, such as a registered company, may commit torts and have torts committed against it. A company may be held to account in tort either directly or under the principle of vicarious liability. Where it is directly liable, this is because the company can be equated with a human agent, who is so much in control of the company that his actions can be seen as the actions of the company. **Vicarious liability** is where the 'master' is held responsible for the acts of the 'servant'. This rather old-fashioned terminology of masters and servants has been transcribed to the modern employment situation, where an **employer** is held liable for the torts of an **employee** committed in **the course of employment**. Wrongful acts by an **independent contractor** do not, as a general rule, give rise to vicarious liability. The reason for this is that a contractor is self-employed and is thus responsible for his own acts.

3   INTENTIONAL TORTS TO PERSON AND PROPERTY

Historically, a claimant would bring a form of action called **trespass** against a defendant where the defendant had intentionally and directly harmed the claimant's person, or his personal property or his land. These so-called forms of action were abolished long ago, but the term trespass has survived in modern English terminology to denote a tortious, intentional interference with the claimant's interests.

3.1   Intentional interference with the person

Intentional, direct interference with the claimant's person is also referred to as **trespass to the person**. The main forms of intentional interference with the person are battery, assault and false imprisonment.

•   **Battery**: this is where the defendant does an act intending to interfere with a person, even if there is no intention actually to injure that person. This act directly and physically affects the person of the claimant. Some sort of physical contact between the parties is required; throwing a stone at the claimant from a distance would still be classed as contact. Actual physical harm need not result, however. The hostile poking of a finger at someone's arm would be enough. The claimant must have been interfered with, without his consent, and that act must have gone beyond the kind of contact that can normally be expected in daily social life.

•   **Assault**: an assault is committed if the defendant causes the claimant to fear that he is going to commit a battery against him. The tort of assault is a separate tort from that of battery. However, it is easy to confuse the two terms because assault and battery are frequently associated, the former often leading to the latter.
     Note: in order to avoid this confusion of terminology, some states in the USA that have a statutory definition of assault that includes battery, now no longer refer to assault but refer instead to **menacing**.

•   **False imprisonment**: this tort is committed by intentionally and directly placing a total restraint on the liberty of the claimant. For example, intentionally locking someone up in a room or a toilet.

3.2   Intentional interference with property

Intentional interference with property covers both interference with personal property and land. Land is **real property**. **Personal property** is property other than real property and in particular **goods** and **chattels**. The terms goods and chattels are not identical. The term chattels is broader than that of goods; it covers all forms of **tangible property** that is not classed as real property. It includes goods, cheques, negotiable instruments, and money. The term **goods** covers most forms of personal property, but not a **chose in action**, or money (in the sense of currency) or securities. A civil action in **trespass** can be brought to protect both land and chattels; the tort of **conversion** only protects chattels.

3.2.1 Intentional interference with chattels

The tort consists of an intentional and direct act by the defendant that interferes with the claimant's possession of the chattel. As noted above, essentially the type of property referred to by the word chattel is personal property but not real property. However, the term chattel does cover an interest in real estate; a leasehold is termed a **real chattel**. The word 'real' in real chattel indicates that a lease is an estate in land, but in the past a lease was not a ground for a so-called real action. This meant that a leasehold could not be classed as real property and for this reason it falls under the category of personal property. Intellectual property rights, such as copyrights and patents, are also personal property. They are often described as **incorporeal chattels**.

3.2.2 Conversion

Conversion is a tort that goes beyond the tort of **trespass to chattels**. In both the torts of conversion and trespass to chattels, there must be intentional and direct interference by the defendant with the chattels of the claimant. However, in the case of conversion that interference goes so far as to amount to a denial of the claimant's right to possess the chattel. A good example of the tort of conversion is where goods are sold, but the seller did not have the right to sell them.

3.2.3 Intentional interference with land

The tort of **trespass to land** is to protect the claimant's right to the peaceful possession of his land. A trespass to land is typically committed when a person intentionally enters on the land of another, without that other's permission. Even negligently entering the land of another can amount to trespass, as can refusing to leave when requested to do so by the claimant.

3.3 Defences to the intentional torts

There are various defences available to one accused of an intentional tort to the person or property. These may be summed up briefly as follows:
- consent: this may be either express, for example giving someone the right to enter on your land, or implied, for example the usual type of physical contact that can be expected in sports;
- inevitable accident: as when a person comes onto the claimant's property as the result of a car accident;
- defence of the person: a person may use reasonable force to protect himself;
- defence of property: a person may use reasonable force to protect his property.

For example, if a trespasser has been asked to leave but refuses, reasonable force can be used to eject him;

- necessity: it is lawful to protect someone or his property from threats of harm, for example, to administer medical treatment to someone who is unconscious and cannot, therefore, give his consent;
- lawful arrest, search and seizure also fall under this defence.

4   Negligence

In the early twentieth century, an expansion of the concept of what was tortious was taking place. Courts were wrestling with the concept of **negligence**. In general, intentionally interfering with another person's rights had long been accepted as tortious conduct. The question that now arose was whether negligent behaviour that caused harm to a person was a proper ground for a legal action. While the English courts came to acknowledge that various instances of negligence could be tortious, in the early years of the twentieth century there was no coherent theory of a tort of negligence.

It was an American court rather than an English court that led the way. In the USA the landmark case of MacPherson v Buick Motor Co. 1916 established the modern common law approach to negligence: liability depended upon establishing a breach of a **duty of care** owed by one party to the other. The existence of a separate tort of negligence, based upon a duty of care, was only conclusively established in England in 1932 with the case of Donoghue v Stevenson. Donoghue v Stevenson remains the basis of the English law of negligence, and the terminology used in this case is still the terminology of negligence used in English law up to the present day.

Note: it was not only common law jurisdictions that were struggling with the concept of negligence at the beginning of the last century. In the Netherlands, for example, the courts at the turn of the twentieth century used a very strict interpretation as to what constituted a wrongful act, as can be seen in the 1910 case 'Zutphense waterleiding'. In that case, a defendant was not liable simply because she had refused to turn off a water pipe, even though this had caused damage to the claimant's property. However, a few years later a much wider interpretation of what was wrongful conduct was evident in Lindenbaum-Cohen 1919. That case laid down that it could be tortious to behave in a way inconsistent with the care that is proper in social interaction with respect to persons and goods.

4.1   Requirements

In ordinary English, negligence is the word used to describe a careless act, or lack of attention, that causes harm to another. The English legal term **negligence** is far more specific; the tort of negligence is not merely carelessness. The defendant must have breached a duty of care that has been fixed by law, and that breach must have caused the claimant loss or injury. In general, a claimant must prove that the defendant was at fault. In order to succeed in a claim for negligence, a claimant must show that three requirements have been satisfied:

1   There must be a **duty of care** recognised in law. In order to establish whether there is a duty of care, there are two sources: the common law and statutes. Common law duties of care are laid down in case law, which means precedents must be consulted. Various statutes also lay down what are referred to as **statutory duties of care**. Both common law and statutory duties of care may be relevant to a given situation, for example, an employer owes an employee a duty at common law to take reasonable care, but he must also comply with various statutory duties of care.
2   There must be a **breach** of the duty of care.
3   There must be damage resulting from that breach. That damage must not be too **remote** a consequence of the breach.

4.1.1 Duty of care at common law

In the common law the emphasis in negligence is on establishing a duty. It is vital to understand what the legal term **duty of care** implies. As mentioned above, in English law, the terminology defining a duty of care is very much the product of one major court case, that of Donoghue v Stevenson 1932 (see the Appendix for the head-note of this case). The ratio of that case established that a manufacturer owes a duty of care to the ultimate consumer of his products. This recognised what is now called product liability (see below). The case was in retrospect more significant than this narrow ratio decidendi on manufacturers and ultimate consumers would seem to imply. General principles were laid down which could be applied to see whether a duty of care would arise at common law and to whom it was owed.

The test laid down in that case to establish whether a duty of care is owed or not was formulated by Lord Atkin. It is called the **neighbour principle** because whether there is a duty depends upon whether the claimant is a neighbour in the legal sense of that word. Lord Atkin described a neighbour as a person "so closely and directly affected by my act that I ought reasonably to have him in contemplation as being affected". A person is under a duty to take **reasonable care** to avoid acts or omissions, "which you can **reasonably foresee** would be likely to injure your neighbour".

The neighbour principle has remained generally applicable. However, today other factors are also taken into account. Present case law indicates that it is usual to take three criteria into account when establishing whether there is a duty of care:

1   reasonable foreseeability;
2   **proximity**;
3   whether it would be fair, just and reasonable to impose a duty.

The literal meaning of the word **proximity** is 'closeness'. There must be a sufficiently close relationship between the claimant and the defendant to amount to proximity, but there is no clear legal definition of what that term means. Indeed, judicial opinion has suggested that proximity is not a definable concept but simply a description of circumstances. Neither is it clear what amounts to 'fair, just and reasonable'. That these words are open to interpretation was admitted by Lord Bridges in the Caparo case 1990 when he stated the concepts of proximity and fairness are "not susceptible of any such precise definition as would be necessary to give them utility as practical tests, but amount in effect to little more than convenient labels to attach to the features of different specific situations." A reluctance to define key terms may seem strange to some civil law lawyers, but this unwillingness to tie terminology to strict definitions is a characteristic of the common law system. The terms **reasonably foreseeable**, **proximity** and **fair, just and reasonable** simply do not reflect precise legal concepts.

For this reason, although there is now a three-stage approach to establishing a duty of care, the old problem of defining what is reasonably foreseeable remains unresolved. Different factors may be relevant in determining reasonable foreseeability, depending on the type of harm suffered. A set of facts may make physical injury to a person reasonably foreseeable, but that same set of facts will not necessarily make psychological injury reasonably foreseeable.

4.1.2 Duty of care and nervous shock

With respect to **nervous shock** or psychiatric injury cases, the English courts have been reticent to allow claims for nervous shock unless the psychiatric injury was connected to a claim for physical injury. There is still no liability for causing emotional distress or grief unless this leads to a recognisable medical condition, such as depression, personality change or post-traumatic stress disorder. If a defendant is to be held liable for nervous shock, then injury by way of nervous shock must in itself be reasonably foreseeable. For example, due to his careless driving, a motorcyclist killed himself in an accident. A woman who did not see the accident, because she was standing on the other side of a tram, but heard the noise and saw blood on the road suffered nervous shock which caused her baby to be still-born. It was held she could not claim against the deceased's estate for negligence because the deceased could not have foreseen nervous shock to a person who had not directly witnessed the accident.

Proximity may be taken into account in assessing whether the nervous shock suffered was **reasonably foreseeable**. A person who is not the victim of the negligence, but has a close relationship to the victim and as a result suffers nervous shock, may be able to recover damages. This is certainly the case where such a person was present at the accident, there was proximity in the sense of the relationship and also in terms of time and space. Case law also indicates that an action can be brought even if the claimant was not at the scene of the accident or in the vicinity but was confronted with the **immediate aftermath** of the accident and the claimant witnessed this directly with his own unaided senses.

Note 1: policy may play a role in determining a duty of care. Courts may be influenced by the fear of 'opening the floodgates', in other words, increasing the number of potential claims, or where the court considers that liability may not be in the public interest, for example where the defendant is a policeman. It is very likely that not only English courts are influenced by similar considerations.

Note 2: it is common for English lawyers to insert a clause in contracts excluding liability for common law duties of care. It is, however, not possible to exclude liability for negligence that has caused death or personal injury.

4.1.3 Duty of care and economic loss

The law of negligence has traditionally not given the same level of protection to economic loss as it has to physical injury, unless the economic loss is the result of physical injury. With respect to economic loss that results from **negligent misstatements** or **negligent acts**, even if a person could reasonably foresee such harm he will not necessarily be liable to the claimant.

A false statement may cause economic loss to one who acts upon it. A false statement may also be referred to as a 'misstatement' or, more specifically in the context of the tort of negligence, as a **negligent misstatement**. Should a person be held liable for negligent words that caused another financial loss? The answer to that question was given by the case of Hedley Byrne & Co. Ltd v Heller and Partners Ltd (1964), which is still cited as the standard case in English law. Hedley Byrne were advertising agents who asked their bank to check on the credit-worthiness of one of their clients, Easipower. Their bank asked the client's bank and a favourable reference was received. Hedley Byrne relied on this advice and lost a lot of money when Easipower went into liquidation. Hedley Byrne actually lost this case because the bank had expressly stated that the advice was given "without responsibility". However, the court accepted the principle that a negligent misstatement could be tortious.

What the court made clear is that a duty of care for a negligent misstatement will only arise in certain circumstances. It is not enough to show that the maker of the statement could have reasonably foreseen that financial loss would result if the statement was untrue. It would be unfair to impose a duty of care on everyone who makes a careless statement. The statement may have been made casually, for example during an informal occasion, without any intention that it should be acted on.

The Hedley Byrne case provided important terminology as to when a duty of care would arise for a negligent misstatement. To establish a duty of care for a negligent statement causing financial loss, there must be a **special relationship** between claimant and defendant, so that the claimant could reasonably be expected to **rely** on the statement. This special relationship of reliance arises typically in a **quasi-contract** setting; a formal setting where the relationship is similar to a contractual relationship. For example, the defendant is in the business of giving professional advice based on expertise. It is reasonable for the claimant to presume that the defendant is knowledgeable, and the defendant knows that it is likely that the claimant will act on the advice given. Unless the defendant has made it clear that he will not accept responsibility for the advice given, the defendant may have assumed a duty of care. In English law, a duty may be owed simply because of a voluntary **assumption of a duty**. In the Hedley Byrne case, the **disclaimer** used by the bank made it clear that no duty of care had been voluntarily assumed. Such a disclaimer today, however, will not necessarily exclude liability unless it is reasonable, given the circumstances, to rely on the disclaimer.

With respect to financial loss caused by **negligent acts**, the general principle is that pure financial loss caused by a negligent act rather than a negligent statement is not actionable as there is no duty of care for such loss. The main reason for this is to avoid open-ended liability.

Note: instead of referring to financial or economic loss, the term **pecuniary** may be used.

4.2 Statutory duties of care

Certain duties of care have now been laid down in statute form. For example, not only common law duties of care, but also statutory duties of care regulate an employer's liability towards his employees. It is the common law duty of every employer to ensure the health and safety of his employees while at work, as far as is reasonably practicable. This includes providing a competent staff with adequate training, a proper plant and equipment, a safe place of work and a safe system of work. Various statutes regulate specific aspects of health and safety.

There may be strict liability where there is a statutory duty of care. **Strict liability** means liability even without fault. The defendant may neither have acted intentionally nor negligently, yet he will still be held responsible. For example, statute governs an employer's liability for defective equipment. Under this statute, an employer will be in breach of a duty of care where a workman has suffered personal injury in the course of his employment as a consequence of a defect in the equipment provided. That the equipment was defective due to the fault of a third party, does not alter the liability of the employer.

4.3 Breach of duty

If it has been established that the defendant did owe the claimant a duty of care, the next hurdle for the claimant is to show that the defendant **breached** that duty of care. The test for determining breach is **objective**. The standard is one of **reasonableness**; whether the defendant has acted as a **reasonable man** would have acted in the situation. So has the defendant failed to do something that a reasonable man would have done, or has he done something that a reasonable man would not have done?

Note: the term 'reasonable man' has long been in use, but it is considered by some to be politically incorrect. Reference may also be made to the more gender-neutral **reasonable person** test.

There is no general definition in English law of what a reasonable man is and what he is not. The court reaches its decision based on the actual facts of the case. Therefore, previous decisions on similar facts will not bind the courts. From case law, it is clear that the judge will take certain factors into account:

- the degree of risk to the claimant created by the defendant's conduct;
- the seriousness of the harm the claimant may suffer;
- the social utility of the defendant's action, for example, was he a fireman or policeman;
- the expense and practicability of taking precautions against the risk.

The **burden of proof** rests on the claimant. The claimant must show that the defendant did not act in a reasonable way. In accordance with the general rules for civil trials, he must show that on the **balance of probabilities** the defendant was negligent and this negligence caused his injuries. It can be very difficult for the claimant to prove that the defendant failed to take reasonable care. An important rule in this respect is that of **res ipsa loquitur**: the facts speak for themselves. This rule of evidence applies where it would be hard to explain how the claimant was injured unless the defendant was negligent. Negligence is presumed in the absence of an alternative explanation by the defendant, for example, when a lorry has gone out of control and killed someone. The evidential burden of proof is then reversed, as the defendant must now prove that his negligence did not cause the claimant's injury.

4.4   Causation and remoteness of damage

This question arises if it is proved that the defendant is in breach of a duty of care. In general, the claimant must prove that the defendant's act caused the damage and the damage suffered was foreseeable. This involves two issues: **causation** and **remoteness** of damage.

In order to establish **causation**, there must be a clear link between the claimant's loss and the defendant's conduct. The claimant must be able to show that without the defendant's negligence, he would not have suffered harm. This is often referred to as the **but for test**: would the claimant not have suffered damage but for the events brought about by the defendant? An example of the 'but for' rule in operation is the case of the night watchman who became sick during the night, but no one in the hospital was prepared to examine him. He died of arsenic poisoning a few hours later. It was held that the negligence of the hospital had not caused the death, as had he been examined immediately he would still have died from the arsenic poisoning.

Even if the claimant can establish a link between the defendant's breach of a duty of care and his injury, that injury must not be a too **remote** consequence of the breach. Remoteness of damage acts as a cut off point beyond which the defendant will not be liable. Only damage that was **reasonably foreseeable** at the time of the negligent conduct can be recovered by the claimant. The type of injury suffered by the claimant must have been reasonably foreseeable, even if the extent of that injury could not have been foreseen. This means that if the injury is the type of injury that could be foreseen by a reasonable person, a defendant may be liable for all the injury of that type that occurs. The case of a lorry driver who contracted frostbite illustrates this point. The lorry driver was told to drive his lorry on a long journey during winter, even though his employer knew that the heating system had broken down. The employer argued that it was not reasonably foreseeable that the lorry driver would suffer frostbite. The court held that as frostbite was the type of injury associated with prolonged exposure to severe cold, the employer was liable as the type of injury was foreseeable, even if the extent was not.

Any peculiarities of the victim that make the extent of the claimant's injuries worse than could have been expected, do not generally lessen the responsibility of the defendant. The **thin skull rule** is that you 'take your victim as you find him'. Therefore, if the victim has an unusually thin, egg-shell skull, which means that the injury he sustained was more severe than would have been sustained by a person with a normal skull, the defendant will be liable for the full extent of that injury as long as the type of injury suffered could have been reasonably foreseen.

The injury suffered by the claimant may be held to be too remote if an unforeseen, intervening act **breaks the chain of causation**. Where there is a sequence of events, every act in the sequence is relevant and the court must decide on the operative cause of the injury. A **novus actus interveniens** (or **nova causa interveniens**) is the name given to an intervening act that breaks the chain of causation. If this intervening act is the direct cause of the injury, and beyond the control of the defendant, he will not be liable for the claimant's loss. It is not a novus actus interveniens, however, if the original injury is still having an effect. For example, in one case a lady's neck was injured by the defendant. She was fitted with a surgical collar and this meant that she was unable to use her bifocal glasses properly. This led to further injuries. It was held that the additional injuries were not a novus actus interveniens but attributable to the original injury caused by the defendant.

4.5   Defences

Clearly, it is a defence to argue that one, or more, of the three elements required to bring a successful claim in negligence has not been proved. However, if the claimant has established all the elements necessary for negligence, one possible line of defence is **contributory negligence**. Alternatively, it could be argued that the claimant had voluntarily assumed the risk, this latter defence being known by the Latin phrase of **volenti non fit injuria**.

4.5.1 Contributory negligence

Although the claimant's injury was partly caused by the defendant's conduct, the claimant himself is also at fault and therefore partly to blame for his own injury. There has been an unreasonable failure on the part of the claimant to look after his own safety. For example, although the defendant was responsible for a car crash, the injuries suffered by the claimant were aggravated because he was not wearing a seat belt at the time, even though fastening a seat belt is a legal obligation. **Contributory negligence** does not mean that a claimant is barred from bring a claim (although in the past it did). He can still bring a claim, but the damages recoverable will be reduced by the extent to which he can be held liable for his injuries.

Note: as mentioned above, at one time in England if contributory negligence succeeded as a defence, the plaintiff could recover nothing. The term contributory negligence has retained this earlier usage in the USA. In states that still allow the defence of contributory negligence, a plaintiff would receive no compensation if the defence is proved. As an alternative to this harsh rule, the concept of **comparative negligence** (or comparative fault) emerged in the USA. It means the negligence of the plaintiff is compared to the negligence of the defendant. The level of the reduction in damages that results from this comparison varies from state to state.

4.5.2 Volenti non fit injuria

Here, the claimant knows of the risk and has freely accepted to run the risk of being injured by the defendant's negligence. In effect he has given his consent to taking that risk. In the past, this defence was used to defeat claims made by employees who had been injured in the course of their employment. The employer argued that a man working in a steel mill knows there is always a risk of being in contact with molten metal and by accepting the work, he had willingly accepted the risk of harm. The defence of volenti by an employer is not allowed in these cases anymore.

    Volenti, unlike contributory negligence, provides a complete defence. If the defence of volenti is successful, it will totally defeat the claimant's claim. This has led to courts being reluctant to accept the defence of volenti, preferring to interpret the claimant's behaviour as contributory negligence. This approach explains the decision in a case where a woman agreed to a lift home, even though she knew the driver was drunk, saw he was driving badly, had opportunities to leave the car, did not and was injured in a crash. The court still held it was contributory negligence rather than volenti. The scope of the defence has been cut down considerably over the years. Nonetheless, it may still be a defence in certain situations, for example, it can be used by the occupier of premises where a visitor has been injured, but the visitor had willingly accepted the risk of injury (see below) and in sport related injuries.

Note: the defence of volenti is often referred to in the USA by the phrase **assumption of the risk**. Some states have abolished assumption of the risk as a distinct defence, treating it either as a matter in assessing whether there was a duty of care owed by the defendant or as comparative negligence.

5   STATUTORY PRODUCT LIABILITY

In England, Donoghue v Stevenson is the basis at common law for stating that a manufacturer can be liable to the ultimate consumer of a product for defects in its manufacture. Until 1987, any product liability case would have to be brought using the tort of negligence and the case of Donoghue. It was therefore necessary to prove fault, even though it was acknowledged that a duty of care was owed to the ultimate consumer. Proving fault on the part of the manufacturer was often difficult for the consumer.

In order to offer consumers more protection, a European Community directive was issued in 1985. When implemented in English law, this directive became the **Consumer Protection** Act 1987. There is now **strict liability** for a defective product, which means that if the consumer uses **statutory product liability**, rather than common law negligence, the consumer need not show fault. However, the claimant is required to show the following:

*   a **product**: product is defined in the statute as any goods or electricity and includes property that forms a part of another piece of property, either as a component or as raw material;
*   **damage**: by way of death, personal injury or damage to other personal (non-commercial) property above a fixed minimum value;
*   a **defect** or defects in the product, making the product not safe;
*   **causation** in that the defect in the product caused the damage.

The person held responsible is the producer of the product rather than the person who supplied it. The manufacturer is considered responsible as the producer, if he is either the manufacturer of the total finished product or that of a faulty component. Also responsible is an own brander who has held himself out as the producer or the importer into the EU. A supplier is only liable where he cannot identify the manufacturer or importer, or his own supplier.

Certain defences are available to the producer. Perhaps the most generally useful is that of the **state of the art defence**. The argument here is that, at the relevant time, the state of scientific and technical knowledge was such that the producer could not possibly have known that the product was defective. The claimant's damages will also be reduced if the defendant can show **contributory negligence**.

Note 1: it could be supposed that statutory product liability, with its access to strict liability, has superseded negligence where fault must still be shown. This, however, is not the case. The tort of negligence can still be used for product liability cases, and indeed must be used where the damage caused is to commercial property rather than a consumer's property.

Note 2: in the USA, the doctrine of strict liability for defective products developed from case law. The doctrine was outlined in a case involving an exploding coca cola bottle back in 1944. Since then, all states have adopted the principle that manufacturers are strictly liable for personal injuries caused by defective products. There is no need for the plaintiff to show negligence. Strict liability arises either because of a defect in the manufacture of the product or a defect in the design of the product. A design will be considered defective if it cannot objectively be considered to be reasonable. There may also be liability for an information defect, if an appropriate and adequate warning was not attached to the product. The criteria for judging defectiveness can vary from state to state.

6   OCCUPIER'S LIABILITY

In general, an **occupier** owes a **duty of care** to all visitors. The basic test for whether a person is the occupier is whether he controls the **premises**. The duty of care means here that the occupier must take reasonable care to see that the visitors will be reasonably safe using the premises for the purpose for which they have been invited by the occupier to be there. However, an occupier must be prepared for children to be less careful than adults.

A visitor is someone with express or implied permission. In some cases, a duty of care can extend even to uninvited visitors. There is a duty of care to non-visitors if the **trespass** would be dangerous, in particular with respect to child trespassers. The duty is to take such care as is reasonable in the circumstances. In some cases, a warning of danger may be sufficient, whereas in other cases more physical protection will be required, such as fencing.

7   NUISANCE

The tort of **nuisance** relates to land. It may be distinguished from negligence in this respect, as the scope of negligence extends beyond only interests that are connected to the use and enjoyment of land. On the other hand, negligence is primarily concerned with physical harm and is not geared up to offering protection to a claimant complaining of noise and smells, whereas that is an essential characteristic of the tort of nuisance. Furthermore, negligence requires the claimant to show a duty of care owed to him by the defendant in that particular situation, whereas in nuisance the duty consists simply in not interfering with the claimant's land.

7.1   Private nuisance

To bring an action in **private nuisance**, the defendant's act must interfere in some unreasonable way with the claimant's use or enjoyment of his land. Unlike **trespass to**

land, this tort is caused by indirect rather than direct interference. The damage suffered by the nuisance must be **reasonably foreseeable** and therefore not too **remote**.

Interference could be in various forms. The nuisance could cause actual **physical damage** to the property, for example by a fire spreading from the neighbouring land. On the other hand, it may simply be an interference that prevents the claimant's enjoyment of his property, for example through smells, noise or vibrations. This latter form of interference is often referred to as **amenity damage**. Many traditional common law nuisances, like noise and fumes, are now also classed as **statutory nuisances**. A nuisance covered by statute, for example one falling under environmental protection legislation, empowers the local authority to take action to bring an end to the nuisance.

Neighbours have a duty not to cause each other harm. A person who has an interest in the land affected by the nuisance may bring an action. This person may be an owner or an occupier. The defendant may not necessarily be the one who actually caused the nuisance, but he may be responsible for the nuisance created by someone else (**vicarious liability**). Fault of some kind, on the part of the defendant, is usually necessary. The main remedy for nuisance cases is an **injunction** to prevent the continuance of the nuisance. It may be the case, however, that both an injunction and **damages** are sought.

7.2   Public nuisance

Public nuisance is a crime as well as a tort. It is an act or omission which materially affects the reasonable comfort of a class of 'her majesty's subjects', in other words, where a group of people are inconvenienced, for example by a discharge of oil into a harbour or by the obstruction of a road. In order to bring an action in tort, the claimant must be able to show that he has suffered particular damage, more so than the rest of the community. This **special damage** can arise from personal injury, damage to property or loss of business profits. However, any such damage must be a **foreseeable** consequence of the nuisance.

7.3   Rule in Rylands v Fletcher

As its name suggests, this rule was laid down in a case back in 1868. At one time, the rule was considered to be part of the law of nuisance. It is now generally considered to be a separate tort. It is still referred to by the name of the old case.

The rule in Rylands v Fletcher deals with a specific situation where a person can be held liable under the principle of **strict liability** for carrying on dangerous activities. He will be held liable if he has brought onto his land, or keeps there, anything that could cause 'mischief' to a neighbour were it to escape. This thing capable of causing mischief must constitute a non-natural use of the land, and the damage must be a natural consequence of the escape. In the Rylands v Fletcher case itself, the damage was brought about by the defendant's contractors damming a stream to create a reservoir to provide water for a mill. The contractors failed to fill in the old mine shafts with the result that the mines on the neighbour's property were flooded. Whether something is likely to do mischief if it escapes is a question of fact to be decided in each individual case. As the rule in Rylands v Fletcher is a rule of strict liability, proof of negligence or wrongful intention on the part of the defendant is not required but actual damage must be shown.

Note: the rule in Rylands v Fletcher has been debated in American courts. Restatements on torts have imposed strict liability on one who carries out 'abnormally dangerous' activities.

8   Discrimination torts

Statutes have regulated sexual, racial and disability discrimination. An employer may be **vicariously liable** for discrimination during the **course of employment**, unless he can show that he took reasonable precautions to prevent such discrimination. However, it is open to argument whether an employee committing racial or sexual harassment can be said to be doing this during the course of employment.

9   Defamation

The tort of defamation provides a remedy to both individuals and organisations where **defamatory statements**, made by another, have had an adverse effect on their reputation. As a result, damage has been suffered. There are two forms of defamation: **slander** and **libel**. An action is based on libel where the defamatory statements are in a more permanent form, for example in writing. Slander is usually in the form of an oral defamatory statement.

9.1   Requirements

In order to bring a successful action for defamation, the following three elements must be established:

1   The statement was **defamatory**. Vulgar abuse is not necessarily a defamatory statement. The test used in English law to determine whether a statement is simply abuse or is defamatory was devised in 1936. It stated that it would be defamatory if the statement 'lowered the plaintiff in the estimation of right-thinking people'.

2   The **defamatory statement** must have referred to the claimant. This is normally not an issue if the claimant is specifically mentioned by name. However, a defendant may still be liable, even if he did not actually intend to refer to the claimant. For example, the defendant may have thought the name was fictitious. Nonetheless, if someone who is actually called that name, and is considered by others to be the subject of the defamatory statement, he will have the right to bring an action if his reputation has been damaged.

3   The statement must have been **published**. Published is used as a legal term in this context to indicate that the statement has been brought to the attention of a third party. A husband and wife are still considered to be one for this purpose.

9.2   Defences to defamation

A number of special defences are available to the defendant being sued for defamation:

- **Justification**: the fact that a statement has been made which damages the claimant's reputation does not make that statement in itself defamatory. There is no defamation if the defendant is simply telling the truth, no matter how this affects the claimant's reputation. The defendant will, however, be required to prove that he was telling the truth.
- **Fair comment**: this defence recognises the need to find a balance between the protection of someone's reputation and the general right of freedom of speech. It is a defence to claim that the words were fair comment upon a matter of public interest. The 'comment' refers to the requirement that the statement is one of opinion, not one of fact. The proper defence for a statement of fact is justification. The statement does not have to be correct, but it must express an honest opinion on a matter of public interest. If it was not made in good faith, but in malice, the defence will be lost.
- **Absolute privilege**: if the statement is covered by absolute privilege, this is a complete defence. Even if there was a malicious motive for making the statement, the defence still stands. Typical examples of defamatory statements that are subject to absolute privilege are those made in the course of parliamentary proceedings, judicial proceedings or between husband and wife.
- **Qualified privilege**: unlike absolute privilege, the defence of qualified privilege will be lost if the defendant can be shown to have been malicious in making the statement. Qualified privilege may arise where one party has a legal, moral or social duty to make the statement, and the other party has a duty to receive the statement. Typical examples of statements that may be subject to qualified privilege are reports of public meetings, testimonials and references.
- **Unintentional defamation**: in general, at common law no intention is necessary in order to prove defamation. As seen above, using a name believing it to be fictitious will not avoid liability if someone has been harmed. A statutory defence was, therefore, created for publishers who had inadvertently published a defamatory statement. The publisher must make amends by placing a correction and an apology.

10   ECONOMIC TORTS

Pure economic loss is less well protected by English law than physical injury leading to economic loss. As noted above under the tort of negligence, liability arises for financial loss resulting from a negligent misstatement where a duty of care can be established. However, what is the situation where the economic loss was not caused negligently but intentionally? There is no general principle that imposes liability for causing deliberate economic harm to another, even if that economic harm is quite severe. Unlike in some other legal systems, there is at present in English law no general tort of unfair competition. **Unfair competition** is the violation of accepted fair trade practices. Nonetheless, there are various common law torts that a claimant can call upon for protection. These include the torts of deceit, malicious falsehood, passing-off, inducing breach of contract, intimidation and conspiracy.

- **Deceit**: the defendant must have made a **fraudulent misrepresentation** to the claimant. This misrepresentation may be made either knowingly or **recklessly**, but the intention is that the claimant will act on the misrepresentation. Damage results to the claimant as a consequence.
- **Malicious falsehood**: this is also referred to as **injurious falsehood**. Here the defendant must make a false statement about the claimant or his property that is calculated to cause damage to the claimant. The motive behind this statement must be malicious: the maker of the statement does not believe it is true. The statement must then be made known to a third party or parties.
- **Passing-off**: essentially this is where a competitor passes off his own goods or services as being those of the claimant, for example by infringing the claimant's **trademark**. This passing-off misleads the claimant's customers into presuming they are buying the claimant's goods or services. The tort has been used increasingly as a way of combating unfair competition, but the exact scope of the tort is not entirely clear.
- **Interference with contract**: a person may interfere with a contract either by persuading a party to the contract not to carry out his duties under that contract or by acting in a way that interferes with the performance of that contract. **Inducing breach of contract** is the term for an action brought against a defendant who has **induced** or persuaded a party to a contract to breach that contract. At present, the exact nature of what comprises an inducement is not entirely clear. With respect to acts, either direct or indirect, that prevent the performance of the contract, it is probably the case that the defendant must have used unlawful means to prevent the performance.
- **Intimidation**: in this tort the defendant has threatened to commit an unlawful act. The threat is intended to cause damage to the claimant and actual damage does indeed ensue.
- **Conspiracy**: it is unlawful to associate with others if the sole or primary object of that association is to cause injury to another person, even if the means used are not in themselves unlawful. Where the conspiracy is intended to promote

the conspirators' interests rather than injure another, then wrongful means must be proved.

Note 1: EU law has also affected English competition law. The EC Treaty states that agreements which have as their object or effect the prevention, restriction or distortion of trade within the common market are prohibited. Also prohibited is the abuse of a dominant position (see chapter 3).

Note 2: the USA has traditionally paid more attention to banning restrictions on competition (**antitrust law**) than to unfair competition law. The law of unfair competition is mainly governed by state law. In addition to the common law torts, such as deceit and interference with contract, there may also be statutory unfair competition law as in California.

11   REMEDIES IN TORT

Claims must usually be brought within a certain time; this is called a **limitation period**. The limitation period varies according to the legal basis of the claim and the type of damage suffered by the claimant. Claims brought after the specified time will not be heard as they are said to be **statute barred**.

The aim of compensation in tort is to restore the injured party to the position he would have been in if the tort had not been committed. This approach is not without its critics: it means that relief is based upon what the claimant has actually lost rather than what the claimant actually needs, so damages are higher for a high earning claimant. The injured party is, however, under a **duty to mitigate**, which means he must do all that is reasonable to avoid making more losses than necessary.

11.1   Damages

One of the most common and important remedies in tort, as well as in other civil actions, is damages. The word **damages** means financial compensation awarded to the claimant for the injury he has suffered. This term is sometimes misused by foreign lawyers as they fail to see the distinction between damages and damage. Damage means harm done: it does not become damages with an 's' if there has been more than one sort of harm done. This misuse can cause confusion in sentences like "Damages will be limited to the sum of € 1,000 for the damages".

Damages may be **awarded** in the form of one **lump sum** or a **structured settlement**. The latter term refers to a lump sum followed by periodic payments. A **discount rate** applies where a lump sum has been awarded which takes into account future losses and expenses, as that lump sum can earn interest in the meantime.

Damages awarded for personal injury fall into two categories: straightforward **pecuniary** loss, such as the loss of earnings and expenses, and **non-pecuniary** loss, such as the loss of enjoyment in life due to pain and suffering, both physical and mental, and **loss of amenity**. Where the victim of the tort has been killed, the dependents may claim for any financial harm they suffer because of the demise of the tort victim.

Most damages are **compensatory damages**, in other words, the award is calculated to recompense the claimant for the harm suffered. There are other sorts of damages:

*   **Nominal damages** are awarded where the claimant has been successful but has suffered very little damage.
*   **Contemptuous damages** is the term given to the compensation where the claimant has been technically successful, but the claim had little merit.
*   **Exemplary** or **punitive damages** are given in English courts to punish the defendant or make an example of him; the claimant receives more than simple compensation for the harm suffered. An action for libel is an example of the type of case in which these damages may be awarded. To some lawyers outside the common law system, it may seem strange that punitive or exemplary damages may be awarded in civil cases. It should be pointed out that there are limited situations in which punitive or exemplary damages can be awarded.
*   **Aggravated damages** are also awarded where the defendant has behaved intentionally and has caused the claimant distress. Here the damages awarded are more than compensatory but less than punitive.

11.2   Injunction

An **injunction** is an equitable remedy and therefore discretionary. It will not be awarded if damages would be an adequate remedy. However, in certain tort cases, for example nuisance cases, an injunction is usually the remedy the claimant wants. A **prohibitory injunction** prohibits a person from doing something. In nuisance it would prohibit the tortfeasor from continuing the nuisance. A **mandatory injunction** requires the direct performance of a positive act. For example, if the nuisance is caused by trees situated in the tortfeasor's garden blocking the road, the tortfeasor could be ordered to chop down the obstruction. Injunctions may be granted on a temporary or permanent basis. An **interim injunction** *is* granted before the outcome of a trial. A final injunction, referred to either as a **perpetual** or **permanent injunction** may be granted upon the completion of a trial.

Tort case discussions

1   Mary is a florist who supplies flowers to various companies for their reception area, payment being at the end of the calendar month. One of these companies is Evasion Ltd. It has not paid for its flowers for months. Mary is unaware of this due to the inefficiency of her secretary.
Smith supplies magazines to companies for their reception area. He wants to do business with Evasion Ltd. He asks Mary whether the company pays its bills on time. Mary says that it does. Consequently, Smith supplies Evasion Ltd with magazines. However, having received no money after three months, he finds out that Evasion Ltd has been declared insolvent. He wants to sue Mary as he had relied on her advice. Would Smith's action in tort be successful?

2   John has just graduated with a degree in computer science and has applied for a job with a software company. He asks his old university lecturer, Dr. Peters, for a reference. Dr. Peters knows that John is a good candidate, but he wants his own son to get the job. So he writes to the software company saying that John was consistently late for class, showed little initiative and spent more time on women than on his studies. These statements were in fact untrue. John does not get the job. Can John bring an action in tort against Dr. Peters?

3   Richard has an orchard at the back of his house. He decides to cut down the trees and fences off that area. He then buys two tigers, which he keeps in a pen in the old orchard. Richard does not clean out the tiger pen very often as he is rather scared of the animals. The neighbours complain about the smell and the howling of the animals. The tiger pen is badly maintained and one day the smaller tiger manages to escape. The tiger mauls Richard's neighbour, causing him injuries to his face and hands, and ruins his flower-beds. What claims can the neighbour bring against Richard?

Tort knowledge questions

1   Tort overlaps two other major branches of law. Which branches are these?

2   Explain the concept of vicarious liability in tort.

3   Donoghue v Stevenson 1932 was the first major negligence case in English law. In that case Lord Atkin laid down 'the neighbour principle'. What is the neighbour principle?

4   In the area of law known as statutory product liability, manufacturers of products can be held 'strictly liable' for defects in their products. Explain what this means.

5   Explain how the operation of res ipsa loquitur in negligence cases alters the usual burden of proof.

6   What is the difference between the defences of contributory negligence and volenti non fit injuria?

7   In the tort of nuisance, what is meant by the term amenity damage?

8   The tort of defamation comprises two torts. What are they and in what way do they differ?

9   Explain what is meant by joint and several liability in tort.

10   What are the two major remedies in tort?

Chapter 5 **Contract law terminology**

Contract law vocabulary

Ab initio: Latin term meaning from the beginning. A contract terminated ab initio returns the parties to the pre-contractual position.

Acceptance: this is the acceptance of an offer either by words or conduct. There must be unconditional assent.

Accord and satisfaction: the accord is the agreement to discharge a contract, and the satisfaction is the consideration needed.

Adequate: the legal term adequate refers to the requirement of **consideration** for the formation of a contract. That consideration does not have to be adequate means the consideration given by one party does not have to be equal to that given by the other party.

Affirm: if a contract has been affirmed, in other words accepted, by a party once he knows of a defect, the right to rescind the contract is lost.

Agreements to agree: are not binding but simply an expression of the intentions of the parties.

Anticipatory breach: where a party makes it clear before the performance date is due that he will not perform his obligations under the contract.

Bars to rescission: it is not always possible to rescind a contract. The right is lost where there has been affirmation, restitutio in integrum is impossible or third party rights have intervened.

Battle of the forms: this term applies to the situation where parties have exchanged their own standard contracts and it is unclear whether the conditions laid down in the offer or the acceptance govern the contract.

Bilateral discharge: where both parties have not performed under the contract, discharge by agreement takes place by an exchange of promises not to enforce the original contract.

Binding: an agreement between two or more parties that is binding in law is a legally enforceable agreement.

Breach of contract: the refusal or failure by a party to a contract to perform an obligation imposed on him under the contract. Damages are available for any breach, but if the defaulting party has committed a very serious breach, the innocent party has the right to choose whether to end the contract as well as the right to claim damages.

Business efficacy rule: a court may be prepared to imply in a term if the agreement was clearly intended to create a legal relationship and, unless a term is implied in, the contract cannot function.

Capacity: refers to the ability of a natural or legal person to enter into a contract.

Caveat emptor: Latin phrase meaning 'let the buyer beware'.

Collateral contract: one party enters into the main contract on the basis of a promise made by the other party.

Collective agreements: these take the form of an agreement between trade unions and an employer.

Common mistake: the mistake is common where both parties mistakenly believe the same thing, and the mistaken assumption was based on a reasonable ground.

Condition: is a fundamental term of the contract. If it is breached, the **innocent party** may not only claim damages but may also opt to treat the contract as ended.

Condition precedent: is a condition stating that a right will not be granted until some future event.

Condition subsequent: is a condition stating that the contract can be modified or set aside if some event occurs later.

Consensus ad idem: Latin term referring to the need for a meeting of minds in order for there to be contractual agreement between the parties.

Consequential loss: unusual or special loss that would not necessarily be caused by the breach.

Consideration: the bargain. Each party gives value to the other either by exchanging promises or by a promise given in exchange for an act. A one-sided promise is not a binding contract.

Consumer: a person not acting in the course of business. There are special rules that apply to contracts where one of the parties is acting as a consumer.

Construction: where the court interprets the meaning of words.

Contra proferentem rule: an exclusion clause is interpreted strictly, so if there is any ambiguity in the wording of an exclusion clause, the clause will be construed as narrowly as possible against the one relying on the clause.

Contract: a contract is a legally enforceable agreement.

Contracts in restraint of trade: are those preventing the free exercise of trade or business. They are prima facie void unless it can be shown that the provision is reasonable as between the parties and not against the public interest.

Counter-offer: where not all the terms of an offer are accepted, then there is no acceptance but a counteroffer.

Damages: in contract law, financial compensation which should put the claimant in the position he would have been in if the contract had been performed properly.

Deed: a written document that has been signed by the parties and witnesses.

Discharge: release from the obligations under a contract. Discharge may be by performance, agreement, breach or frustration.

Discharge by agreement: both parties agree to end the contract.

Discharge by breach: a contract may be discharged by breach where the party in default has repudiated the contract either before performance is due or before it has been fully performed, or where there has been fundamental breach.

Discharge by frustration: parties are excused from the contract if, through no fault of either party, after the formation of the contract it becomes impossible to carry out the contract or the contract has become commercially sterile or futile.

Discharge by performance: the obligations under the contract have been carried out.

Divisible contract: in this case a contract can be divided into a number of specific parts.

Doctrine of impossibility: term often used in the USA for the doctrine of frustration.

Duress: violence or threats of violence in order to make someone enter into a contract. The contract is arguably void from the outset. If it is seen as voidable, it can be set aside. **Economic duress** may also make a contract voidable.

Entire contract: a contract that is not divisible into sets of obligations.

Ex post facto warranty: if the innocent party chooses to continue the contract, even though a condition has been breached, then the condition is treated as a warranty and the obligation is then referred to as an ex post facto warranty, and only damages may then be claimed.

Exceptio non adimpleti contractus: Latin phrase referring to a principle in the civil law, which allows the innocent party to suspend his own performance of the contract until the other party has fulfilled an agreed obligation.

Exclude: to rule out liability for contractual failure.

Exclusion or limitation clause: term to exclude or limit the liability of a party for breach of contract, misrepresentation or negligence.

Executed consideration: where one party performs an act in fulfilment of a promise made by the other, as in a unilateral contract.

Executory consideration: the term used to refer to an exchange of promises to perform acts in the future.

Expectation damages: damages the innocent party can claim in a breach of contract action, where the damages take into account the profit the innocent party should have received if the defaulting party had performed the contract as agreed.

Express terms: terms explicitly stated by the parties, either oral or written.

Firm offer: in English law this simply means that the offer is unequivocal. It does not mean that the offer cannot be withdrawn.

Force majeure: most contracts include a force majeure clause. This lists events considered to be outside the control of the parties and for which the parties cannot be considered to be in breach.

Fraudulent misrepresentation: the person knew that the statement was untrue, or was reckless as to whether it was true.

Frustrating event: an event, beyond the control of the parties, that has made it impossible to carry out the contract or commercially pointless to do so.

Frustration of the common venture: a contract can be discharged by frustration where there is no physical destruction of the subject-matter, but the essential commercial purpose of the contract no longer exists.

Fundamental term/breach: a term is fundamental if it goes to the root of the contract. If it is breached, the breach is referred to as fundamental breach.

Good faith: see **principle of good faith**.

Guarantee: a legally enforceable promise that the goods are of good quality and will work properly. This is sometimes referred to as a warranty.

Honour clause: this clause makes clear that there is no intention to create legal relations.

Illegality: certain types of contracts are illegal and therefore void.

Implied terms: terms that can be read into the contract, either by custom, statute or by the courts.

In lieu of: instead of, for example damages instead of rescission.

Incorporation: the exemption clause must have been incorporated into the contract either by including it in a signed document or by giving notice of it where there is no written document.

Indemnify: to reimburse someone for the damage that he has suffered, a statement of liability to pay compensation for a loss or for a wrong in a transaction.

Indemnity: an order of rescission may be accompanied by the court ordering an indemnity. An indemnity is not the same as damages; it is simply to put the parties back in the pre-contractual position, so that the innocent party is neither better off nor worse off than before.

Induce: to encourage or persuade someone. It is used here in the sense of encouraging someone to enter into a contract.

Inequality of bargaining power: one party to a contract may have a dominant bargaining position and the other party has little bargaining power and therefore little choice. As a consequence, the bargain is very one-sided.

Inequitable: unfair, against the principles adopted by the court of equity.

Injunction: with respect to contract law, usually a court order to stop a negative stipulation in the contract from being broken. It is a discretionary remedy and will not be ordered if damages are a sufficient remedy.

Innocent misrepresentation: the maker of the statement had reasonable grounds for believing that it was true.

Innocent party: the term refers to the party to a contract who has suffered loss because the other party is in default.

Innominate term: a term is classed as innominate where it is uncertain whether it is to be treated as a condition or as a warranty.

Intention to create legal relations: there must be an intention to create a legally binding agreement.

Invitation to tender: although a tender is an **offer**, an invitation to tender will usually be an invitation to treat.

Invitation to treat: this is a stage in negotiations where one party is inviting others to make an offer, which he is free to accept or reject. An invitation to treat is not an offer.

Just apportionment: statute law makes provision for a fair adjustment of costs incurred under a contract discharged by frustration.

Lapse: no longer valid. An offer is said to lapse when the time in which the offer could be accepted has expired.

Last shot rule: where parties have exchanged their own standard contracts, the last shot rule means that the conditions laid down in the acceptance will be the ones to determine the contract.

Letter of comfort: this type of letter is usually written in support of someone who is applying for a loan and offers the potential offeror reassurance.

Letter of guarantee: this letter takes the form of a declaration to guarantee the payment of a debt incurred by another if that other fails to repay.

Letter of intent: this letter is not a contract. Its terms are not legally binding. In the common law, it is considered simply to be an attempt to put a preliminary understanding into a written form.

'**Lie where they fall**': at common law there is no just apportionment for costs incurred when a contract is discharged by frustration. It is generally not possible to recover money due or paid before the frustrating event.

Liquidated damages: where the parties themselves, rather than the court, have determined the level of damages.

Liquidated damages clause: a proper attempt to pre-estimate the loss that would result if the other party breaches the contract.

Main purpose rule: it is presumed that an exemption clause is not intended to defeat the main purpose of the contract.

Mandatory injunction: a court order requiring the defendant to act.

Merchant: the term merchant is used in the American UCC to indicate a professional contracting party or one skilled in an occupation.

Minor: a minor is a person under the age of majority, the age of majority being eighteen years in English law.

Misrepresentation: where the representation is a false statement, it is called a misrepresentation. Misrepresentations can be fraudulent, negligent or innocent.

Misrepresentor/misrepresentee: the misrepresentor is the one making the false statement, the misrepresentee is the one to whom the false statement is made.

Mistake: where the mistake is of an operative and fundamental character, which goes to the very substance of the contract, the contract will be **void**.

Mistake as to identity: this is usually a unilateral mistake where one party is mistaken as to the identity of the other party.

Mistake as to quality: mistake as to the quality of the subject-matter of the contract is not usually sufficient to make the contract void.

Mitigation: the innocent party must take reasonable steps to minimise his loss.

Mutual mistake: is where the parties are at cross-purposes, the offer being made in one sense and accepted in another.

Naturally arising: damages may be claimed for losses that arise naturally from the nature of the contract.

Negligent misrepresentation: a lack of reasonable care was taken in making the statement.

Nominal consideration: something of minimal value exchanged in order to make the other party's promise legally enforceable.

Non-consumer: a person acting other than as a consumer, carrying out some form of commercial activity.

Non est factum: in general, a person is bound by the terms of a document that he has signed, even if he has not read it or understood it. The non est factum defence forms an exception to this rule in certain circumstances.

Notice of default: notice is given to the defaulting party that he is in breach of contract, and a period of time is usually specified within which the defaulting party must fulfil his obligations. Notice is not a general requirement in English law but parties are free to agree to give such notice.

Of the essence: words used in a contract to show that a particular term is of fundamental importance.

Offer: an offer shows a willingness to enter into a contract without further negotiations. (Compare **invitation to treat** which is merely a step in negotiations.)

Offeror/offeree: the one making an offer is called the 'offeror'. The person to whom an offer is made is called the 'offeree'.

Parol evidence rule (four corners rule): where a contract is embodied in a written document, then extrinsic (parol) evidence is not admissible to add to, vary, subtract from or contradict the terms of the written document. The rights and duties created by the written agreement must be looked for only within the four corners of the writing itself.

Partial performance: where the performance is not exact and complete.

Past consideration: past consideration is not valid, as it refers to a promise to do something that has already been done before the promise was made.

Penalty clause: the penalty is meant to punish the other party for breach, or deter him from breaching the contract. In English law, penalty clauses are in principle unenforceable.

Peppercorn rent: where nominal consideration has been given in order to make the agreement legally binding.

Performance: to carry out obligations under a contract.

Postal rule: in English law, where acceptance is to be communicated by post then acceptance is complete when the letter is posted, even if the letter is never delivered.

Pre-contractual: this term indicates a period of negotiation prior to entering into a contract.

Presumption: the law makes certain assumptions based on a set of facts. In order to override a presumption, a party must bring forward further convincing evidence.

Previous course of dealing: an exclusion clause may have been incorporated because the parties have contracted before on the same consistent terms.

Prima facie: Latin term meaning 'at first sight'.

Principle of good faith: here negotiations and contractual relations should be characterised by honesty and fairness, by the intention to carry out contractual obligations, and with no intention to seek an unfair advantage or purposefully act to the detriment of the other party. This principle is not operative in the common law of contract.

Privity of contract: a contract only confers rights and obligations on the parties to the contract. There are, however, exceptions to this rule both in statute law and common law.

Promisor/promisee: the promisor is the one making the promise; the promisee is the one to whom the promise is made.

Promissory estoppel: promissory estoppel is an equitable principle. It may make a one-sided promise binding where there is an existing legal relationship and the promisor has promised not to enforce a legal right. Having induced reliance on this promise, it would be inequitable not to enforce the promise.

Proximate: damages are awarded for a loss that clearly results from an event of default.

Purchaser: an alternative term for buyer.

Quantum meruit: the claim of quantum meruit is for 'as much as he deserves'.

Reasonable: in order to prevent the abuse of exclusion clauses there has been statutory intervention demanding that an exclusion clause must be reasonable. This also gives protection to non-consumers.

Reasonable man/person: an objective test to establish the behaviour or expectations of a reasonable person.

Rebut: to refute or oppose, for example to rebut a claim or a presumption.

Remoteness of damage: the loss suffered by the innocent party must be either a natural cause of the breach or reasonably within the contemplation of the parties as the probable result of a breach. If not, the damage is too remote and no damages can be claimed.

Representation: it is a statement that induces the contract but does not itself form a part of that contract.

Representor/representee: the representor is the one making the representation, the representee is the one to whom the representation is made.

Repudiation: the other party makes it clear, either explicitly or implicitly, that he will not perform or continue to perform the contract.

Rescission: the representee can opt to have a voidable contract set aside. He is said to **rescind** the contract. Where there has been a misrepresentation, the contract can be terminated retrospectively. The contract is void and the parties are put back in the position they were in before the contract was made.

Restitutio in integrum: Latin term meaning 'to restore something to its original state'. Where it is not possible to go back to the original state, the equitable remedy of rescission is not available.

Revoke: an act of annulment, such as withdrawing an offer.

Rights and obligations: the terms of the contract set out the legal rights and obligations of the parties.

Rule in Pinnel's case: the payment of a lesser amount than is owed cannot discharge the obligation to pay the full amount, even if the creditor has agreed to accept the lesser amount, unless there is fresh consideration.

Rule of construction: interpretation of a clause, such as an exclusion clause, in order to reflect the parties' intention when making the clause.

Rule of law: unlike a rule of construction, this must be applied whether it would mean giving effect to the parties' intention or not.

Set aside: to annul or make void. A voidable contract is valid until it is set aside.

Signatory: one who signs a document.

Simple contract: a contract that does not have to be in any particular form.

Sit on the breach: there is a duty on the claimant to take all reasonable steps to mitigate loss. He should not simply do nothing and let the situation deteriorate even further.

Special notice: if a claimant wants to claim damages for losses that do not arise naturally from the contract but could reasonably be supposed by both parties to be a probable result of a breach, then he must give the other party special notice of such probable losses.

Specific performance: a court order to make a person carry out his obligations under a contract. This is a discretionary remedy and will not be ordered if damages are a sufficient remedy.

Statement of fact: to be classed as a misrepresentation, the statement must be a statement of fact not of opinion.

Statement of opinion: in general a statement of opinion is not classed as a misrepresentation unless it is not actually held or it implies a factual basis.

Substantial performance: substantial performance means that the contractual obligations are as good as fulfilled except for a few minor aspects.

Sufficient: where the law recognises the consideration as having some value, the consideration is termed sufficient.

Suspension of performance: in the common law, there is no general principle allowing an innocent party to suspend his own performance because the other party is in breach.

Tender: a tender is an offer to provide goods or services for a specified price. An invitation to tender is usually not an offer but an invitation to treat.

Termination: a contract is terminated when it is brought to an end. The term termination should be used rather than rescission where the contract is discharged by **breach**.

Terms: the promises and stipulations that are part of a contract. Not all the terms in a contract are of equal importance. English law categorises terms as conditions or warranties.

Third party: one who is not a party to the original contract.

Trade usage: where the contract is silent on the matter, a term can be incorporated into a contract reflecting local custom or trade usage in a particular sector.

Uberrimae fidei: this Latin term means of the utmost good faith. In contracts that are uberrimae fidei there is a duty of full disclosure.

Uncertainty: if a term of a contract is uncertain it may defeat the contract if that term is of fundamental importance, although there are exceptions to this rule.

Unconscionability/unconscionable inadequacy: this doctrine is more developed in American contract law than in English contract law. It allows a contract to be set aside where there is an **unconscionable bargain**. This is a bargain that is so detrimental to one of the contracting parties as to be an affront to what can be considered reasonable.

Undue influence: refers to improper pressure other than violence to make someone enter into a contract.

Unfair contract terms: refers in particular to the use of exclusion clauses.

Unilateral contract: in this type of contract there is no exchange of promises. Instead, one party provides consideration in the form of a promise and the other party provides consideration in the form of an act.

Unilateral discharge: where there has been performance or partial performance by only one party, there can only be discharge if the other party draws up a deed or provides fresh consideration.

Unliquidated damages: the quantification of damages is at the discretion of the court.

Vendor: an alternative term for seller.

Vitiating factor: a vitiating factor is a defect that was present in the agreement at the time the contract was concluded. The defect is sufficiently serious to have the contract set aside. Vitiating factors include misrepresentation, mistake, duress and undue influence.

Void: a void contract is one that was never legally valid and without legal effect.

Voidable: a voidable contract is a valid contract, but it contains a vitiating factor. That means it can be made void if one of the parties takes steps to rescind the contract.

Waiver: where one party voluntarily gives up his right to insist upon precise performance under the contract.

Warranties and indemnities: here a warranty refers to a statement made by one party promising the other party that the facts are as stated. It is usually connected to a promise to indemnify the promisee for any loss he sustains from having relied on the promise if the promise is false.

Warranty: is a term of lesser importance than a condition. Its breach would not give the innocent party the option to end the contract, but it would give the innocent party the right to claim damages. In the USA, warranty is used in the sense of warranties and indemnities and in particular in the context of the sale of goods where representations made by the seller, either express or implied, become part of the contract of sale. This creates a warranty, which means that the goods must conform to these representations. If they do not, the innocent party can bring an action for breach of warranty.

Contract law terminology in context

1   INTRODUCTION

There is something of a culture clash between the English law of contract and contract law in civil law systems. To many lawyers in civil law systems, English contract law appears harsh and rigid. And English lawyers often look upon the contract law of their continent neighbours as too vague and discretionary.

It would be fair to say that English contract law is based upon the presumption that ordinary, adult individuals are capable of making their own bargains and knowing what is in their own interests. The common law is primarily concerned with the need for legal certainty in interpreting contractual terms: the law will enforce what has actually been agreed and it will not try to ascertain the mental state of the parties. Consequently, common law courts adopt an objective approach to contracts, interpreting contracts literally and strictly according to their terms. The intention of the parties is inferred from the contract itself. By contrast, when Dutch courts interpret contracts they take into account not just a linguistic analysis of the contract, but also other factors, such as the reasonable expectations of the parties given the nature of the contract and what would be fair and reasonable.

This different approach to contract law means that some principles, generally taken for granted in civil law systems, do not exist or only exist in an underdeveloped form in English common law. For example, the **principle of good faith** has no role to play in the English common law of contract. The principle of **unconscionability** is known in English law but is not of major significance. In many instances, where the lawyer in the civil law system would be calling upon such principles, English common law is silent. There are times, however, when the 'harshness' of the English common law is mitigated by the principles of equity (see chapter 1). These principles of equity are the nearest equivalent to the concept of 'fair and reasonable'.

Note: American contract law is generally based on the English common law of contracts. However, in some instances the traditional common law approach has been modified. The Uniform Commercial Code (UCC) is one such example. It contains provisions which deviate from English common law (see below). One such deviation is that contracts that fall within the ambit of the UCC are subject to the principles of good faith and unconscionability.

2   THE FORM OF A CONTRACT

Not all agreements are contracts. A **contract** is a specific type of agreement. It may be defined as an agreement between two or more parties that is **binding** in law, in other words, it is a legally enforceable agreement. This means that the agreement generates **rights and obligations** that may be enforced in the courts. A non-contractual agreement may still be honoured by the parties out of a sense of moral or social obligation, but no legal sanctions are available.

The common law in general allows freedom with respect to the form in which a contract may be made. Contracts can be by word of mouth, written or partly written and partly oral. In some cases it is even possible to infer a contract from the conduct of the parties. The term **simple contract** is used to describe a contract that does not have to comply with any requirements of form. A simple contract may, nonetheless, be in writing. This is not because it is a legal requirement, but because a written agreement provides better evidence of what was agreed between the parties than an oral agreement.

However, some contracts are only binding if in a certain form: a written form. In English law, a **deed** (a written document, signed by the parties and witnessed) is necessary to transfer the legal title in land from one party to another or create a lease of more than three years duration. A written contract is also required for transferring copyright, hire purchase agreements, transfer of shares, cheques, bills of exchange and promissory notes. In English law, a contract of employment does not have to be in writing, but a written statement of the main terms and conditions of employment must be provided. A contract that is not in the required form will be invalid.

Note: the same attitude to freedom with respect to the form in which a contract is made is found in civil law systems too. Under Dutch law, for example, there is no general requirement that a contract should be in writing; in principle it is 'form free'. However, just as in the common law, there are a number of exceptions to that principle.

3   FORMATION OF A CONTRACT

If an agreement is to be in the form of a contract, English law demands that certain basic elements must be present. For the formation of a contract, three elements are necessary:
1   offer and acceptance;
2   intention to create a legally binding relationship;
3   the presence of consideration.

3.1 Offer and acceptance

A contract rests on agreement. There must be a **consensus ad idem**. This Latin term denotes a meeting of minds. As in civil law systems, the process of offer and acceptance must, in general, show agreement on the fundamental terms of the contract. Whether there is agreement is judged objectively in the common law. What is examined is the external appearance of the contract, not the mental state of the parties at the time of contracting.

3.1.1 Offer

The person who makes the offer is called the **offeror**, the person to whom it is made is called the **offeree**. An **offer** may be defined as a statement of willingness to contract according to the terms proposed with the intent that it will become a binding contract if accepted. For an offer to be legally effective, it must comply with certain requirements:
- the offer must be unequivocal;
- the offer must be communicated;
- the terms in the offer must be certain;
- the offer must not have terminated.

Note 1: the term **firm offer** can cause confusion, as the implication of this term is different in the civil law. The word 'firm' used in the context of English law only describes an unequivocal offer; it does not mean that the offer cannot be withdrawn. In English law an offer creates no legal rights *until* it is accepted. One consequence is that, unlike in the civil law, an offer may be **revoked** despite the fact that the offeror had promised to keep the offer open for a specified period of time. An offer described as a 'firm offer' can, therefore, be revoked any time before acceptance if there is no **consideration** (see below). There will be consideration if the offer is given in exchange for something else, for example, the option on the offer is purchased.

Note 2: the same traditional common law rule with respect to the right to revoke an offer any time before acceptance generally applies in the USA. However, the classic common law position is not upheld in contracts that fall within the ambit of Article 2 of the UCC, which applies specifically to written offers by a **merchant** (being a professional or one skilled in that occupation) to buy and sell goods. Here a firm offer made in a commercial setting cannot be revoked for up to three months, even if there is no consideration.

3.1.2 Invitation to treat

It is necessary to distinguish an offer from an **invitation to treat**. An offer may be made by words or conduct that shows a willingness to enter into a contract without further negotiations. An invitation to treat, however, is merely a step in negotiations where a party is simply inviting offers that he is free to accept or reject. For example, an agent rang up a person who was selling a house and asked: "what is the lowest price you would accept for your house?" He was told "not less than £400,000", to which he replied "I accept your offer of £400,000." It was held that the sum of £400,000 was an invitation to treat and not an offer. Advertisements are generally regarded as invitations to treat. At an auction, the auctioneer does not make an offer to sell the goods, but an invitation to treat. By contrast, each bid is an offer.

3.1.3 Tender

There is also a distinction between a **tender** and an **invitation to tender**. A tender is an offer. An invitation to tender will usually be an invitation to treat. Although an invitation to tender will not normally amount to an offer to contract with the party submitting the most favourable tender, if it can be shown that this was clearly the intention of the parties it will be enforced.

3.1.4 Communication of the offer

In English law, an offer does not have to be addressed to a specific person. It can be made to the public at large, for example, offering a reward to anyone who finds a lost cat. This type of contractual arrangement, where the offeree's performance of the specified act is the acceptance of the offer, is known in the common law as a **unilateral contract**. However, an offer cannot be accepted by someone who is unaware of its existence.

Note: the term **unilateral contract** is sometimes misused by civil law lawyers. It should not be used to describe an agreement where only one party offers value. This type of agreement is not considered to be a contract in English common law.

3.1.5 Certainty of terms

If a term in a contract is **uncertain**, it will depend upon how fundamental that term is to the contract as to whether the contract will fail. A minor term that is unclear will not render a contract invalid; lack of clarity with respect to a **fundamental term** may well be fatal to the contract. In certain instances, however, even where a fundamental term is unclear the contract will stand: in contracts for the sale of goods if the parties have not agreed a price, the price will be interpreted as referring to a 'reasonable price'.

3.1.6 Termination of an offer

An offer is terminated when it has been **revoked**, or it has **lapsed** or been met with a **counter-offer**. The revocation of an offer means that the offer has been withdrawn by the offeror. The offeror must, however, bring this to the attention of the offeree. An offer is said to lapse after the time limit for the offer has expired or, if there was no time limit, after a reasonable interval. It is also terminated where the offeree does not accept all the terms of the offer and instead makes a counter-offer.

3.2   Acceptance

Acceptance is unconditional assent, communicated to the offeror by the offeree, to all the terms of the offer. Where there is not unequivocal acceptance, for example where one of the terms is rejected, this is termed a **counter-offer**. A counter-offer is a rejection of the original offer and there can be no contract until the counter-offer is accepted. For example, in a case where the seller had made an offer to sell his farm for £1,000, but the other party offered £950, it was held that there was no contract when the other party later decided to accept the seller's offer of £1,000 because this was not acceptance of the original offer as that original offer had been extinguished by the counter-offer.

Note: as already noted, the UCC contains some provisions that deviate from the traditional English common law. Relevant here is the provision that a contract will not necessarily be defeated because the acceptance contains terms in addition to or different from the terms of the original offer.

3.2.1 The postal rule

The offeror is free to stipulate how the acceptance should be given although acceptance must actually be communicated. Consequently, there can generally be no acceptance simply by silence. Unless a specific method of acceptance has been specified, an offer can be accepted either by words or conduct. The contract will come into being when and where the acceptance is received.

Civil law practitioners should be aware of a peculiarity in English law which has to do with acceptance sent through the post. The **postal rule** states that acceptance is complete when the letter is posted, even if the letter never reaches the offeror. This rather eccentric rule can be overridden by an express clause stating that acceptance sent via the post will only be effective when received; the usual rule in civil law systems.

3.2.2 The 'battle of the forms'

This term applies to situations where offer and acceptance by the contracting parties are made on their own standard, printed contracts. As a result, it can be unclear which set of conditions applies: those conditions set down in the offer or those set down in the acceptance? A common approach to resolving this problem is the so-called **last shot rule**. This means that the conditions laid down in the acceptance will govern the contract. For example, where the contract is a sales contract and there has been one offer by the seller and one acceptance by the buyer prior to the performance of the contract, the buyer's terms will be the relevant ones.

Note: an alternative word for 'seller' is **vendor**. A buyer may also be referred to as a **purchaser**.

3.3   Intention to create legal relations

Not all agreements are intended to create legally enforceable rights and obligations. If it is concluded that the intention of the agreement was not to create a legal relationship, then there is no contract. In English common law, there are certain presumptions that help to determine whether such an intention was indeed present.

3.3.1 Presumptions

With respect to domestic or social arrangements, it is presumed that the agreement was not intended to be binding, for example arrangements between parents and children. This **presumption** can be **rebutted** if there is clear evidence of an intention to create a contractual relationship.

In the case of commercial agreements, it is presumed that there is an intention to create a legally binding relationship. Similarly, to rebut this presumption there must be very clear evidence that there was no intention to create legal relations. Factors to be taken into account in this respect include whether an **honour clause** has been used, a clause that would typically use words like 'binding in honour only'. It is also important to distinguish a **letter of comfort** from a **letter of guarantee**. For example, where one party does not wish to give a formal guarantee that it will cover a loan taken out by a third party, it may issue a letter of comfort that is intended to give reassurance to the creditor. Where it is clear that the letter of comfort is not offering a guarantee, it will usually be interpreted as not giving rise to contractual obligations.

There is also a presumption that **collective agreements** are not intended to be legally binding. These are agreements made between trade unions and an employer. They deal with conditions of employment, such as rates of pay and conditions of work. It should be noted that provisions in collective agreements will be legally binding if they have been **incorporated** into an individual contract of employment.

3.3.2 Pre-contractual liability

Another question to be determined is whether there was any intention to create legally binding relations in a **pre-contractual** phase. As part of negotiations, it is quite usual to draw up **agreements to agree** such as a **letter of intent**. In common law jurisdictions these agreements are in principle not binding. It is seen as a declaration of interest in entering into a contract in the future, but in itself it is only a preliminary stage in negotiations. No legally enforceable rights can therefore be obtained from a letter of intent unless the parties expressly stipulate otherwise. For example, a clause could be inserted which states:

> "Except with respect to paragraphs 5 and 8 above, which shall constitute a legally binding agreement between the parties, this letter neither constitutes an offer nor a binding obligation."

In civil law jurisdictions, a letter of intent may trigger legal consequences. For example, in the Netherlands, in certain circumstances a letter of intent may be treated as a legally enforceable contract.

In legal systems where the doctrine of **good faith** is recognised, breaking off contractual negotiations may give rise to legal consequences. The Italian Civil Code, for example, expressly states that there is a duty to negotiate in good faith. In the Netherlands, where the concept of reasonableness and fairness also plays an important role, once negotiations have clearly gone beyond an initial stage, the party that breaks off the negotiations may have to reimburse the costs of the other party and, if the negotiations have reached an extremely advanced stage, breaking off negotiations may no longer be allowed.

There is, in general, no duty to negotiate in good faith in English law. There is no liability, either in contract or in tort, for pulling out of negotiations at any stage and for whatever reason. Where English law is applicable, a party entering into such negotiations should therefore arrange with the other party, in a specific contract, that the one pulling out of negotiations will reimburse the other party for any losses suffered as a consequence of the withdrawal.

Note: some other common law jurisdictions, such as the Australian and American, show more respect for the concept of good faith. The American UCC imposes a duty of good faith and recent Australian case law indicates a development in that direction.

3.4   Consideration

In the common law, **consideration** is a vital element in the formation of a contract. Consideration is best defined through the language of buying and selling. One party must show that he has bought the other party's promise either by doing some act in return for it or by offering a counter-promise. English law requires a simple contract to be a bargain. The court enforces a bargain, not a one-sided promise. This means that a promise to make a gift is generally unenforceable in the common law of contract because there is no consideration. To make a promise enforceable, the promise should either be exchanged for **nominal consideration**, such as £1, or be made in the form of a **deed**.

3.4.1 Types of consideration

Executory consideration is the term used to refer to an exchange of promises to perform acts in the future, for example a promise to deliver goods in return for a promise made by the other party to pay for the goods. **Executed consideration** is where one party performs an act in fulfilment of a promise made by the other, for example in a unilateral contract where one of the parties has offered a reward for finding his cat and the other party has found the cat.

A promise made by one party must be given in response to a promise made by another party. Where a promise is given to pay for something done in the past, this is classed as **past consideration** and it is not valid. For example, if work has already been carried out free of charge and only when it is completed is a promise given to pay for it, this promise to pay would be past consideration. In general, fresh consideration will be necessary in order to make the agreement binding. An exception to this rule is where the claimant can maintain that the work was carried out because of an implicit promise by the other party to pay.

3.4.2 Nature of consideration

The value of the consideration given by one party does not have to be equal to the value of the consideration given by the other party. The consideration must have some value, but the value could be minimal. In other words, consideration does not have to be **adequate**. Here the legal term adequate means equal to the promise given. Where the law does recognise the consideration as having some value, the consideration is termed **sufficient**. The courts will not defeat a contract simply because one of the parties has made a bad bargain. For example, given that the contract has been entered into freely, if one party pays rent of £1 per month this would be sufficient consideration, even if the ordinary market rate for renting that property would be £100 per month rather than £1 per month. This type of nominal consideration is sometimes referred to as a **peppercorn rent**.

There are certain limits as to what will be seen by the courts as sufficient consideration. A promise to carry out a duty that is already owed to the **promisee** will not be sufficient consideration, for example where there is an existing contractual obligation to carry out that promise. Only if the circumstances have changed dramatically may it be possible to show that a new contract has actually been entered into.

Another rule for assessing sufficiency was laid down in an old case determined in 1602. It is called the **Rule in Pinnel's case**: payment of a lesser amount than is owed cannot discharge the obligation to pay the full amount, even if the creditor has expressly agreed to release the other party from the original obligation and accepts a lesser amount. In English law, there would be nothing to prevent the creditor from suing for the rest of the money at a later date, as the agreement was not supported by consideration from the debtor. However, such an agreement for part-payment will be binding if there is fresh consideration from the debtor. Consideration will be sufficient if the creditor receives something of value from the debtor in return for abandoning his right to the full amount. If a lesser amount is paid before the date on which the sum is due to be paid, this will be sufficient consideration as it is of benefit to the creditor. Substituted performance if accepted by the creditor will also suffice, for example, the creditor accepts a chattel instead of money.

Note: it could be the case that there is an **inequality of bargaining power** between the parties to a contract. One party to a contract may have a dominant bargaining position and the other party has little bargaining power and therefore little choice. As a consequence, the bargain is very one-sided. In English law, there is no general principle that a contract based upon an inequality of bargaining power should be set aside. However, the doctrine of **economic duress** may make a contract voidable if someone was forced to enter into a contract and there was no true consent on his part. In certain circumstances, a weaker party may find a remedy for an **unconscionable bargain** under the equitable principle of **undue influence** (see below). The doctrine of **unconscionability** is not as well developed in English law as in the USA. In the American UCC, for example, the term **unconscionable inadequacy** describes a contract where the bargain is so one-sided as to be absolutely unreasonable. Although the UCC accepts the traditional common law position that a contract can be grounded on an inequality of values, an unconscionable contract or term should not be enforced especially where one party is a consumer.

3.4.3 Promissory estoppel

In very particular circumstances, the common law rules on consideration can be side-stepped by calling upon the equitable concept of **promissory estoppel**. The doctrine provides a means of making a promise binding without consideration, but its application is limited. There must be an existing contractual relationship between the parties and a clear and unambiguous statement by the **promisor** that he will not enforce a legal right under that contract. The legal effect of the estoppel is to stop one party not keeping his promise where the **promisee** has clearly relied on the promise, and it is reasonably foreseeable that the promisee would rely on that promise. It would then be **inequitable**, in other words unfair, for the promisor to go back on his word.

For example, in one case a landlord gave his tenant six months notice to make repairs otherwise the lease would be ended. During that period, the landlord initiated negotiations with the tenant for the sale of the lease. The tenant did not repair in this period. When negotiations broke down, the landlord claimed the lease was ended because the repairs had not been made within the six months notice period. The court held that the opening of negotiations by the landlord amounted to a promise not to enforce the notice while negotiations continued, and the tenant had relied on this promise and made no repairs. The tenant was entitled to equitable relief in the sense of being given extra time. His obligation to repair was suspended because of the promise but not extinguished.

Note: the scope of the doctrine of promissory estoppel is not entirely clear. The position was always that the doctrine could only be used as a defence, but not as a cause of action. Nonetheless, in both American and Australian courts estoppel has been used in several recent cases not as a defence but as a cause of action.

4   CAPACITY

In the context of contract law, the term **capacity** refers to the ability of a natural or legal person to enter into a contract. There are three special cases with respect to contractual capacity: corporations, persons of unsound mind and **minors**.

Corporations are legal persons and may enter into contracts and be sued for breach of contract. However, an incorporated body, such as a registered company, only has the right to enter into contracts within the scope of its objects clause. The implementation of a EU directive now makes it possible for a company to be bound by a contract that is outside the objects clause (see chapter 6). A contract entered into by a person of unsound mind can be set aside if the person's condition was clear to the other party. Finally, minors, otherwise referred to as children, are protected by the law from entering into unfavourable transactions.

5   PARTIES TO THE CONTRACT

The general rule is that no-one is entitled or bound by the terms of a contract if he is not an original party. This is called the doctrine of **privity of contract**. The principle is still the determining factor in English common law, although there are a number of exceptions at common law. Since 1999, the doctrine of privity has also been affected by a statute. This statute allows a named or designated third party who is to benefit from the contract to enforce it.

6   CONTENTS OF THE CONTRACT

A contract consists of the promises that the parties have made to each other. These promises are legal obligations and are legally enforceable. The undertakings stipulated in a contract are grouped together under the word **terms**. They may be oral or written. Terms may be express or implied and will determine the extent of the party's rights and duties.

6.1   The parol evidence rule

Civil law lawyers often remark on the fact that common law contracts are so extensive: what a Dutch contract can say in four pages, takes an English or American contract twenty pages! The reason that Anglo-American contracts are so bulky is because of the **parol evidence rule**, otherwise referred to as the **four corners rule**.

At common law, where a contract is embodied in a written document, and that written document looks as if it should be treated as the entire contract, no external evidence will be admissible to vary the terms of the written contract. This means that it is not possible to vary the terms of a written document by bringing in oral, or other, evidence to show a contrary intention. The rule reflects the emphasis of the common law on contractual certainty rather than ascertaining the actual intention of the parties. It is a harsh rule; even though its abolition has been recommended on various occasions, it is still unwise to place any reliance on an oral agreement if that oral agreement is not in keeping with a formal written document. The parol evidence rule can, however, be circumvented. One example is where a party can maintain that the contract was partly oral and partly written, so that the parties did not intend the written document to be the sole evidence of the agreement. Another example is the existence of a **collateral contract**: where one party can show that he entered into the main contract because of a promise made by the other party. A collateral contract must have all the elements of an independent valid contract.

The parol evidence rule leads to more extensive contracts because the contract drafter must try to anticipate all possible eventualities. In this way, extrinsic evidence would be irrelevant anyway as a means of interpreting the contract as the solution to any dispute between the parties could be found within the four corners of the contract itself.

6.2 Pre-contractual phase

In a pre-contractual phase, certain statements may be made during negotiations. Some of these statements will later reappear as terms of the contract. However, not all statements made in the pre-contractual phase will become part of the final agreement. A statement may simply have been made in order to encourage or **induce** the other party to enter into the contract, but it was made without the intention that it should become part of the contract itself.

A **representation** is the name given to a statement that induces the contract but does not itself form part of it. As will be seen below, the remedy for a false representation will lie in an action for **misrepresentation** and not in breach of contract, as it is not a term of the contract. It should be pointed out that in certain specific circumstances a misrepresentation may be classed as a term of a contract (see below). Where a misrepresentation can be classed as a term of the contract, the injured party can sue either for misrepresentation or for breach of contract.

6.3 Classification of contract terms

A **term** is a promise or undertaking that is part of the contract itself. The importance of a contractual term can vary: it may be of fundamental importance, going to the very root of the contract, or it may be of only minor importance. In English law, the terms of a contract are classified either as conditions, which are fundamental terms of a contract, or as warranties, which are minor terms.

6.3.1 *Condition*

A **condition** is a fundamental term. Its performance is so integral to the contract that, if it is not carried out, the **innocent party** has the right to treat the contract as **repudiated**. Not only does the innocent party have the right to claim damages but also to treat the contract as ended. If the innocent party does choose to continue the contract, then the condition is treated as a warranty and the obligation is then referred to as an **ex post facto warranty**, and only damages may then be claimed.

Note 1: a contract may describe a term as being a condition to indicate that the term is of fundamental importance. Alternatively, an obligation may be said to be **of the essence**.

Note 2: the word 'condition' describes the status of a term. This may appear odd to lawyers in civil law systems, who are more familiar with the use of the word condition to denote an external event which suspends or cancels an obligation. This use of the word is also found in English contract law. A **condition precedent** is a condition saying a right will not be granted until something is done. In English law, agreements made subject to some future event may produce a variety of results. There may be no contract at all, either because the parties have agreed not to be bound until some future event, for example the execution of a formal contract, or because the condition is uncertain. On the other hand, it may be that the whole existence of the contract is suspended until the happening of the stated event. A **condition subsequent** is a condition stating that the contract can be modified or set aside if some event occurs later.

6.3.2 *Warranty*

The word **warranty** is used to indicate that a term in the contract is of lesser importance. A warranty is described as a term collateral to the main purpose of the contract. The breach of a warranty does not give the innocent party the right to treat the contract as **discharged** but would allow the innocent party to claim damages. Commercially, there may be reasons for treating what would normally be seen as a condition as a warranty in order to avoid the repudiation of the contract. With respect to contracts for the sale of goods, even if there has been a breach of a major term, the parties will often agree to treat it as a breach of a warranty.

Note 1: the word **warranty** is used in English law in various ways, not only to denote a contractual term of lesser importance. It is commonly used in the sense of **guarantee**, for example that the product has a warranty for a period of one year. The word may also be found in the main body of the contract itself, usually under a heading **warranties and indemnities**. In this context, a warranty refers to a promise made by one party that the other party can rely upon the existence of a certain fact, and does not have to investigate this fact himself, for example where a manufacturer warrants to a distributor that no third party has the right to use any trademarks used by the manufacturer. It is normally connected to a promise to **indemnify** the promisee for any loss he sustains from having relied on the promise, if it should turn out to be untrue.

Note 2: in the USA, the term warranty is also used to refer to a promise made by one party to the other party so that the other party can rely upon the existence of a certain fact, and does not have to investigate this fact himself. In particular, the term warranty will be found in the context of the sale of goods where representations made by the seller, either express or implied, become part of the contract of sale. This creates a warranty, which means that the goods must conform to these representations. If they do not, the innocent party can bring an action for breach of warranty.

6.3.3 Innominate term

It is sometimes difficult to determine whether a term is a condition or a warranty. In that case it may be referred to as an **innominate term**, meaning an intermediate term. In assessing the nature of a contractual term, two approaches are possible:
*   concentrate on the effect of the breach. For example, in a case where a ship was chartered, there were a number of delays in sailing because the engines were old and the staff incompetent. The defendants alleged that the plaintiff had breached a 'condition' that a seaworthy ship would be provided and repudiated the contract. The plaintiff argued that the breach was of a warranty, which only gave the defendant the right to claim damages, but not to repudiate the contract. The court found for the plaintiff, stating that by looking at the events that had occurred as an effect of the breach, the defendant had not been deprived of the whole of the benefit of the contract;
*   concentrate on the nature of the term itself. For example, is it the case that such a term is commonly used in contracts of a particular sort and has, in the past, been held to be a condition? This would support a party's contention that it was intended to be a condition.

Note: in the USA, the courts generally use an objective test to determine the status of a contractual term. A **reasonable person** test is used to establish what would have been the commercial expectations of a reasonable person.

6.4   Express terms

Express terms are those terms that have been specifically agreed upon by the parties, being terms the parties either said or wrote. Sometimes an express term in the contract is described as being a 'condition' or a 'warranty'. That does not necessarily mean that the court has to accept that classification of the term.

It may be necessary for the court to determine whether a **representation** made in a pre-contractual phase has become incorporated into the contract as a term. A number of factors are taken into account, such as whether the party making the statement promised that it was accurate, whether the innocent party would have entered into the contract had the statement not been made, or whether one of the parties had special knowledge and skill with respect to the subject-matter of the contract. It may also be argued that the contract was intended to be partly written and partly oral, or that it was a collateral contract.

6.5   Implied terms

As mentioned above, at common law the emphasis is on the legal certainty of contracts and the expectation is that individuals can take care of their own interests. It is, therefore, not the practice of the courts to insert new terms into contracts. Their task is to interpret those terms that exist already. Nonetheless, English law does recognise that terms can be implied into a contract in certain situations.

6.5.1 Trade usage

A term can be incorporated into a contract reflecting local custom or **trade usage** in a particular industry if the contract is silent on the matter. For example, where a crane hired by a construction company sank into the mud, it was held that the hirer should bear the cost of retrieving it as this term could be implied from trade usage. Such a term cannot be implied if it would be contrary to an express term in the contract.

6.5.2 Statutory implied terms

Legislation implies terms into certain types of contracts. In particular, statutory implied terms are important in contracts for the sale of goods. For example, in English law it is an implied term that the seller has the right to sell the goods, that goods correspond to their description, that they are of satisfactory quality and are fit for their purpose. Most implied terms are conditions. These implied terms may not be **excluded** in a **consumer** transaction. Where the parties are not consumers, they may agree to exclude most of these implied terms, but only in so far as is reasonable.

Note: the UCC has provisions similar to those set down in the English sale of goods legislation. There is a warranty of title, that the seller has the right to sell the goods. If the description of the goods is basic to the bargain, then there is an express warranty that the goods will conform to their description. There is an implied warranty of merchantability and an implied warranty of fitness for a particular purpose. The Code lays down specific rules as to whether a warranty may be excluded or modified.

6.5.3 Terms implied by the courts

In general, the court will not read terms into a contract but only interpret the terms that are there. In certain circumstances, the court will be prepared to imply in a term if the agreement was clearly intended to create a legal relationship and the nature of the contract itself requires the term because otherwise the contract cannot function. An implied term will then give the transaction so-called **business efficacy**. For example, in a landlord and tenant case, it was held that there was an implied term that the landlord would maintain the stairs and lift so that the tenant could reach his flat on the upper floor.

6.6 Exclusion clauses

The purpose of an **exclusion clause** is to exclude all liability of the party for breach of contract, misrepresentation or negligence. A variant of the exclusion clause is the **limitation clause**, which does not seek to exempt a party from all liability but to reduce that liability. Typically, a limitation clause places a financial limit on the liability of a party, for example limiting the liability for a defective product to the obligation to replace the product in question.

In order to prevent parties relying on unfair exclusion clauses, there are judicial rules of construction and specific statutes in English law. The first stage in assessing the validity of an exclusion clause is to examine the judicial rules. If an exclusion clause is not invalid at common law, the second stage of the test is to see whether it complies with the statutory provisions.

6.6.1 Judicial rules

These rules were developed by the common law. The courts looked to see whether an exclusion clause had been incorporated into the contract. If it had been incorporated, it was then a matter of construction whether it covered the liability in question or not. In English law a **rule of construction** is supposed to give effect to the parties' intention by interpreting the contract, whereas a **rule of law** must be applied whether it gives effect to the parties' intention or not.

- **Incorporation**: the exclusion clause must have been incorporated, either as a part of a written, signed document or, if the exclusion clause is not in a written document, by displaying it on a notice. Where the exclusion clause is on a notice, reasonable precautions must have been taken to bring it to the attention of the other party. With respect to written documents, there is generally no obligation to bring an exclusion clause to the attention of the other party. A person who signs a contract in which there is an exclusion clause will be bound by it, even if he has not actually read it, unless the signature was the result of fraud or misrepresentation. An exclusion clause will not stand if it is only brought to the attention of the party after the contract itself has been concluded and does not form a part of that contract.

An exclusion clause may have been incorporated by a consistent **previous course of dealing** between the parties on the same terms. This is the case where parties have consistently made use of the same terms, and the exclusion clause was incorporated in a standard contract. This is also common practice in civil law jurisdictions, such as in the Netherlands.

- **Contra proferentem rule**: if an exclusion clause has been incorporated, it must still cover the breach in question. An exclusion clause will be interpreted strictly and if there is any ambiguity in the clause this will be construed to the disadvantage of the party relying on the clause. The Latin term 'contra proferentem' is one familiar to civil law lawyers.
- **Main purpose rule**: an exclusion clause may fail if it would defeat the main purpose of the contract. For example, the court held that an exclusion clause did not cover the situation where a carrier had delivered the goods to a party who had no right to receive them, even though the exclusion clause stated that the carrier's liability ceased once the goods had been removed from the carrier's ship. It was a rule of construction that the exclusion clause was not intended to defeat the main purpose of the contract.
- **Fundamental breach**: can a party rely on an exclusion clause to exempt him from liability for fundamental breach of the contract because the wording of that exclusion clause clearly covers liability for fundamental breach? Over the years the approach of the English courts has varied: at one time the position seemed to be that it was a rule of law that an exclusion clause could not be used to exclude fundamental breach, at another time that it was only a rule of construction. The question now seems to have been resolved: it is a rule of construction.

6.6.2 Legislation

Even if an exclusion clause has survived the common law rules, it may still fail to comply with statutory provisions. English legislation on **unfair contract terms** provides a comprehensive set of rules to regulate the use of exclusion clauses. English law makes a distinction between contracts involving **non-consumers**, where the contract arises from the course of a business, and contracts involving **consumers**, where one of the parties is not acting in the course of business. Consumer protection has become an increasingly important element in legislation. Exclusion clauses must be **reasonable**. However, in certain types of consumer contracts an exclusion clause will be **void**, for example in a sale of goods contract where an attempt is made to exclude liability for providing goods that are of unsatisfactory quality or not fit for their purpose. Even if the parties to a contract for the sale of goods are not consumers, then unfair contract terms legislation requires that the exclusion clause must still be reasonable.

Note 1: liability for negligence causing death or personal injury cannot be excluded.

Note 2: EU law has created a certain level of harmonisation within the EU with respect to laws regulating consumer contracts. It is also via EU law that the principle of good faith has crept into English law. With respect to consumer contracts, a term is unfair if it is contrary to the requirements of **good faith**.

7   REASONS TO HAVE A CONTRACT SET ASIDE: VITIATING FACTORS

A contract may appear at first sight to be perfectly valid. However, it later emerges that there was a defect in the contract that was present at the time of agreement. This defect is sufficiently serious to have the contract **set aside**. A **vitiating** factor is a factor that can invalidate a contract. Misrepresentation, mistake, duress and undue influence are vitiating factors. The contract may be **void or voidable**. A void contract is one that was never legally valid or without legal effect. A voidable contract is one that can have legal effect but could be made void if the representee **rescinds** it.

7.1   Misrepresentation

A **representation** is a statement that was made to induce the **representee** to enter into the contract but does not itself become part of the contract. A **misrepresentation** is a false representation. A misrepresentation is actionable, not as breach of contract, because it is not a term of the contract, but under the rules applicable to misrepresentations. If the misrepresentation can be construed as a term of the contract, for the reasons given in section 6.4, then a claim lies either for misrepresentation or for breach of contract.

To be classed as a misrepresentation, the statement must be a **statement of fact**. It must have been made before or at the time of the contract and had the effect of inducing the other party to enter into the contract. If the **misrepresentee** has not relied upon the **misrepresentor's** statement, because he was unaware of it, or did not believe it or had decided to depend upon his own skill and judgment, there is no operative misrepresentation. For example, where the purchaser of a mine had not relied on the seller's estimate of its capacity, but on that of his own expert, it was held he had not been induced to enter the contract on the basis of the misrepresentation. A **statement of opinion** is not a misrepresentation, although a statement of opinion can also be a misrepresentation if not actually held, or it implies a factual basis because of the knowledge and expertise of the party making it.

A lot of advertising slogans fall outside the rules on misrepresentation as the statements are not capable of verification, for example, 'we are offering you the holiday of a lifetime!'. However, advertising statements that imply a factual basis could incur legal consequences as misrepresentations or under trade description legislation.

In general, in English law silence is not a misrepresentation. There are important exceptions to this rule where a party is under a duty to disclose. In contracts **uberrimae fidei** (of the utmost good faith) there is a duty of full disclosure, for example where shares have been purchased based on a company prospectus or the contract is one of insurance. A court is free to conclude that there was a duty of disclosure where one party is in a stronger position than the other to know the truth.

7.1.1 Types of misrepresentation

In breach of contract, the state of mind of the one responsible for the breach is legally irrelevant at common law. The question is whether there has been a breach or not and the reason for that breach is of no importance (see below). That is not the case, however, with respect to the law on misrepresentations, where the state of mind of the misrepresentor is relevant.

There are three types of misrepresentation: fraudulent, negligent or innocent:

1   **Innocent misrepresentation**: here the maker of the statement had reasonable grounds for believing that it was true.
2   **Negligent misrepresentation**: a lack of reasonable care was taken in making the statement.
3   **Fraudulent misrepresentation**: the person knew that the statement was untrue, or was reckless as to whether it was true.

7.1.2 Remedies for misrepresentation

A misrepresentation makes the contract **voidable**. Not only the common law, but also legislation and equity offer the innocent party a remedy. In some instances, the remedy available will depend upon whether the misrepresentation was innocent, negligent or fraudulent.

•   **In equity**: an innocent party can **rescind** the contract in all types of misrepresentation. **Rescission** is a remedy where the representee has shown that he does not intend to be bound by the contract. The contract is said to be terminated **ab initio**; hence the parties are returned to the position they would have been in if the contract had never been made. The basic idea of rescission is that the innocent party gets back what he gave if he gives back what he received. As rescission is an equitable remedy, based on principles of fairness, it is discretionary and it will not be granted where it would be inequitable to do so. Consequently, there are certain so-called **bars to rescission**: if a contract has been **affirmed** the right to rescind is lost, or if **restitutio in integrum** is impossible (because it is impossible to go back to the original position), or where **third party rights** have intervened. Furthermore, a party who is in breach of contract will have lost the right to rescind that contract.

    In equity, rescission may be accompanied by an **indemnity**, which is to cover the necessary costs of obligations created by the contract. An indemnity is not the same as damages; it is simply to put the parties back in the pre-contractual position, so that the innocent party is neither better off nor worse off than before.

- **At common law**: in addition to, or as an alternative to, rescission it is possible to sue for **damages** in tort if the representee was induced to enter into a contract by a fraudulent or negligent misstatement, but not if he entered into the contract because of an innocent misrepresentation. He can claim damages in the **tort of deceit** for a fraudulent misrepresentation and in the **tort of negligence** for a negligent misstatement (see chapter 4 for these terms).
- **Legislation**: under statue, damages can be claimed for negligent and innocent misrepresentations. With respect to a negligent misrepresentation, damages may be claimed in addition to rescission or **in lieu of** rescission. Damages may be claimable for an innocent misrepresentation instead of rescission if this would be equitable.

7.2   Duress and undue influence

At common law, a contract can be set aside if it was entered into under **duress** or **undue influence**. **Duress** means either actual violence or the threat of violence was used to make the other party enter into the contract. It is not entirely clear in English law whether the contract will be **void** or **voidable**. **Undue influence** refers to improper pressure other than violence. For example, threats to prosecute, or where advantage is taken of a special relationship of a fiduciary nature, such as that between a parent and child, or solicitor and client. Where undue influence can be shown, the contract is **voidable**. A crucial element with respect to undue influence is whether the agreement was signed after independent advice had been obtained, for example by the claimant's own lawyers. If it has, it is less likely that a contract will be set aside for undue influence.

7.3   Mistake

The old rule of **caveat emptor** (let the buyer beware) still applies in private sales where the parties are bargaining equals. Certain types of mistake will not affect the validity of a contract, for example, an error of judgment where there was no misrepresentation, or a mistake about the time needed to perform a contract.

However, where the mistake is operative and fundamental, as it goes to the very heart of the transaction, the contract will be considered as **void** from the outset. Mistake will render a contract void where the defence of non est factum can be raised, where there is a mistake as to the identity of the contracting party or where the parties are both acting under a mistaken assumption or are at cross-purposes.

- **Non est factum**: in general, a person is bound by the terms of a document that they have signed, even if they have not read it or understood it. The non est factum defence forms an exception to the rule. To qualify for this defence, the signed document must be fundamentally different from the one the **signatory** believed himself to be signing, the signatory must have taken reasonable care in signing the document and fraud must have been used to induce the signature.

- **Mistake as to identity**: this is usually a unilateral mistake where one party is mistaken as to the identity of the other party. The contract is void if the innocent party can show that the identity of the other party was crucial to the transaction.
- **Common mistake** and **mutual mistake**: here both parties are mistaken. The mistake is common where both parties mistakenly believe the same thing, and the mistaken assumption was based on a reasonable ground. Mutual mistake is where the parties have misunderstood each other, in other words, the parties are at cross-purposes. That means that there is no real offer and acceptance as the offer is made in one sense and accepted in another. Consequently, there is no meeting of minds. The mistake must go to the substance of the contract. A **mistake as to quality** is rarely seen in English law as fundamental. For example, a claimant had contracted to buy napkins belonging to Charles I. It turned out that they were in fact Georgian napkins. It was held that whether the contract was void depended upon whether the parties were simply buying and selling antique napkins or whether the claimant specifically wanted a personal relic of Charles I; in the latter case the mistake would be fundamental.

7.4   Illegality

A contract will not be enforced if its purpose is illegal; this includes contracts for criminal purposes or those that are considered injurious to society. For example, the contract will be **void** if it is prohibited by statute, on grounds of public policy, or it promotes sexual immorality.

7.5   Contracts in restraint of trade

Any contract that restricts freedom of trade is **prima facie void**. However, such a contract, or clauses with that effect, will be legally enforceable if justified. The party seeking to rely on a contract in restraint of trade must be able to show that the restrictions are reasonable as between the parties and are not against the public interest, for example where the contract is to protect legitimate trade secrets or business connections.

8   DISCHARGE OF CONTRACTUAL OBLIGATIONS

Discharge means a release from an obligation. In contract law, it means the parties are free of their mutual obligations under the contract and, therefore, the contract comes to an end. Discharge can be achieved in a variety of ways: by performance, express agreement, breach or under the doctrine of frustration.

8.1 Discharge by performance

The general rule is only a complete **performance**, exact and precise, will discharge a party's contractual obligations. This rule is particularly disadvantageous for a party who has entered into what is called an **entire contract**. An example of an entire contract is where the agreement is for a lump sum for the work done. In that case, if one party has only carried out part of his contractual obligations, but not all, the nature of the contract excludes the possibility of part payment.

However, there are two exceptions to complete performance that give the defaulting party some relief. The exceptions apply where there has been substantial performance or where the contract is divisible.

- **Substantial performance**: substantial performance means that the contractual obligations are as good as fulfilled except for a few minor aspects. These aspects must indeed be so minor that it would be inequitable not to allow the party in default to recover any of the contractual payment. The innocent party can then claim damages for those aspects that the defaulting party had not fulfilled.
- **Divisible contract**: in this case a contract can be divided into a number of specific, separate parts. For example, the agreement is not for a lump sum, but for payment by instalment. It is then possible for the party in default to recover payment for that specific part of the contractual obligations that he has carried out. Most building contracts are now done this way: a specific sum is paid on the completion of a certain stage in the building.

8.2 Discharge by agreement

A contract may be **discharged by agreement** in several situations. The parties may have agreed that the original contract should end automatically if some event occurred or after a fixed period of time. A contract may also be discharged where there is a new agreement that replaces the old contract. However, in general consideration is necessary to make an agreement to discharge or to vary terms. Where neither party has performed under the contract, each party can agree to release the other from his obligations under the contract. There is **bilateral discharge** where both parties exchange promises not to enforce the original contract. This mutual **waiver** forms the consideration.

The situation is more complicated where there has been performance or partial performance by one of the parties. There can only be discharge if the party who has not performed either draws up a deed or provides fresh consideration. This fresh consideration need not be adequate but it must be of value (see above). **Unilateral discharge** requires **accord and satisfaction**. The word accord refers to the agreement to discharge, and the word satisfaction to the consideration needed. This rule also applies if the parties wish to vary the terms of their agreement.

It is also possible that one party offers to **waive** his rights to performance as stipulated in the contract, for example where he is prepared to accept a late delivery of goods. A waiver can be legally enforceable *without* consideration. In this respect the common law doctrine of waiver is similar to the equitable doctrine of promissory estoppel. The one who granted the waiver is not allowed to change his mind about it and demand performance in accordance with the original terms of the contract. The waiver is binding on him, even though there is no consideration from the defaulting party. For this reason, the following clause is usual in English contracts:

> "Any waiver by either party of a breach of any provision of the Agreement shall not be considered as a waiver of any subsequent breach of the same or any other provision."

8.3   Discharge by breach

There will be **breach of contract** where a party has failed to perform his obligations under the contract, or has performed them defectively. At common law, contractual liability for breach is strict and the motive for that breach is, in general, irrelevant. For example, if a party to the contract has a bad cold and is not able to carry out the obligations under the contract at the stipulated time, he may still be in breach even though he cannot be held responsible for having come down with a bad cold. The court is not interested in why the defendant did not carry out his obligation, nor whether he had tried his best to carry out those obligations. The question is simply 'is it breach or is it not breach?' In those civil law systems where fault plays a more significant role, this may seem a very harsh approach.

8.3.1 Termination

The innocent party always has the right to sue for damages for breach. However, where the breach is of a very serious nature, the innocent party may have the option of continuing with the contract or treating it as discharged. If the innocent party chooses to treat the contract as terminated by breach, he is then released from his own obligations under the contract. The innocent party has the right to treat the contract as discharged where there is:

*   **Repudiation**: the party in default has repudiated the contract by making it clear, either explicitly or implicitly, that he will not carry out his obligations under the contract. If a party makes it clear that he will not perform his obligations under the contract before the performance date is due, this is called **anticipatory breach**. The innocent party does not have to wait until the date due for performance, but has an immediate right of action.
*   **Fundamental breach**: the defaulting party has not explicitly or impliedly repudiated his obligations, but has breached a term of the contract that is of fundamental importance. This means that a condition has been breached.

In order to treat the contract as discharged in English law, an innocent party does not need to go to court to terminate a contract. Nor is there any general legal obligation to give the other party notice of default as in Dutch and German contract law. **Notice of default** must be given, however, if this has been specifically agreed upon between the parties and provided for in the contract. An agreement to give each other notice of default is quite common commercial practice in common law jurisdictions.

8.3.2 Termination or rescission?

Rescission is a remedy for setting aside a voidable contract, such as one entered into because of a misrepresentation. The primary and technically correct meaning of the term rescission is that the contract is retrospectively cancelled **ab initio**, i.e. the contract is destroyed as if it never existed. Discharge by breach in English law, on the other hand, does not affect the rights and obligations of the parties that have already come into existence. As Lord Wilberforce pointed out, "it is now quite clear, under the general law of contract, that acceptance of a repudiatory breach does not bring about rescission ab initio". The contract is discharged, not rescinded. For this reason, the more correct terminology with respect to discharge by breach is **termination** rather than rescission.

When translating foreign language contracts into English, care should be taken in the use of terminology with respect to provisions regulating breach of contract. It is necessary to be aware of the distinction in English law between **rescission** and **termination by breach** of contract.

It is common to find the term rescission used in Dutch contracts, written in English, to describe a remedy available in Dutch law. In Dutch law, the innocent party may, in principle, have a contract dissolved ('ontbinden') if the other party can be held responsible for breach of contract. As in English law, this does not affect the rights and obligations that have already come into existence as dissolution does not have a retroactive effect. If so wished the parties may agree to revert to the pre-contractual situation ('ongedaanmakingsverbintenissen'). This is often translated by the word rescission. As noted above, the proper use of rescission in English law is as a remedy for a voidable contract. If the contract drafter wishes to use the word to describe a Dutch legal concept, he must make that very clear.

8.4 Discharge by frustration

Parties are excused from performance if through no fault of the parties events that occur *after* the formation of the contract make it impossible to perform the contract, or that the contract becomes commercially sterile or futile. Where the events that have occurred are outside the control of either party, the contract will then be **discharged by frustration**.

A contract may be discharged by frustration for a variety of reasons. For example, the destruction of the subject-matter of the contract, changes in the law that would make the performance of a contract illegal, the death or permanent ill-health of one party where it is a contract for personal services, or the inability to achieve the main object of the contract as circumstances have dramatically and radically changed since the signing of the contract. The commercial purpose of the contract is said to be defeated where there is no physical destruction of the subject-matter, but the essential commercial purpose no longer exists. This rule is referred to as **frustration of the common venture**, for example in the case where a cargo ship stranded on rocks on its way to pick up its cargo, and would be out of commission for some time, the other party was free to charter another ship as the original contract had been frustrated.

8.4.1 Limits of the doctrine of frustration

The doctrine of frustration does not apply where a change in circumstances has simply made the contract more difficult to perform and less profitable than was anticipated at the time of the contract. For frustration to apply, there must be a radical change of circumstances so that contract has become fundamentally different from the original undertaking, not just more onerous to perform. For example, where a building contract took longer and cost more to perform because of labour shortages it was held there was no frustration. Nor will there be discharge by frustration if the parties have included an express term in the contract dealing with the event which occurred, or if one party foresaw or should have foreseen the frustrating event given his special knowledge. If the frustration was self-induced it will be breach rather than frustration.

8.4.2 Consequences of frustration

Civil law lawyers should be aware that in English law the effect of discharge by frustration on the parties depends on the type of contract involved. There are statutory provisions that apply to certain types of contracts, such as shipping contracts, insurance and contracts for the sale of specific goods. Under statute, provision is made for a **just apportionment** of losses. Money paid before the **frustrating event** is recoverable. Money due to be paid after the frustrating event no longer has to be paid. Expenses incurred before the frustrating event may be deducted from the money that has to be returned, and compensation may be paid on a **quantum meruit** basis (see below) for work carried out before the frustrating event, which is of benefit to the other party.

All other contracts than those specified by statute fall under the ambit of the common law. The common law position is that a contract is not discharged **ab initio** (from the outset), but only after the frustrating event. With respect to work done before the frustrating event, the losses are said to **lie where they fall**, in other words, it is generally not possible to recover money due or paid before the frustrating event.

Note 1: even though this doctrine of frustration is more usually referred to as the **doctrine of impossibility** in the USA, impossibility is no longer the only reason for discharging the contract. The modern American doctrine of impossibility also takes into account 'commercial impracticability', where performance has become impracticable because of an extreme or unreasonable difficulty, expense, injury or loss making the contract a fundamentally different one from that anticipated by the parties. This more liberal approach as to what constitutes frustration has developed in many common and civil law jurisdictions. The level of relief given for changed circumstances varies.

Note 2: it is usual for commercial contracts, whether common law or civil law, to include a **force majeure** clause. This clause includes a list of events considered to be outside the control of the parties, such as labour disputes, acts of God, war, riot, compliance with a law or governmental order, accident, breakdown of machinery, fire or flood.

9   REMEDIES FOR BREACH OF CONTRACT

Various remedies may be available to the innocent party where there has been a breach of contract. At common law, the innocent party can claim damages and, if the contract has been repudiated by the other party or if the breach is fundamental, he can treat the contract as discharged. He may also apply for an equitable remedy where this would be appropriate. Equitable remedies include **quantum meruit**, **specific performance** and **injunctions**. Equitable remedies are **discretionary**. They will only be awarded where damages are not a suitable alternative.

9.1   Damages

The legal term **damages** means financial compensation. The object of damages in contract law is to put the claimant in the position he would have been in if the contract had been performed properly. Damages will compensate the innocent party for any loss suffered by the breach. In English contract law, it is not the idea to punish non-performers by awarding damages in excess of the loss suffered, but only to compensate for those losses that have actually been caused by the failure of the other party to carry out his obligations. Nonetheless, an award of damages may include full **expectation damages** where appropriate. This means that a claimant may claim for an expectation loss, which is a loss in the sense that the claimant expected to have it, for example, he expected to make a profit on the contract. Damages should not, however, make a claimant better off than he would have been if the contract had been performed. Damages may also be refused if the court finds them too speculative. In general, the claim is made for **unliquidated damages**, as the quantification of damages is a matter for the discretion of the court.

9.1.1 Liquidated damages and penalties

Sometimes the contract itself will include a clause which stipulates how much must be paid in damages by the defaulting party in the event of breach. These clauses are of two types:

- **Liquidated damages clause**: here the parties have attempted to estimate in advance what their losses would actually be in the event of breach. The damages are then assessed by the parties, rather than left to the discretion of the court. This is called **liquidated damages**. If the court is convinced that the clause is a genuine pre-estimate of loss, the court will enforce the clause. If the sum stipulated by the parties is accepted as liquidated damages, this sum will be awarded, whether the actual loss is greater or smaller.

- **Penalty clause**: a penalty clause is where one party intends to punish the other party for breach of contract, or deter him from defaulting, by making him pay a penalty. Where a clause is considered to be a penalty clause, it will be ignored by the court, as the claimant may only recover his actual loss. The court will then award damages on the usual principles for assessing **unliquidated damages**. It is likely that the court will construe a term as a penalty clause if the stipulated sum is much greater than any likely loss. In recent years, English courts have been reticent to classify stipulated damages clauses as penalty clauses where the contract concerned is between commercial parties.

9.1.2 Remoteness of damage

The consequences of a breach of contract may be far-reaching, extending beyond the obvious losses associated with the breach of contract. For example, the original breach of contract may force the innocent party to be in breach of contract to someone else, and that someone else may in turn be in breach to yet another person. The original breach could lead to a whole chain of people being in breach. To prevent damages spiralling out of control, there must be a cut off point for **remoteness**. Damages must be **proximate**.

The rules in English law on **remoteness of damage** are based upon an old case from 1854, Hadley v Baxendale. Here a miller gave a broken driving shaft to the defendant to be delivered to the repairers. The defendant delayed taking the driving shaft to the repairers and the miller sued for loss of profits during the unnecessary delay. As the defendant could not have known there was no spare driving shaft, the court held that the damage was too remote. The rule laid down in this case is that a victim of breach can recover for losses in two instances:

1   for those **naturally arising** from the nature of the contract; or
2   if the losses do not arise naturally from the contract, they may be reasonably supposed to have been in the contemplation of both parties at the time they made their contract as the probable result of the breach. To show that the parties were aware that such losses could result from the breach, **special notice** must have been given. The term **consequential loss** is often used to

refer to unusual or special losses. Liability for consequential loss is often excluded in contracts.

9.1.3 Mitigation of loss

There is a duty on the claimant to take all reasonable steps to **mitigate** loss. In other words, the innocent party must take reasonable steps to minimise his loss. For example, if a seller has had his goods improperly rejected by the other party, he must try to sell them for the best price available elsewhere. He must not **sit on the breach**.

9.2   Quantum meruit

The claim of **quantum meruit** is for 'as much as he deserves'. It is a claim for reasonable remuneration, unlike damages which are awarded as compensation for loss. The claim can be made where **partial performance** was voluntarily accepted by the other party, or where one party has been prevented by the other from completing performance.

9.3   Specific performance

Specific performance is an order to make a party perform his obligations under the contract. At common law, an innocent party does not have the legal right to demand that the other party performs his obligations. Specific performance is discretionary and will not be ordered if damages are a sufficient remedy. To justify an order for specific performance, the subject-matter of the contract must be unique and consequently not readily available elsewhere, for example, it is a specific painting or land. The court must be able to supervise the performance and it must be equitable to grant the order. Just as in civil law jurisdictions, it will not be granted where the contract is for personal services, such as a contract of employment.

9.4   Injunction

An injunction is a court order prohibiting a person from doing something (a **prohibitory injunction**) or requiring a person to do something (a **mandatory injunction**). With respect to contract law, an injunction usually works as a form of specific performance, by prohibiting the breach of a clause.

A **prohibitory injunction** will stop a party breaking a negative stipulation in the contract, for example where a contractual clause states that a party will not work for anyone else in a certain capacity for a specified period of time. Warner Bros was granted a prohibitory injunction in its claim against the film actress Bette Davis, when she breached the agreement only to work for Warner Bros and not for any other company without their consent for a set time. An injunction may also be ordered to prevent breaches of restrictive covenants, for example, covenants not to disclose confidential information or not to set up in competition with one of the parties.

Note: there are several other types of injunction: **freezing injunction, interim injunction** and **final injunction** (see chapter 2 and chapter 4 for these terms).

9.5   Suspension of performance

The right of the innocent party to suspend performance where the other party is in default is a familiar one in the civil law. In civil law systems, such as the French, German and Dutch, the principle of **exceptio non adimpleti contractus** generally applies: **suspension of performance** in the event of breach.

At common law, there is no general principle allowing suspension of performance by an innocent party. On the contrary, suspension of performance will in turn be breach of contract. There are, however, certain specific circumstances in which suspension by the innocent party is permissible. This is the case where the parties have provided for suspension of performance in the contract, or where terms are considered to be interdependent, for example in a sales contract where non-payment by the buyer allows the seller to withhold delivery.

Contract law case discussions

1   Prince Charles is to be crowned King of England. The date set for his coronation is the 1st of July. There will be a splendid coronation day parade down the Strand in London to mark the event. Consider the position of the parties in the following scenarios:

• Miss Smith has a friend who works in a shop overlooking the Strand. Her friend tells her that the shop assistants' lunch room is above the shop and they will have a wonderful view of the parade from there. Miss Smith asks her friend whether she can come and sit with her in the lunch room, so that she can see the parade too. Her friend agrees and Miss Smith arranges a train ticket and a hotel in London to stay overnight. When she arrives, her friend apologises but says she cannot come to the lunch room as her boss says it is not allowed. Miss Smith wants to sue her friend for the price of the train ticket and her hotel. Will Miss Smith be successful?

• Prince Charles becomes seriously ill and has to postpone his coronation day. This means that the coronation day parade planned for the 1st of July is cancelled. Miss Jones had already booked a hotel room overlooking the Strand for the 1st of July. When she hears that the coronation day parade has been postponed, she wants to cancel her hotel reservation. She rings up the hotel on the 30th of June, but the hotel replies that in the contract she signed for the room, if a reservation is cancelled less than 24 hours in advance, the full amount for the room must be paid. Miss Jones argues that having a room in the hotel is now utterly pointless and that she will neither take up her reservation nor pay for the room. What is Miss Jones's legal position?

2   Mr. Jones is a second-hand car dealer. Miss Smith wants a second-hand car but tells Mr. Jones that she is only interested in buying a car which has done less than 10,000 miles. He offers Miss Smith a 1994 Ford Escort for a reasonable price. During the trial run, Miss Smith tells him she likes the car, the price is acceptable, but she repeats that she only wants the car if it has done less than 10,000 miles. Mr. Jones says: "Of course it has not done more than 10,000 miles. Look at the milometer!" The milometer shows 7,000 miles. One month later, Miss Smith learns that the previous owner of the car altered the milo-

meter and that the car has done at least 30,000 miles. Advise Miss Smith as to her legal position.

3   Miss Smith books a hotel for a holiday in York. When she arrives, she signs a contract for the room. The contract states the room number, the number of days Miss Smith will stay and the price of the room. During her stay, Miss Smith's pearl necklace is stolen from her room. When she complains, the hotel manager points out that there is a notice in her room stating that the hotel will not be liable for any items stolen from the hotel rooms. Advise Miss Smith.

Contract law knowledge questions

1   There are certain basic requirements before an agreement will be treated as a contract. Which three basic elements must be present for the formation of a contract?

2   What is the doctrine of privity of contract?

3   In what way does the doctrine of promissory estoppel affect the usual common law rules on the formation of a contract?

4   Consideration does not have to be adequate but it must be sufficient. Explain the terms 'adequate' and 'sufficient'.

5   In English law, contractual terms are classified according to their importance. Name these categories and explain how the status of a term affects the innocent party's position if there has been breach of contract.

6   What is the purpose of excluding and limiting terms in a contract?

7   Explain the term 'rescission'.

8   What is a vitiating factor?

9   What is meant by the term 'discharge by frustration'.

10 Explain what is meant by 'remoteness of damage'.

Chapter 6　Company law terminology

Company law vocabulary

Adjudication order (or **bankruptcy order**): order by which the court declares a person bankrupt.

Administrative receiver: a qualified insolvency practitioner appointed to take control of the assets, such as those subject to a floating charge, for the benefit of creditors with these assets as security.

Administrator: this is a qualified insolvency practitioner appointed by an **administration order** in an attempt to save the company as a going concern rather than wind it up.

Agent: a person given the authority by a principal to enter into contracts on his behalf.

Alternative director: this is a person appointed by a director to act in his place.

Annual accounts: a detailed record of a company's financial situation that must be produced each year.

Annual general meeting (AGM): meeting of the shareholders of a company which takes place once a year.

Articles of association: document which regulates the way a company's internal affairs are managed. It consists of regulations governing the rights of the members and the internal structure of the company.

Articles of incorporation: document filed in the USA to incorporate a company.

Articles or deed of partnership: written agreement setting out the structure of a partnership. It is not a legal requirement.

Assets: property owned by a person or company that has monetary value.

Auditor: a member of a recognised body of accountants who examines (or audits) company accounts. **Auditing** is the process by which the financial situation of the company is examined in order to draw up the annual accounts.

Authorised share capital: this is the amount of capital a company can raise by selling its shares.

Bankruptcy: where an individual is unable to pay his debts.

Board of directors: this board comprises the individual directors. It is the ultimate decision-making body of a company and determines the delegation of power.

Bond: a certificate issued by the government or public company promising to repay borrowed money at a fixed rate of interest at a specified time and to repay the original sum in full after a specified term. In the UK, the term debenture is used to denote a domestic secured bond.

Breach of directors' duties: where a director has acted in a way inconsistent with the duty of care and skill and fiduciary duties owed to the company.

Bylaws: in the USA, the structural aspects of the corporation are set out in bylaws, which do not have to be filed.

Called up share capital (paid-up capital): the sum that shareholders have already paid in return for shares.

Capital: the net worth of a company; money, property and any other assets.

Certificate of incorporation: this is issued to a registered company on incorporation.

Chairman: an appointed director who presides over meetings of the board of directors and general meetings.

Charge: a charge on property means that the property is not free but it has a certain liability attached to it.

Class meeting: is where a class of shareholders meet to decide matters which affect their particular class of shares.

Class rights: rights attaching to different classes of shares.

Close corporation: a form of corporation found in the USA consisting of a single individual or a very small group of individuals. It is typically managed by the stockholders themselves.

Company: in English law, an association of persons formed for the purposes of an undertaking or business carried on in the name of the association. It is legally incorporated and is a legal person, separate from its individual members. In the USA, the word applies to a wide range of activities and can be used to describe private corporations as well as partnerships.

Company constitution: in English law, the constitution of a company is governed by two main documents, the memorandum and articles of association.

Company secretary: in England, every company must have a company secretary who is responsible for the administration of the company's affairs.

Conflict of interest: where there is a conflict of interests between a director's personal interests and those of the company, those of the company must prevail.

Contributory: is someone who is liable to contribute to the assets of a company on a winding up.

Corporate governance: term often used to describe the way in which companies are directed and controlled.

Corporate veil: the legal recognition of the company's independence from its owners and management.

Corporation: in English law, a legal body, such as a limited company or public authority, which has been incorporated. It is often used to indicate a large company. Likewise, in the USA, the term also means an association of shareholders that has a legal identity entirely separate and distinct from those who compose it.

Creditor: one to whom a debt is owed. A **debenture holder** is a creditor, whereas a shareholder is a member of the company.

Crystallise: a floating charge is said to crystallise, in other words be triggered, if the debtor is in default.

Debenture: a document acknowledging a debt for a capital sum that is to be repaid on a certain date, with interest payable at a fixed rate. In the London financial markets, the word debenture is used primarily to denote a secured loan. Reference may be made to a naked debenture, which is a debt without security. In the USA, a debenture is usually an unsecured loan.

Debenture holder: is a creditor of the company.

Debenture stock: credit certificates issued in a similar way to an issue of shares.

Debenture trust (or **indenture**): a deed setting out the terms of the loan.

Defunct: a defunct company is a company that has ceased to trade.

Derivative action: an action by a minority shareholder (or minority shareholders) is a derivative action if the shareholder is suing in the name of the company.

Director: in English law, there is no legal definition of director but, according to legislation, the term director includes any person occupying the position of director, by whatever name called.

Directors' duties: include the duty of care and skill and fiduciary duties.

Disclosure: to disclose involves revealing details about an act or transaction. Directors are under a duty to disclose any personal interest that could lead to a conflict of interest situation.

Disqualification order: order by which a person is not allowed to act as a company director. The grounds for a disqualification order include: a conviction for an indictable offence, breaches of company law, fraud, unfitness to manage a company. An order on the grounds of unfitness can only be made if the company is insolvent.

Dissolution: here the term refers to bringing a business organisation to an end.

Dividend: a sum paid to shareholders by a company when in profit, the amount being in proportion to their shareholding.

Duty of care and skill: the so-called **business judgment rule** means that a director must not be negligent in the management of his company, but that he will not be liable for mere errors of judgment.

Elective resolutions: certain formalities are relaxed for private companies. Private companies may pass elective resolutions for a limited number of specific purposes, for example to dispense with the holding of annual general meetings.

Event of default: an event either specified by statute or specified in a debenture document that means a charge on property secured by the debenture is activated.

Executive director (inside director): this is usually a full- time officer employed by the company to manage company business.

Extraordinary general meeting: in addition to the AGM, shareholders may be asked to vote on special business if required by a sufficient number of the members.

Extraordinary resolution: this must be passed by a majority of at least 75% and fourteen days prior notice must have been given to the shareholders.

Fiduciary duties: a director is under an obligation to exercise his powers for the benefit of the company and not for his own benefit. He owes a general duty of trust, honesty and integrity towards the company.

Filing: in the USA, reference is made to **filing** rather than registering.

Firm: partnerships are referred to in English law as firms and the name under which their business is carried on is called the firm name. In the USA, the word company is used synonymously with firm, whereas in English law a firm is never a company.

Fixed charge: a charge on a particular asset or property.

Fixed interest securities: securities with a fixed rate of interest, such as a bond.

Floating charge: this type of charge attaches to a class of assets, which in the ordinary course of a company's business would be changing from time to time. It 'floats' above the property until some event occurs which triggers the charge. A similar charge is available in the USA: this may be referred to as a **floating lien**.

Flotation: also known as an **initial public offering**. This is where the shares in a company are issued for the first time on a stock market by means of an offer document called a **prospectus**.

Fraudulent trading: where a person continued trading even though he knew the company could not pay its debts.

Group accounts: group accounts must be drawn up by a holding company where there is a parent/subsidiary relationship.

Hire purchase agreement: a form of credit agreement where the payment is in instalments.

Holding company (or **parent company**): the business of a holding company consists wholly or mainly in holding shares or securities in one or more companies within the group, which are its subsidiary companies.

Incorporation: the issue of an incorporation certificate creates an independent legal personality.

Insider dealing/trading: using confidential information about a company in order to buy or sell its securities at a profit.

Insolvency practitioner: is someone qualified to conduct the affairs of companies that are in default or insolvent, for example an administrative receiver or a liquidator.

Insolvent: a company is insolvent if it can no longer pay its debts. **Insolvency** procedures will then be followed.

Issued capital: that part of a company's authorised share capital that has actually been issued to the shareholders.

Joint and several liability: partners may be collectively liable and individually liable.

Legal person: once registered, a company becomes a separate person in law. This artificial legal person can own property, commit crimes and torts and conclude contracts.

Lien: in general a charge upon the property of another until the debts associated with that property have been paid off.

Lifting the veil (US **piercing the veil**): process by which the courts may lift the veil of corporate secrecy and look at the underlying economic reality.

Limited liability company: in England, a registered company where the shareholders' liability in the event of a winding up is limited to any amount that has not yet been paid for their shares. It is the most usual form of trading company. The American limited liability company is not the direct equivalent of the English limited liability company as it is something of a hybrid between a corporation and a partnership.

Limited liability partnership: is a separate legal entity, giving its members the benefit of limited liability while retaining the internal structure of a partnership.

Limited partnership: one where a distinction is made between general partners and limited partners. Limited partners have invested in the company but have no active function. These limited partners are not personally liable for the debts of the partnership beyond the capital they have invested already.

Liquidation: process by which a company is brought to an end, often because of insolvency.

Liquidator: the one appointed to supervise the winding up of a company. A **receiver** may become the **provisional liquidator** until the creditors have met to decide upon a permanent liquidator.

Listed company (or a **quoted company**): is one that is listed on the Stock Exchange.

Listing particulars: document offering shares or debentures to the public where the company is listed already.

Loan capital: capital that has been obtained on credit.

Majority shareholder: one who holds sufficient shares in a company to influence the decision-making.

Management: those who direct or run a business.

Managing director (or **chief executive officer**): a director in charge of the management of a company.

Members: the members of a company are the **shareholders**.

Membership contract: special contract which binds the company to the members and regulates the relationship between the members.

Memorandum of association: legal document regulating a company's external activities. It states the company's name, objectives, registered office, domicile, the amount of the company's nominal capital and the number and amount of shares.

Minority action: an action brought by a single shareholder or small number of shareholders.

Minority shareholder: one who does not hold sufficient shares in a company to command an influential position.

Minutes: an official written record of the discussion points and decisions made during a meeting.

Moratorium: a **suspension of payments** is initiated for a fixed period so that no-one except the administrator can deal with the assets of a company during that period.

Natural person: this is a human being rather than an artificial person, such as a registered company. A natural person has the right to participate in a wider variety of legal transactions than a legal person.

Negative pledge clause: it prohibits the company from using any assets as security in the future if that would be disadvantageous to the existing debenture holder's security.

Negotiable: where a document, such as shares and debentures, may legally be transferred to another.

Nominal value: the face value of a share rather than its market value.

Non-cash asset of the requisite value: non-cash asset covers a wide range of property, tangible and intangible. Requisite value refers to a value exceeding a certain percentage of the company's net assets as determined in its last accounts.

Non-executive director (outside, independent or **non-management)**: this is not a salaried employee and he is not actively involved in daily management.

Novation: a new party to a contract is substituted for an original party with the agreement of the remaining party. The existing contract is replaced by the new contract.

Objects clause: a clause in the memorandum of association setting out the purpose for which the company was incorporated.

Officer (of a company): one invested with authority for a particular position. In English law, a director is an officer of a company as is a company secretary.

Official receiver: a government official appointed by the court to act as an interim receiver or a **provisional liquidator**.

Order of priority: the liquidator must pay creditors according to a list of priorities. Certain factors can interfere with this list, such as a retention of title clause, a lien or a trust device.

Ordinary course of business: a partnership will be bound by contracts entered into by an individual partner if covering the usual type of business conducted by the firm.

Ordinary resolution: a simple majority vote by shareholders.

Ordinary share (or equity share): holders of ordinary shares are entitled to be paid a dividend depending upon how well the company is doing. The ordinary shares of English companies nearly always give their holders the right to vote in general meetings and on important matters regarding the running of the company.

Owners: the owners of a company are the **shareholders**.

Partnership: the relationship between persons carrying on a business in common with a view to profit. It is unincorporated and therefore not a separate legal person.

Partnership property (or **capital**): is property that is jointly owned by the partners. Assets that have not been transferred to the partnership remain the property of the individual partners.

Personal liability: where an individual is held liable, for example, a sole trader is held liable for the debts of his business.

Petition: certain actions are commenced by petition, for example, a winding up petition is presented to the court in order to liquidate a company.

Pre-emption rights: the right to purchase (shares) before others.

Preference share: this is a share that pays a dividend at a fixed rate. This fixed amount of dividend is paid out before ordinary shareholders are paid a dividend.

Preferential creditor: one paid out before certain other categories of creditors in a winding up.

Pre-incorporation contract: where a person enters into a contract on behalf of a company which has not yet been formed.

Premium: when shares are issued above their nominal value, the whole of the premium is placed in a share premium account.

Private company: a company that may not offer its shares and debentures to the public.

Promoter: one who organises the setting up of a new company.

Prospectus: document in which shares or debentures are offered to the public for the first time.

Provisional liquidator: see **liquidator**.

Proxy: here, person appointed by a shareholder to vote in his place at a company meeting.

Public company: a public company must have a minimum subscribed share capital. It may seek finance by offering its shares and debentures to the public. If it is a public limited company, it is one incorporated with limited liability.

Quasi loans: where the company pays for certain personal items of the director, although the director repays later.

Ratify: to approve officially, for example, a contract outside the objects clause can be ratified and the clause can then be altered by special resolution.

Receiver: when the company has failed to repay a debt to a creditor, a receiver will take control of the property in question for the benefit of the creditor. He is not appointed to wind up a company.

Reckless: taking an unjustifiable risk.

Register: to be noted on an official list, such as the Companies Registry.

Registrar: the Registrar of Companies keeps an official record of all incorporated businesses.

Relief: a remedy or assistance provided by the court.

Representative action: where a member (or members) brings an action to enforce a personal right.

Reserve capital: a part of the uncalled share capital set aside as a fund for paying unsecured creditors should the company be wound up.

Resolution: a formal proposal, usually voted upon at a meeting.

Restrain: attempt to prevent someone carrying out a certain action, for example to prevent a director entering into a contract beyond the scope of the objects clause.

Retention of title clause (also referred to as a **Romalpa clause**): this is a clause inserted into a contract of sale stipulating that the seller remains the legal owner of the goods he sells until the buyer has paid for the goods in full.

Self-dealing rule: if a director has an interest in a contract between the company and a third party, he must disclose this to the company, as a possible conflict of interest situation.

Shadow director: a person is termed a shadow director if he controls the other directors, even though he is not officially a director of the company.

Share capital: the total amount which a company's shareholders have contributed or are liable to contribute as payment for their shares.

Shareholder: one who holds shares in a company.

Shares: interest held by a shareholder in a company, measured by a sum of money for the purposes of liability and dividend. There are various types of shares. Two of the most common are preference shares and ordinary shares.

Sole proprietorship: the American term for a sole trader.

Sole trader: an unincorporated, one-man business, where the owner of the business is personally liable for any losses arising from his business.

Special resolution: a company resolution, which is only valid if approved by 75% of the votes cast at a meeting. Twenty-one days notice must be given.

Stock: in England, stock is used to describe a member's holding expressed in monetary terms rather than in terms of the number of shares held.

Stockholders: in the USA, shareholders are referred to as stockholders (as they own one or more shares of stock).

Subscriber shares: the first shares issued when a new company is formed.

Subsidiary: a subsidiary company is one that is held by a parent company.

Supervisory board: in some countries, companies may have a supervisory board that advises and supervises the board of directors. The USA and England do not have a two-tier system of management, although they may well use advisory committees.

Trading certificate: once registered, a public limited company has to wait for a trading certificate before it can commence business.

Trustee in bankruptcy: this trustee manages the assets of a bankrupt and pays off the creditors according to their priority.

Ultra vires: Latin phrase meaning to act in a way which exceeds legal powers or authority. Contracts outside the scope of the objects clause used to be ultra vires and therefore void. This position has been changed by EU law.

Uncalled share capital (unpaid capital): if the shares that have been issued have not required the shareholders to pay for them in full, the amount outstanding is unpaid capital.

Underwriter: a person (or institution) who takes up shares or debentures not taken up by the public.

Undischarged bankrupt: a person subject to a bankruptcy order that is still in force.

Unincorporated: a business organisation that is not incorporated is not a separate legal person.

Unissued share capital: the difference between the nominal value of a company's authorised share capital and the nominal value of the issued share capital, minus any amounts of issued capital that have not been called up by the company.

Unsecured trade creditor: a category of creditors without security. This category does not have a high position on the order of priorities in a winding up.

Voluntary arrangement: rather than enter into winding up proceedings, a company can make a voluntary arrangement with its creditors for repayment, if supervised by a qualified insolvency practitioner. A **composition** or a **scheme of arrangement** can be drawn up.

Winding up: process by which a registered company is dissolved. A winding up can be **compulsory** or **voluntary**. A voluntary winding up may be either a **members' winding up** or a **creditors' winding up**. A compulsory winding up is by court order upon the presentation of a **winding up petition**.

Written resolution: this dispenses with the need for a meeting by a private company.

Wrongful trading: where a person went on trading although he ought to have realised that the company could not pay its debts.

Company law terminology in context

1 INTRODUCTION

With respect to English company law terminology, two points are worth noting. Over recent years, the European Union has sought to harmonise the company law of the Member States. This has affected English law in various ways. For example, an EU directive on objects clauses altered the common law position that a contract outside the scope of the objects clause was automatically **void** (for this term see chapter 5). Now, such a contract, once concluded, will usually not be treated as void. Nonetheless, there are still differences between the Member States. For example, a textbook on English company law will not deal with the function and rules relating to supervisory boards, whereas any Dutch or German legal textbook will. The reason is simple: the supervisory board has no role to play in English law but in Dutch or German law a supervisory board must be set up once a company reaches a certain size.

There are also differences in terminology between England and the USA, which students and practitioners should be aware of to avoid confusion. The word **company** itself is used rather differently by English lawyers than by American lawyers. In English law, the word company has a specific meaning, denoting an incorporated entity, a registered company. In the USA, company may be used in a more general way. The word company has been held to cover private corporations, joint stock companies and partnerships. Take a sentence from an American law book: "Start-up companies are often formed as proprietorships or general partnerships." This sentence would never appear in an English legal textbook as a company by definition could not be a sole trader or a partnership. In English law, a **firm** is not an incorporated entity. A sentence such as that from a book written by the eminent American lawyer Richard Posner, on the 'Economic Analysis of the Law', therefore reads strangely for an English lawyer: "The theory of the firm tells us why so much economic activity is organized in firms but not why most of those firms are corporations." Just to add to the confusion, one relatively recent form of business organisation in the USA is the limited liability company. A limited liability company is the most usual form of registered company in England. However, the form of business organisation in the USA that is most similar to the English limited liability company is not the limited liability company but the corporation, as the American limited liability company is something of a hybrid between a corporation and a partnership.

With respect to the process of incorporation, English law could be said to be more similar to Dutch law than to American law. Incorporation in both England and the Netherlands requires fairly weighty documentation, outlining the structure of the company, and a procedure that can easily take several months. In general, incorporation is a simpler matter in the USA. The requirements of the states vary, but the state of Delaware is famous for its speed in incorporating businesses, with documentation that is sometimes no longer than a page.

Note: in this chapter, references to the term 'company' will be used in the English legal sense of the word to mean only an incorporated, separate legal person.

2 UNINCORPORATED BUSINESS ORGANISATIONS

Businessmen have to choose whether to operate as a sole trader, or in a partnership or a company. One of the main distinctions in the classification of business enterprises is between enterprises that are **incorporated** and those that are **unincorporated**. Incorporation makes a business a **legal person**. A business organisation that is not incorporated is not a separate legal person. This means that, as it is not a legal person, an unincorporated business may be equated with the **natural person** or persons who comprise the organisation.

2.1 Sole trader

A **sole trader** is basically a one-man business, where the owner himself has usually put up the capital for the business. If a person operates a business alone, the business and the owner are one. In other words, the sole trader carries full responsibility for his business. The sole trader is entitled to the profits of the business but he is also responsible for its losses. If the business is in debt, then the sole trader is personally liable for those debts and his private property can be called upon in order to satisfy the creditors.

Note: a sole trader is called a **sole proprietorship** in the USA.

2.2 Partnership

A **partnership** is just a term used to describe the relationship between persons carrying on a business in common with a view to profit. Partnerships are referred to in English law as **firms** and the name under which their business is carried on is called the firm name. There are no legal formalities as to how a partnership should be set up. It is usual, and indeed advisable, to do this in the form of a written agreement, called a **deed** or **articles of partnership**, but a written agreement is not a legal requirement. However, if the name of the firm does not consist of the names of the partners (which may be shortened to 'and co'), the name the firm has chosen to trade under must be registered. For practical purposes, proceeding may be brought by or against the firm in the firm's name.

Note 1: the abbreviation 'and co' is short for 'and company'. A business organisation ending with 'and co' is not a company but a firm.

Note 2: in English law, the word firm is connected in particular to partnership and it cannot be used to describe an incorporated company. The words **company** and **firm** cannot, therefore, be used synonymously in English legal terminology as a firm cannot be a company. In the USA, it is common to find the two words used interchangeably. This is because, under statutory construction, the term company has been held to include partnerships. Take the following example from an American textbook on corporate governance: "Furthermore, when one firm controls a number of other firms held in the form of subsidiaries, the parent firm is referred to as a holding company." Such a sentence would not be possible in an English legal textbook.

2.2.1 Legal structure of a partnership

As a partnership is unincorporated, it is not a separate person in law. It is formed by the individual partners who are natural persons. Unlike a registered company, a partnership does not have to comply with many legal formalities, for example, a partnership does not have to be **registered**.

In English law, every partner is an **agent** of the firm and can act to bind the firm and his other partners for the purpose of the business of the partnership. A partner has an agent's power to bind the partnership by his acts carried out within the **ordinary course of the business**. Then the partnership is bound by contracts made within the agent's actual and apparent authority. The actual authority is the express power given to the agent. Apparent authority is the authority the agent appears to others to hold.

The individual partners in the firm pay tax under the income tax system, the amount of tax depending upon their respective shares in partnership profits and losses. Partners can raise funds for the firm from outsiders and secure loans on partnership property. However, a firm may not secure a loan and raise finance by using a **floating charge**. This form of borrowing is not available to a partnership.

2.2.2 Liability of the partners

As every partner is an agent of the firm, if a partner breaches a contract or commits a tort in the course of the firm's business, all the other partners are liable. Partners may be **jointly and severally liable**.

The individual partners are also accountable for all the firm's debts. Every partner is jointly liable with the other partners for all the debts and obligations incurred in the period in which he is a partner. By suing in the firm's name, a creditor can join all the partners in an action. This means he will be paid out of the **assets** of the firm as a whole. **Partnership property** is property that is jointly owned by the partners. Assets that are not transferred to the partnership remain the property of the individual partners. Creditors of the partnership have the right to call upon the private property of the individual partners if the partnership property is insufficient to meet the debt.

Note 1: a hybrid form of partnership is the **limited partnership** ('LP'). This is a partnership in which the general partners manage the business of the partnership, but one or more silent partners contribute capital to the partnership (so-called limited partners). These limited partners have no say in the running of the partnership. As long as they have not participated in its management, if the partnership fails, their personal liability for its debts is limited whereas the general partners remain personally liable for the debts.

Note 2: yet another form of partnership is the **limited liability partnership** ('LLP'). Limited liability partnerships came into existence in English law in 2001, following an Act of Parliament of the year before. The LLP is a separate legal entity, giving its members the benefit of limited liability while retaining the internal structure of a partnership. In the USA, the form of the LLP may vary somewhat from state to state, but generally it is so structured that the partners are not personally liable for any malpractice by the other partners, although they do remain personally liable for many types of debt.

3   REGISTERED COMPANIES

In English law, a company is an association of persons formed for the purposes of an undertaking or business carried on in the name of the association. It must be registered and is then legally incorporated. The registered company is a legal person, separate from its individual members and management.

Note: the American legal term **corporation** is the one used in the USA to describe an association of shareholders, which is a legal entity entirely separate and distinct from those who own and manage it. American corporations are further sub-divided into C and S corporations: a C corporation is the regular corporation and the S corporation must conform to certain special criteria, such as it must be of domestic origin and have no more than seventy-five stockholders. English terminology also refers to corporations to indicate a limited company or public authority that has been incorporated. The English often use the term corporation to indicate a large company.

3.1 Types of registered company

There are three types of registered company:
1   limited by shares: the shareholders' liability is limited to any amount that has not yet been paid for their shares;
2   limited by guarantee: the shareholders' liability is limited to the amount they have guaranteed to contribute if the company is wound up;
3   unlimited: here the shareholders are fully liable for the debts of the company if the company is wound up.

The most popular form is the **limited liability company** (which is the one used as a standard company in this chapter). If a company is a limited liability company, shareholders cease to incur liability to contribute to the debts of the company once the shares held by the members have been fully paid up. That means that the **nominal value** of the share has been paid to the company (this is the face value of a security rather than its market value).

Note 1: in the USA, the term company applies to a wide range of activities and can be used to describe private corporations, joint stock companies as well as partnerships. The American **limited liability company** ('LLC') is not a direct equivalent of the English limited liability company. The precise format of an LLC can vary from state to state. In general, it can be said that an LLC is a separate legal entity, usually a board of directors is not a requirement, it is often set up for a limited duration, and the LLC itself is not taxed but the profit is taxed when distributed to the members as income.

Note 2: shareholders may also be referred to as **members** of the company or **owners** of the company.

3.2 Legal person

A company's incorporation creates three separate pillars: the **company**, its **membership** and its **management**. Once registered, a company becomes a separate person in law. As a legal person, it can own property, commit crimes and torts and conclude contracts. The **shares** held represent the members' interest in the company and their legal rights and duties are laid down in the company's constitution (see below). The shareholders are the owners of the company, but they are not responsible, in their capacity as shareholders, for the day-to-day running of the company: that is the task of management.

While each individual company has a separate legal identity, it is common to find groups of companies headed by a **holding company** (or **parent company**). The business of a holding company consists wholly or mainly in holding shares or securities in one or more companies in the group, which are its **subsidiaries**. Under statute, in English law a holding company must produce **group accounts**. A group relationship is defined as a parent/subsidiary relationship.

At first sight, an obligation to produce group accounts would seem inconsistent with the concept of each company being a separate legal entity. After all, the company as a separate legal person independent from its membership and management is an essential element of company law. The legal recognition of the company's independence creates what is often referred to as the **corporate veil**. Usually, this veil cannot be lifted. However, as shown by the requirement of group accounts, there are times when the company's separate legal personality can be put aside. The process by which the court looks behind the veil of corporate secrecy is called **lifting the veil** (or in the USA **piercing the veil**). One reason for doing so is where fraudulent practices are suspected. This may lead the court, for example, to identify a company within a group with another company within that group, such as identifying a subsidiary with its holding company so that the court can treat it as if it had no separate legal identity.

3.3   Formation of a company

The creation of a new company needs a **promoter**. There is no specific definition of a company promoter in English law, but from case law it seems he must have contributed some essential element towards the incorporation. A promoter is subject to certain legal duties. He owes **fiduciary duties** to the company he is promoting. This means that a promoter should not make secret profits. Once the company starts trading, the role of the promoter is at an end.

There are various types of promoters. The promotion of a public or large private company is often undertaken by a professional agency. It is also possible for an incorporated company to act as the promoter of a yet to be incorporated company. The promoter of a small company is often the owner of the pre-incorporated business. Once the company is set up, it may be that the former promoter becomes a director of the company.

The promoter's task is to set up a registered company. The promoter will deal with administrative aspects, such as registering the **memorandum** and **articles of association**, but he may also be active in acquiring capital for the company and entering into preliminary agreements. This may require the promoter to enter into **pre-incorporation contracts**. A pre-incorporation contract is where a person enters into a contract on behalf of a yet unformed company. A company cannot be bound by a pre-incorporation contract since it does not exist at the time of the contract. Within the EU, the position is that the promoter who entered into the contract can be held personally liable for that contract, unless the agreement provides otherwise.

Note: often in civil law countries, for example the Netherlands, a company can simply ratify a contract made on its behalf before incorporation. In English law, retrospective ratification is not allowed. In order to take over the pre-incorporation contracts, a company must follow a process known as **novation**. This process requires that the original contract is replaced by a new one, in which the company name is substituted for the original contracting party (usually the promoter).

3.4   Registration

To become incorporated, the company must **register**. In England, a number of documents must be delivered to the **Registrar** of Companies. These include:
* the company's **memorandum of association**;
* the company's **articles of association**;
* a statement giving particulars of the company's first directors and secretary;
* a statutory declaration by a solicitor or a person named as director or secretary that the statutory regulations for registration have been complied with.

Once registered the company will be issued a **certificate of incorporation**. A private company may then commence business, but a public company has to wait for a **trading certificate**.

Note 1: in the USA, reference is made to **filing** rather than registering.

Note 2: the filing of a corporation can be achieved more quickly and more simply in the USA than registering a company in England. Only one document needs to be filed (see section 3.6.2). Certain other requirements that are usual in Europe in general, such as a minimum level of share capital and minimum subscribed shares before incorporation, are not necessary in the USA.

3.5   Public and private companies

In English law, an important distinction is made between a public company and a private company. This distinction is found in many civil law countries, for example Germany and the Netherlands.

Note: the corporate laws of the USA have been traditionally geared up to corporations with a large membership. Corporations have generally had the same structure, whether publicly held or privately held. A distinction between public corporations and private corporations has only been recognised in statutes and case decisions relatively recently in the USA. Although provisions may vary somewhat from state to state, the **close corporation** has become a familiar form of incorporation. The close corporation has some, but by no means all, of the features of a private company. A close corporation is one consisting of a single individual or a very small group of individuals. It allows limited liability while dispensing with much of the structure usually associated with a standard corporation in favour of direct management by the stockholders themselves.

3.5.1 Public company

A **public company** may offer its shares to, and borrow money from, the public. To be incorporated, it must have a minimum **authorised share capital**. This is the amount of capital a company can raise by selling its shares. When a new public company launches itself, this is known either as a **flotation** or by the American term **initial public offering** (IPO). A **subscriber** is someone who subscribes for shares in a new company. Subscriber shares are the first shares issued when a new company is formed. If in a flotation the issued share capital is not fully subscribed, an **underwriter** may be liable to take up the unsubscribed shares. Public companies whose shares are dealt with on the Stock Exchange are called **listed companies** or **quoted companies**, meaning they are listed on the Stock Exchange. Smaller public companies that are not quoted on the Stock Exchange can offer their securities on an intermediate market. It must be clear whether the company is a public or a private company. For this reason, the name of a public company must end with the suffix **public limited company**, which is abbreviated to 'Plc'.

3.5.2 Private company

A **private company**, unlike a public company, may not seek finance by offering its shares to, or borrowing money from, the public at large. On the other hand, a private company is exempt from some of the formal requirements of a public company, for example, it is allowed to purchase its own shares. In England a private company does not need a minimum level of share capital to register or commence trading. This is not necessarily the case in other EU countries. In the Netherlands, for example, a private company is also required to have a minimum level of share capital before incorporation, although that amount is less than the amount required for a public company. The name of a private company must end with the word **limited**, abbreviated to 'Ltd'.

3.6 The company's constitution

The constitution of English companies is governed by two main documents: the memorandum and the articles of association.

3.6.1 Memorandum of association

The **memorandum of association** is primarily concerned with the external regulation of the company. It contains a number of compulsory clauses:
- the name of the company, whether it is a limited liability company and the suffix denoting whether it is a private or public limited company;
- the location of the registered office;

- the **objects clause**: this clause states the business or the purpose for which the company was incorporated;
- the nominal capital of the company and its arrangement of shares.

As concerns the objects clause, the basic rule is that a company only has the **capacity** to carry out its business within the scope of the objects set out in the memorandum of association (and associated activities). In English law, the objects clause used to be absolutely crucial to the validity of company contracts. At common law, contracts that were outside the scope of the company's objects clause were **ultra vires** and, therefore, quite simply **void**. Ultra vires means to act in a way that exceeds legal authority. It was no defence on the part of the other contracting party that he did not know the company was acting outside its objects clause.

Changes have been made to the law on ultra vires because of European Union law. A transaction outside the objects clause is no longer void but can be enforced either by the company itself or by the other contracting party. A company can now also change its objects clause by a **special resolution** without restriction.

Nonetheless, it is not the case that the doctrine of ultra vires has become totally irrelevant with respect to object clauses as:

- before a binding transaction has been entered into, a shareholder of the company may **restrain** the company from entering into a transaction that is outside the company's objects clause. Once the contract has been concluded, this possibility is lost;
- if directors exceed their powers, they are in **breach of their directors' duties**. Concluding a contract outside the scope of the objects clause is such a breach. If a member has not been able to restrain a director, the company may be able to sue him for breach of directors' duties;
- the company can choose to **ratify**, in other words approve officially, this breach by a special resolution if it so wishes;
- ultra vires also remains important with respect to directors dealing with their companies or with subsidiaries of their holding company.

An English company still needs to have an objects clause, but it can opt for a general commercial objects clause. A general clause covers the activities of a trading company.

3.6.2 Articles of association

The **articles of association** deal primarily with the internal administration of the company. The document includes articles regulating general meetings, the appointment and powers of directors, the types of shares that can be issued and the class rights attached to shares. In practice the articles and memorandum of association are often attached together.

Together with the memorandum, the articles form the constitution of the company. Acts undertaken outside the provisions of the articles are generally not

binding on the company. For example, in the Guinness distillery case, a committee of three directors was set up to guide a take-over bid. One of these directors was to receive a percentage if there was a successful take-over of the target company. The take-over took place and the director was paid. However, the articles of association did not give a committee of the board the power to enter into an agreement with the director to pay him a percentage of the value of a successful take-over bid. When this payment was later challenged by Guinness, it was held that as this payment was for services outside the scope of a director's normal duties it could only be determined by the board of directors. The company was entitled to claim back the money from the director in question.

Articles are binding but they may, nevertheless, be altered by **special resolution** (75% majority). The courts reserve the power to refuse an alteration unless that alteration would benefit the company as a whole and it has been made in good faith. **Minority shareholders** may **petition** the court if an alteration is unfairly prejudicial to them. However, as long as the amendment benefits the company and is made in good faith, a court will uphold an alteration, even if the amendment is detrimental to individual members.

Note 1: in the USA, generally only one document needs to be filed: this document is often referred to as the **articles of incorporation**. It must state the name, the aggregate number of shares of each class of stock that the corporation is authorised to issue, address of the registered office, name of the registered agent and the name and address of the incorporators. The rules for the internal running of the corporation are set out in a separate document, the **bylaws**, which does not have to be filed.

Note 2: rules similar to those in England concerning incorporation can be found in other EU countries, particularly due to attempts at European harmonisation through EU directives. The number and names of documents necessary for incorporation can vary. For example, the Dutch only have one constitutional document called the 'statuten', which is always translated by the English term 'articles of association'. Nonetheless, the Dutch articles of association contain the same types of clauses as the English memorandum and articles of association. Both countries tend to work with equally extensive and detailed documentation.

3.7   Capital

In general, **capital** comprises all the money or other property owned by a company. However, the term capital can be found used in various contexts:
- **Share capital**: this is capital raised by the issue of the company's shares. It represents the shareholders investment in the company, which becomes part of the company's overall assets. Share capital becomes the property of the company and the shareholder does not become a creditor of the company.

- **Authorised share capital**: the total nominal value of the shares that may be issued by a company. The amount is fixed in the company's memorandum.
- **Issued capital**: that part of a company's authorised share capital that has actually been issued to the shareholders.
- **Unissued share capital**: the difference between the nominal value of a company's authorised share capital and the nominal value of the issued share capital, minus any amounts of issued capital that have not been called up by the company.
- **Called up share capital** (paid-up capital): the sum that shareholders have already paid in return for shares.
- **Uncalled share capital** (unpaid capital): if the shares that have been issued have not required the shareholders to pay for them in full, the amount outstanding is unpaid capital. It is the difference between the nominal value of a company's issued share capital and the value of the company's called up share capital. The outstanding amount represents the extent of the shareholders' liability to the company if the company is wound up.
- **Reserve capital**: a part of the uncalled share capital set aside as a fund for paying unsecured creditors should the company be wound up.
- **Loan capital**: capital that has been obtained on credit.

3.7.1 Shares

An important way of financing a company is by issuing shares. Shares can be defined as the interest held by a shareholder in a company, measured by a sum of money in order to assess the shareholder's liability and **dividend** rights. As a share gives a shareholder a stake in a company, the shareholder also becomes a **member** of the company. A company can issue various types of shares. The two most common types are preference shares and ordinary shares.

- **Preference share**: this is a share that pays a dividend at a fixed rate. This fixed amount of dividend is paid out before ordinary shareholders are paid a dividend.
- **Ordinary share** (otherwise referred to as an equity share): holders of ordinary shares are entitled to be paid a dividend once the preferential shareholders have been paid. This dividend will fluctuate depending upon how well the company is doing. The ordinary shares of English companies nearly always give their holders the right to vote in general meetings and on important matters regarding the running of the company.

Note 1: in the USA, it is common to refer to shareholders as **stockholders** (as owning one or more shares of stock). Preference shares are referred to as preferred stock and ordinary shares are called common stock.

Note 2: in England, **stock** is a term used to describe a member's holding expressed in monetary terms, such as £100 worth of stock as an alternative to one hundred shares of £1 each.

Note 3: the rights of shareholders depend on the **class rights** attached to the shares. The role of shareholders in a company can also vary from country to country. For example, in the Netherlands extensive use has been made of various protective constructions. It is common to find shareholders stripped of any say in the running of a company by using a legal construction known as an 'administration office' (administratiekantoor). This administration office acts as an intermediary between the company and the shareholder. The shares are transferred by the company to the administration office, which in turn issues certificates of shares. It is these certificates of shares that are traded. The administration office remains the actual shareholder, and it is the administration office that has a voice in the running of the company. Certificate holders, in general, only have the right to a dividend.

When a company issues shares, a number of requirements must be fulfilled. If a public company invites the public to subscribe, it must issue a document setting out such information as investors and their clients require in order to make a proper assessment of the standing of that company. This information is contained in a **prospectus** when new securities are being issued and in **listing particulars** if the company is already listed on the Stock Exchange. The information contained in these documents must be true and accurate. It is an offence to create a false or misleading impression as to the market in or value of any investment if the purpose is to acquire, dispose of, subscribe for or underwrite those investments. In English law, criminal liability as well as tortious liability may be incurred both by the company and directors and persons stated to be the issuers of the particulars. It is also an offence for a private company to issue an advertisement offering its securities to the public.

Investors who have been misled by untrue statements in prospectuses and listing particulars have various remedies open to them. Compensation is payable for breach of a statutory duty in failing to meet the information requirements for these documents. Ordinary common law remedies include **rescission** of the contract if the investor entered into the contract because of a **misrepresentation**; **damages** in the tort of **deceit** for a **fraudulent misrepresentation**, and in the tort of **negligence** for a **negligent misstatement** (see chapters 4 and 5 for these terms).

3.7.2 Altering the share capital

Before issuing shares, a company must check its **memorandum** to make sure it has sufficient **authorised share capital** for the issue. In order to issue new shares, it may be necessary to alter the share capital clause. English law lays down certain requirements before this clause may be amended. This is in keeping with one of the basic principles of company law that a company must maintain its share capital. If the share capital is not maintained, this could adversely affect the company's creditors. However, there are a number of exceptions where capital reduction is allowed. For example, a court can order a company to buy its own shares if **minority shareholders** need to be bought out. This is also an exception to the usual rule that a company is prohibited from buying its own shares. Following on from this rule, a company is not allowed to give financial assistance, either directly or indirectly, for the purpose of acquiring shares in itself. Again, there are exceptions to this rule, for example, financial assistance can be provided for a management buy-out scheme or to assist employees in buying shares in the company.

Directors should also bear in mind that the issue may be subject to **pre-emption rights**, in which case the shares must first be offered to the existing members of the company before being offered to non-members. The nominal value of a share is its face value. Where shares are issued at a **premium**, in other words above their nominal value, the whole of the premium must be placed in a share premium account and cannot be used to pay up a dividend. The market value of a share may be a very different value than its nominal value. Information concerning the shares may affect the market value. For this reason, in English law it is a criminal offence for a person to use confidential information about the company in order to buy or sell the securities advantageously. This practice is known as **insider dealing** or **insider trading**.

3.7.3 Loan capital

Share capital is not the only source of finance for a company. Credit arrangements are also vital. The term **loan capital** refers to money borrowed by a company, in its capacity as a legal person. The person or institution lending the money may be either a secured creditor, meaning the lender has some form of security in case the company later defaults on the loan, or an unsecured creditor, in which case the loan is not protected.

A **bond** is a certificate issued by a public company promising to repay borrowed money at a fixed rate of interest at a specified time, and to repay the original sum in full after the specified term. As bonds specify a fixed rate of interest, they are also referred to as **fixed interest securities**. A document that acknowledges a credit arrangement between a company and a creditor is also known as a **debenture**. In England, the term debenture is usually used to describe a secured loan (although the term 'naked debenture' may be used to describe an unsecured loan).

Note: in the USA, a debenture bond is a general obligation of the issuing company and, therefore, unsecured credit.

Where a company borrows money from a single source, for example a bank, there will be a single debenture. Debentures may also be issued in a series, each loan being separate but ranking equally with respect to repayment. There may be an issue of **debenture stock** similar to an issue of shares. However, a **debenture holder** is a **creditor** of the company, whereas a shareholder is a member. Issuing debenture stock is the method used by public companies wishing to raise loan capital on the investment market, as money is raised from different lenders, at the same time, on the same terms. In such a situation there will usually be a **debenture trust** (or **indenture**). This will set out the terms of the loan. There will be a **trustee** who will act on behalf of the debenture holders.

A debenture holder is entitled to be paid back the principal sum lent to the company and the interest on that sum. A company must pay the prescribed rate of interest as stated in the debenture whether it is making a profit or not. If it defaults, a debenture holder may send in a **receiver** to protect his investment. A debenture is transferable, also called **negotiable**, because it can be sold on by its original owner. A company is also free to buy its own debentures, and debentures may be issued at a discount.

Although debentures do not have to be registered, if a loan is to be secured by a **charge** on the property, that charge must be registered. If the charge is not registered it will be void. Charges rank in priority according to their registration date. A charge can take several forms:

1   **Fixed charge**: this charge is similar to an ordinary mortgage. A fixed charge is either equitable or legal (for the distinction see chapter 1). A legal fixed charge is a legal mortgage. An equitable fixed charge is similar, but without a deed the legal title cannot be transferred. To create a fixed charge over a corporate asset, the asset must be identifiable, even if it does not exist at the time of the charge. When registered, a fixed charge gives the holder security over the property subject to the charge, and the company cannot sell or deal with that property in any way without the permission of the fixed charge holder.

2   **Floating charge**: a creditor may secure his loan with a floating charge, which is unique to company law. This type of charge attaches to a class of assets, which in the ordinary course of a company's business would be changing from time to time. Stock, plant, machinery, tools and book debts are examples of the type of property often used to support a floating charge. These assets are used in the ordinary course of the company's business. The company can trade in assets subject to a floating charge. If these assets were covered by a fixed charge, the company would have to notify the charge holder and ask his permission each time it wanted to sell or change an asset.

    A charge may **crystallise** because of an **event of default**, for example the happening of an event specified in the debenture document. Specified events implied by law are the **winding up** of a company and the appointment of a **receiver**. After crystallisation, the company may no longer deal with the assets under the floating charge.

    A contract for a floating charge normally has express provisions that stipulate that:

    •   a company will not deal with the assets otherwise than in the normal course of business, and

    •   a company will not grant a further charge over the charged asset which would rank in priority ahead of the floating charge. This is known as a

negative pledge clause. It prohibits the issuer from pledging any assets in the future if it would be to the detriment of the debenture holder's security.

Note 1: in the USA, where a creditor has a secured loan he may be said to have a **lien** on the property designated to satisfy the debt. A **floating lien** is one term used to refer to a general claim against the assets of a company where there is no detailed specification and few restrictions are set on what the company can do with the assets.

Note 2: debentures can be an attractive form of investment. One reason is that they offer more security than shares. As debenture holders are creditors of the company, they rank in priority before shareholders when a company is wound up.

4   THE MANAGEMENT OF THE COMPANY

The term **corporate governance** is often used to describe the way in which companies are directed and controlled. A company is a separate legal person but it must be managed by people. Whereas the shareholders are its owners, the directors form the management of the company. In practice, particularly in small private companies, each of the shareholders may also be a director. The larger the company, in particular large public companies, the more likely it is that owners and managers are not the same people. In company law, however, the company, its management and ownership are three separate entities.

4.1   Definition of director

In English law, there is no legal definition of **director**. The Company Act does state that the term director includes: "any person occupying the position of director, by whatever name called". This means that a person need not formally have the title 'director' to be one. In practice, the term is applied to anyone who is responsible for the management of a company, because he is on the board of directors and takes part in the decision-making. A director of a company need not be a natural person; a company could act as a director of another company. A director is said to be an **officer** of a company, as is the **company secretary**.

4.2   Appointment of directors

When a company is registered, a form must be sent in stating whom the first directors of the company will be. Once the company is incorporated, these people automatically become the directors. All directors other than the first directors are appointed according to the rules laid down in the articles, usually by the shareholders on an ordinary resolution at the general meeting. Directors are appointed individually for the period specified in the articles.

Unlike a company secretary, a director does not require any formal qualifications. However, not all persons may become directors. They may be barred for a variety of reasons, for example, a candidate is an **undischarged bankrupt** or subject to a **disqualification order**.

4.3   Types of directors

There are various types of director:

- **Executive director** (USA: often referred to as an **inside director**): this is usually a full-time officer of a company, with the task of day-to-day management. The powers of the executive directors are determined by the **board of directors**. Many company directors hold service contracts, in other words, they are salaried employees of the company. Sometimes, in small private companies, each shareholder is an executive director. In that case, it is possible that they are not paid as directors.
- **Non-executive director** (USA: often referred to as an **outside**, **independent** or **non-management** director): a non-executive director is not a salaried employee, nor is he responsible for the day-to-day management of the company. Non-executive directors are usually chosen for their expertise or public recognition in some particular field. They are entitled to director's remuneration (consideration for services, any benefit whether money or otherwise) and business expenses. As they are not salaried employees, the idea is that they have a certain independence with respect to the management of the company. They are expected to keep up with corporate matters, although they may not be expected to attend all board meetings.
- **Chairman**: is an appointed director who presides over meetings of the board of directors and general meetings. He has no special powers but he may have a second or casting vote. The chairman may be, but not necessarily, also the **managing director** (or **chief executive officer**, the **CEO**) of the company. The trend today for public companies in England is to appoint a chairman who is not the managing director, as combining the functions of both chairman and managing director in one person is now generally frowned upon. Whether the CEO should be the chairman is also a contentious issue in American corporate governance discussions.
- **Alternative director**: this is a person appointed by a director to act in his place, for example because of ill health. This must be allowed by the company's articles. The appointment must also be approved by the board of directors.
- **Shadow director**: a person is termed a shadow director if he controls the other directors, even though he is not officially a director of the company.

4.4   Board of directors

There are two power bases in a company: the board of directors and the members in general meeting. The **board of directors** consists of the individually appointed directors. It has general management powers, the scope of those management powers being determined by the company's articles. The board is the major decision-making body of a company. The board should act as one, taking collective responsibility for its decisions. It can also delegate powers to committees of one or more directors, or to a managing director or other executive directors. The board can be called to account by the shareholders in their meetings.

Note: in the USA, it is common for a company to have a board of directors and a senior management team headed by the CEO. The board consists of inside and outside directors. In other countries, for example the Netherlands and Germany, there may be two boards: a board of directors and a **supervisory board**. The task of the supervisory board is to advise and supervise the board of directors. Small companies may elect to have a supervisory board, but large companies must have a supervisory board as well as a board of directors.

4.5   Directors' duties

Although the directors run a company, they cannot treat it as if it were their own property. They owe duties to the company. In general, 'the company' here means the corporate body: the members as the providers of capital. Traditionally directors are said to hold their duties to the company as a whole, in other words to the share-holders as a body and not to individual shareholders. This has now been extended to include a duty to employees. In general, in English law, there is no recognition of a duty owed by directors to creditors while the company is solvent. Once the company is insolvent, it is the creditors, rather than the shareholders, who then control the company assets through **insolvency** procedures.

   Directors' duties are still largely governed by common law and equity, although statute has laid down a number of statutory duties. These statutory duties include various disclosure requirements such as a director's share holding or debentures, disclosure of any substantial non-cash transactions with the company, and the disclosure of any personal interests in company contracts.

4.5.1 The duty of care and skill

This common law **duty of care and skill** is comparable to the American **business judgment rule**. It is basically a duty not to act **negligently** in managing the company. Directors are not liable for mere errors of judgment. The guidelines were laid down in English law in a case back in 1925. The duty of care and skill is fulfilled if directors act within their powers with such care as can be reasonably expected of them, taking into account their knowledge and experience. For example, a director of a life insurance company does not guarantee he has the skill of an actuary or a doctor. The directors must, however, have acted honestly for the benefit of the company.

What is the **duty of care** owed? The standard is flexible. A higher standard is expected of professional directors than the directors of a small family business. The duty of executive and non-executive directors has been held to be the same.

4.5.2 Fiduciary duties

While the duty of care and skill is not particularly far- reaching, much is expected in terms of honesty and integrity from directors. The rules concerning **fiduciary duties** are strict. A director is under an obligation to exercise his powers for the benefit of the company and not for his own benefit. Where there is a conflict of interests between a director's personal interests and those of the company, those of the company must prevail.

This **conflict of interest rule** means that a director must not use any corporate opportunity for his own personal advantage. In many cases, a director who has used a corporate opportunity for himself will be in **breach of directors' duties**. For example, where a director negotiates a contract in the company's name, but then enters into the contract in his own name. This will only be justified if the company has already decided not to enter into the contract without any improper influence having been exercised by the director, and the director subsequently takes it up. A director should take care not to put himself in a conflict of interest situation. For example, in the Guinness distillery case mentioned above, it was held that one of the directors, who stood to gain financially if he recommended a take-over, had acted in breach of his fiduciary duty. He had put himself in a position where his personal interests prevented him from giving independent and impartial advice to Guinness. His duty to the company and his personal interests were therefore hopelessly at odds.

A director is under a duty to **disclose** any personal interests, which could cause a conflict of interest situation, to the company. Again with respect to contracts, if a director has an interest in a contract between the company and a third party, for example because he is a shareholder of the third party, he must disclose this to the company, as a possible conflict of interest situation. This is often referred to as the **self-dealing rule**. There must also be disclosure of any interest held by the director and by connected persons, such as members of his family, in the company, a subsidiary or the holding company. If he is a shareholder of the holding company, that may influence his decision-making with respect to his position as director of the subsidiary. These disclosure requirements apply even where the director is a sole director.

There are also rules to protect the company from undesirable sales or credit arrangements with directors. A company cannot enter into an arrangement with a director for a **non-cash asset of the requisite value**, without the approval of the company in general meeting. This is to prevent directors buying company property at less than its true value. In general, a director would have to pay back to the company any direct profits made in this way.

The position is similar with respect to loans. This includes **quasi-loans** and credit transactions. A quasi-loan is where the company pays for certain personal items of the director, although the director repays later. A credit arrangement could take the form of a **hire purchase agreement** (paid for in instalments). These arrangements are only permissible in English law if under a certain fixed amount and repayable within a set period of time. Loans to directors must also be disclosed in company accounts. It is an offence by both the company and the director to breach these provisions.

4.5.3 Effect of a breach of duty

A director in breach may be **jointly and severally liable** with other directors who are also liable to make good the loss. A director could be **personally liable** in contract law, for example for a breach of warranty of authority. In tort he could be held personally liable for fraud or a negligent misstatement with respect to listing particulars and prospectuses. Statute imposes liability for such matters as an irregular allotment of shares or the improper use of the company name.

In certain circumstances **relief** from breach of duty may be granted. The company could, by ordinary resolution, waive the breach. The court may also grant relief if it finds that the director has acted honestly and reasonably. A company may not **exclude liability** (see chapter 5) for directors' breach, but it can insure directors against it.

4.6 The company secretary

In England, every company must have a **company secretary**. Letters signed by individuals describing themselves as company secretary can be rather perplexing to civil law lawyers who are not familiar with this function. The company secretary is responsible for various administrative duties, including the preparation and keeping of minutes, dealing with share transfers, maintaining a register of members and debenture holders, a register of directors' share interests and sending notices of meetings. As an officer of the company, he owes fiduciary duties to the company in a similar way to directors. He has the power to bind the company in contracts entered into on the company's behalf.

The company secretary is appointed by, and is dismissed by, the company directors. In private companies where there is more than one director, one of the directors may act as a company secretary. In a public company, the company secretary must be properly qualified either through experience as a director or by obtaining the necessary professional qualifications. It is not uncommon for solicitors to become company secretaries.

4.7 Auditor

Auditing is the process by which the financial situation of the company is examined in order to draw up the **annual accounts**. All company accounts have to be audited unless the company qualifies for an exemption, for example because it falls under the category of 'small company', having a turnover of less than the specified amount. An **auditor** is an accountant whose duty it is to investigate and report upon those company's accounts. He must report to the members of the company as to whether the company's accounts give a true representation of the company's financial position. The report must be read at a general meeting and made available to the members. An auditor's report must be attached to a company's balance sheet. His **duty of care** is to the company as a whole, to enable the shareholders as a body to exercise control over it.

Although paid by the company, an auditor must remain independent. He is, therefore, not allowed to be an officer or servant of the company or be employed by someone connected to the company.

5 THE SHAREHOLDERS

Shares represent the interest of the members in the company. The **membership contract** creates contractual rights and obligations between the company and its members and between the members themselves. The main body of this contract is formed by the provisions laid down in the memorandum and the articles of association. Members are bound by these provisions. For example, shares are the shareholders' property and may be sold on. However, if the articles provide for pre-emption rights, stipulating that shares must first be offered to the existing membership, the shareholders would then not be free simply to sell their shares on the open market. The membership contract extends to those who have later bought shares from the original shareholders. This is a departure from the usual rules of contract law, as the **doctrine of privity of contract** means that individuals do not have any rights or obligations arising from a contract to which they were not original parties (see chapter 5).

5.1 Meetings

The directors are responsible for the daily running of the company, but the most important matters that can affect the company must be presented to the shareholders in the general meeting. In England, ordinary shares usually carry voting rights. Every company must hold an **annual general meeting**. It is the duty of the general meeting to act for the benefit of the company as a whole. **Extraordinary general meetings** may also be called to vote on special business if required by a sufficient number of the members. A **class meeting** is where a class of shareholders meet to decide matters which affect their particular class of shares.

A member can appoint a **proxy**, who need not be a member, to vote in his place at a general meeting. Voting can be by a show of hands, one vote per person, or by a poll vote, the voting rights of the members being in proportion to the number of voting shares held. Every company must keep **minutes** of the proceedings of its general meeting and directors' meetings.

5.2 Types of resolutions

Directors may pass directors' resolutions at board meeting. Shareholders may also draw up resolutions, which may be voted on in the annual general meeting. The shareholders vote on the **resolutions** raised during the general meeting. There are various types of resolution:

- **Extraordinary resolution**: this must be passed by a majority of at least 75% and will be used, for example, as a resolution to wind up the company if it cannot pay its debts. Fourteen days notice must be given to the shareholders.
- **Special resolution**: again a 75% majority is required but twenty-one days notice must be given. It would be used, for example, to change a company's articles of association. A special resolution could be passed to lay down how directors should act with respect to a particular matter.
- **Ordinary resolution**: a simple majority vote, for example to remove a director before the end of his term.
- **Written resolution**: this dispenses with the need for a meeting by a private company.
- **Elective resolutions**: certain formalities are relaxed for private companies. Private companies may pass elective resolutions for a limited number of specific purposes, for example to dispense with the holding of annual general meetings.

5.3 Minority shareholders

In effect it is the **majority shareholders** who make the company decisions. It is difficult for **minority shareholders** to prevent a course of action sanctioned by the majority holding. In general, minority shareholders cannot look to the courts for support if they are dissatisfied, as the courts will not interfere in matters of internal management. The general rule is that it is the company which should act as a claimant, not individual shareholders.

There are various exceptions to this general principle at common law and under statute. In certain circumstances, members can exercise control over the board of directors by taking action on behalf of the company to prevent wrongdoing or to enforce their own personal rights. An action by a minority shareholder (or minority shareholders) is either a **derivative action**, if the shareholder is suing in the name of the company, or a **representative action**, if brought by a member to enforce a personal right. For example, if a shareholder complains that the company intends to enter into a contract outside the scope of the objects clause, a minority action is usually permitted to restrain an ultra vires transaction. Fraudulent transactions may also be the subject of a minority action. Nor may a company deny a member his personal rights attached to his shareholding. Statute also stipulates that a member of a company may apply to the court by **petition** for an order on the grounds that the company's affairs are being or have been conducted in a manner unfairly prejudicial to the interest of the members generally or to some part of its members, for example, allotting shares in breach of pre-emption rights, failure to pay proper dividends, or the improper use of company assets for personal interest.

There are various orders the court can make to remedy the situation. It can grant an order regulating the company's affairs for the future, or restricting the company from acting in a certain way. The court can grant a compulsory purchase order, ordering the company or its members to purchase the petitioner's shares. It can authorise civil proceedings in the name and on behalf of the company. Finally, the company may be **wound up** by the court on a petition from a minority shareholder if it would be equitable to do so.

6   The company in default

It may be the case that a company has failed to repay a loan, or the interest on a loan, to a creditor. This is an **event of default**. When a debenture holder wants to enforce the terms of a debenture when there has been default, the remedy is to appoint a **receiver**. Receivers are often solicitors or accountants. A receiver is appointed either by the court or under the terms of the debenture.

There are several different types of receiver. For example, there are administrative receivers, receivers and managers who manage the business of the company where a floating charge covers only a part of the company's undertaking, or a receiver appointed by a lender who has a fixed charge on property. A receiver may or may not be a qualified **insolvency practitioner**, although in English law **liquidators, administrators** and **administrative receivers** must be. A receiver does not have to be a qualified insolvency practitioner to enforce a fixed charge, but must be one to enforce a floating charge. This requires an **administrative receiver** to announce the receivership, take control of the assets subject to the floating charge and realise those assets, paying off creditors in due order. When the receiver has done this, he may leave.

A company does not necessarily go into liquidation after the appointment of a receiver. If it does, the receiver may become the **provisional liquidator** on winding up. The creditors then meet to decide upon a permanent liquidator. An **official receiver** may also be appointed to act as an interim receiver until the liquidator has been appointed.

Note: in English legal terminology there is a distinction between a **receiver** and a **liquidator**. A receiver and a liquidator have separate functions, although physically they may be the same person. A receiver is appointed to help a creditor obtain payment of a debt. He is not there to wind up a company: this is the task of a liquidator.

7   THE DISSOLUTION OF BUSINESS ORGANISATIONS

The term **dissolution** refers to bringing a business organisation to an end. A business may come to an end for various reasons. For example, it may be that the purpose for which the business was set up has been achieved. The most usual reason for dissolution is because the business is **insolvent**. The proceedings for dissolving a business depend upon the type of business in question, whether it is incorporated or not. As a legal person, a company is **wound up** and remains in existence only until the process of **liquidation** is complete. In the case of natural persons, an **adjudication order** declares that they are **bankrupt**. A trustee in bankruptcy is then appointed to supervise the individual's financial affairs.

Note 1: in English legal terminology, the term **insolvent** is generally used to describe a company that cannot pay its debts. The term **bankrupt** is the one generally used for individuals who are unable to pay their debts. This distinction between the use of insolvency for companies and bankruptcy for individuals is not maintained in the USA.

Note 2: in the USA, bankruptcy is governed by federal law. The different types of bankruptcy proceedings are known by the chapters in which they appear in the federal Bankruptcy Code. The Chapter 7 liquidation proceedings are available to corporations and partnerships. A trustee takes control of all assets that are not exempt and pays out the creditors according to the priorities for creditors set down in the Code.

7.1   Dissolution of a partnership

There is no specific term in English law to describe the termination of a partnership. Reference is simply made to the dissolution of a partnership. A partnership can be dissolved either with or without the intervention of the court. The partnership assets will be gathered in and the firm's creditors are first paid from the partnership profits and then from the **partnership capital**. If this is not sufficient to pay all the firm's creditors, outstanding debts will then be paid from the partners' individual property. On the other hand, if there are still assets after all the creditors have been paid off, they will be distributed between the partners, either as arranged in the partnership agreement or under the Partnership Act if there is no agreement.

7.2   Dissolution of a registered company

There are various ways in which a registered company may be dissolved:
*   cancellation of the registration: on the grounds that the company's objectives are illegal, for example, the company was set up for the purposes of prostitution;
*   by an order of the court where the company is transferring its undertaking to another company under reorganisation;
*   by the registrar if the company is **defunct**;
*   by **winding up**.

7.3   Winding up

The **liquidation** of a company is achieved by the process known as winding up. There are two sorts of winding up: **voluntary winding up** and **compulsory winding up**.

1   **Voluntary winding up** is initiated either by the members of the company or the creditors. In a voluntary winding up, the shareholders can resolve to end the company. If the majority of the directors swear a statutory declaration of solvency then the company members can manage the winding up themselves. This is called a **members' winding up**. The members can appoint a liquidator in general meeting. In the case of a **creditors' voluntary winding up**, the directors have failed to swear a statutory declaration of solvency. A meeting of creditors must be called.

2   **Compulsory winding up** (or involuntary winding up) is by court order. A **winding up petition** is submitted to the court by the company itself, or a creditor who establishes a prima facie case or by a contributory. A **contributory** is someone who is liable to contribute to the assets of a company on a winding up. There are various situations in which there will be a compulsory winding up. For example, the company has passed a special resolution that it is to be wound up by the court, the number of members has fallen below the statutory minimum, or the company is unable to pay its debts. Once the petition has been presented, the company may not dispose of any of its property or transfer any of its shares.

7.3.1 The role of the liquidator

A **liquidator** is an insolvency practitioner who is appointed to wind up the company. Once appointed, only the liquidator may deal with the assets of the company. His role is to take control of the company, gather in the assets belonging to the company, realise them and pay off the creditors in order of priority. There is a fixed **order of priority** in a liquidation, with each category being paid in full before moving on to the next category.

Creditors with fixed charges may realise their charges on the company property. Traditionally, the first category in the order of priority has been the liquidator's fees (although this has been recently altered by a House of Lords decision). Then **preferential creditors** such as the Inland Revenue (taxes) and wages to employees, are paid off, followed by floating charge holders and **unsecured trade creditors**. Only when all the creditors have been paid out, will any surplus be distributed to the shareholders. The members rank according to their rights, usually with preference shareholders being paid before ordinary shareholders.

As can be seen from this order of priority, creditors with security are in a better position than unsecured creditors. Most charges on property are registerable, but they must have been registered properly otherwise they may fail. With respect to fixed charges on the same property, the first in time has priority. Floating charges normally rank behind fixed charges in priority, unless there is a **negative pledge clause** in the floating charge stating that the company is not allowed to create a subsequent charge that has priority over a floating charge.

The liquidator may **set aside** (see chapter 5 for this term) transactions that were intended to defraud the creditors. He can apply to the court to recover assets that were disposed of by the company within a fixed period before the insolvency. The liquidator may also set aside transactions made by the company within two years if undervalued, for example a gift made by the company at a time that it was already unable to pay its debts. Some charges may be invalid, for example, if the charge was made in favour of a connected person. A charge will constitute a **preference** if it unfairly prefers some creditors to others.

In certain circumstances, directors of the company may be contributories. A director can be held liable for fraudulent or wrongful trading. **Fraudulent trading** is where a company knows it will not be able to pay its debts when due, or is **reckless** as to whether it can pay them. A director who is guilty of such conduct may be liable to contribute assets. **Wrongful trading** is where a director ought to have realised that the company could not pay its debts. Again, the director could be required to contribute to the assets of the company.

7.3.2 Special creditor rights

That the liquidator pays out creditors according to an order of priorities can be very unfavourable to some creditors. Certain legal constructions have been developed to circumvent the order of priorities and give protection to those who would otherwise find themselves low down on the list.

* **Retention of title** or reservation clause (also referred to as a **Romalpa clause**): this is a clause inserted into a contract of sale stipulating that the seller remains the legal owner of the goods he sells until the buyer has paid for the goods in full. Only then will the title pass. The purpose of this clause is to affect priority, as a supplier of goods with a valid retention of title clause will rank above a creditor secured by means of a registered charge in the event of receivership or liquidation.

- **Lien**: here the lien acts as a charge on the property of another as security for the performance of an obligation. For example, a lien can exist where a person has carried out work on another person's property, such as carrying out repairs. The person carrying out the work has a lien over the property until he is paid for his work. The liquidator cannot take the property until the holder of the lien has been paid off.
- **Trust device**: the trust is a legal construction usual in common law countries (see chapter 1). Funds that have been given to the company for a specific purpose may be held on trust, creating a relationship of trustee/beneficiary rather than that of creditor/debtor. This means that the funds are not part of the assets that the liquidator may call upon to distribute to creditors.

7.4   Alternatives to winding up

There are circumstances in which winding up the company would not be the best option for the creditors. The company could attempt to reach an understanding with the creditors. In some cases, the best option for all concerned may be to rescue the company and get it up and running again.

- **Voluntary arrangement**: this is a legally binding, voluntary arrangement between the company and its creditors. Any such arrangement must be supervised by a qualified insolvency practitioner. Voluntary arrangements may be in the form of a composition or a scheme of arrangement. In a **composition**, an agreement is made with the creditors to settle a debt immediately by repaying only part of it. In a **scheme of arrangement**, a plan is drawn up to offer a way of paying debts and avoiding insolvency.
- **Administration order**: it may be possible to rescue a company by putting its management in the hands of an **administrator**, who again must be a qualified insolvency practitioner. The purpose of an administration order is the survival of the company as a going concern, as a whole or in part. Any petition for winding up would then be dismissed, as would a receiver if the order is granted. The order creates a **moratorium**, or **suspension of payments**, for a fixed period so that no-one can deal with the assets in that specified period. The administrator then runs the business.

Note: in the USA, Chapter 11 of the Bankruptcy Code allows a corporation or partnership to restructure the business finances so that it may continue in operation. A disclosure statement and a plan of reorganisation must be filed with the court. Although the court retains supervision, it is the corporation or partnership itself that remains in possession and control of the assets without the appointment of a trustee.

7.5   Personal insolvency

Personal insolvency refers to the bankruptcy of natural persons. With respect to business organisations, this would be the case for the sole trader who cannot pay his debts or a partner where the debts of the partnership cannot be satisfied. A **bankruptcy order** can be granted against an individual unless he can make a **voluntary arrangement** with his creditors. If the individual is declared bankrupt, then the **trustee in bankruptcy** will gather in the assets of the **bankrupt** and pay off creditors in accordance with rules that are similar to those of a winding up. All of the bankrupt's property vests in the trustee with the exception of certain items of personal property and equipment necessary for his work. An **undischarged bankrupt** remains subject to certain legal restrictions.

Company law case discussions

1   Acme Ltd is an organic fruit and vegetable company, producing fruit and vegetables free of chemical sprays. One of the directors of Acme Ltd wants to enter into a contract with the Farmers Bank to borrow money in order to begin pig breeding. Julie, a shareholder in Acme Ltd and a convinced vegetarian, is outraged. Is there anything she can do to stop Acme Ltd entering into a contract with the Farmers Bank?

2   Mr. Smith is employed by Chapelforth Motors Ltd to work as a salesman. In his employment contract, a clause has been included that states that Mr. Smith will not contact customers of Chapelforth nor compete with Chapelforth for a certain length of time after he has left the company's employment. This agreement is a valid legal agreement.

Mr. Smith is a good car salesman and decides to leave Chapelforth Motors. Almost immediately after he has left Chapelforth, Mr. Smith forms a new company called Cars R U Ltd to carry on a similar business to that of his former employers. He also acts as its managing director. He sends advertisements to the customers he knew from Chapelforth Motors. This business is so successful that he forms another company, Cars 4 U Ltd. He takes a number of cars that belong to Cars R U Ltd to start the new business.

- Chapelforth Motors wants to stop him contacting its customers. Mr. Smith says it is not he who is contacting Chapelforth's customers but Cars R U. What is the position in company law?
- Mr. Smith has taken a number of cars that belong to Cars R U Ltd to start his second company, Cars 4 U Ltd. May he do this?

3   Jones and Smith are the directors of a toy company. The range of toys the company has developed is not doing well. It is clear that the company will soon run out of money. Nonetheless, Jones and Smith launch an expensive advertising campaign for a singing robot, using the services of an advertising agent. Jones also buys his wife a racehorse. A few months later, the company collapses and is unable to pay its debts. The company owes the advertising agent a lot of money. Explain to the advertising agent what happens when a company becomes insolvent and whether he can recover the money that he is owed.

Company law knowledge questions

1   A partnership is unincorporated. What does that mean?

2   What is meant by the term legal person?

3   Explain what is meant by the phrase 'lifting the corporate veil'.

4   What may a public company do that a private company may not?

5   What is the purpose of articles of association?

6   In what way is the doctrine of ultra vires still relevant to a company objects clause?

7   A debenture may be secured by one of two ways: by a fixed charge or by a floating charge. A floating charge is unique to company law. Explain what a floating charge is.

8   What is the difference between an executive director and a non-executive director?

9   What are the fiduciary duties owed by a director to a company?

10 If the company has gone into liquidation, who is appointed to wind up the company and what is his task?

Bibliography

Andrews, Neil, English Civil Procedure: Fundaments of the New Civil Justice System, Oxford University Press, 2003.

Baker, C.D., Tort, Sweet & Maxwell, 1996.

Cheshire, Fifoot & Furmston's Law of Contract, Butterworths, 2001.

Civil Procedure, White Book, Sweet & Maxwell, 1999.

Colin, P.H., Dictionary of Law, Peter Collin Publishing, 2000.

Dunné, J.M. van, Verbintenissenrecht, Kluwer, 2001.

Ellison, John & Tom Harrison, Business Law, Harrison Law Publishing, 2000.

Essential Law Series (Cavendish Publishing) revision aids on: tort (Richard Owen), company law (Nicholas Bourne) and European Community law (Richard Owen).

Franken, H., Encyclopedie van de rechtswetenschap, Kluwer, 2003.

Gifis, Steven H., Law Dictionary, Barron's Legal Guides, 1996.

Glendon, Mary Ann, Michael Wallace Gordon & Christopher Osakwe, Comparative Legal Traditions: Text, Materials and Cases, West Publishing Co, 1994.

Griffin, Stephen, Company Law: Fundamental Principles, Pitman Publishing, 1994.

Harvard Business Review on Corporate Governance, Harvard Business School Press, 1999.

Jolowicz, J.A., On Civil Procedure, Cambridge, 2000.

Keenan, Denis, Smith & Keenan's Advanced Business Law, Pearson Education Limited, 2000.

Kent, Penelope, Law of the European Union, Pearson, 2001.

Kite, Kevin L., Adam Rappaport & Craig A. Sperling, Blond's Commercial Law, S&G Publishing, 1995.

Morrison, Alan B. (ed.), Fundamentals of American Law, Oxford University Press, 1996.

Nutshell Series (Sweet & Maxwell) revision aids on: European Union law (Mike Cuthbert), company law (Francis Rose), consumer law (Sandra Silberstein), English legal system (Penny Darbyshire) and contract law (Robert Duxbury).

Schilfgaarde, P. van, Van de BV en de NV, Gouda Quint, 1998.

Walker, Ronald & Richard Ward, Walker & Walker's English Legal System, Butterworths, 1998.

Weir, Tony, Tort Law, Clarendon Law Series, Oxford University Press, 2002.

Appendix

McLoughlin v O'Brian and others

HOUSE OF LORDS
LORD WILBERFORCE, LORD EDMUND-DAVIES, LORD RUSSELL OF KILLOWEN, LORD SCARMAN AND LORD BRIDGE OF HARWICH
15, 16 FEBRUARY, 6 MAY 1982

Negligence – Duty to take care – Foreseeable harm – Duty to take care to avoid injury to persons who might foreseeably suffer injury from want of care – Driver of motor vehicle – Duty to other road users and owners of property – Nervous shock – Plaintiff suffering nervous shock on hearing that family involved in road accident – Plaintiff at home at time of accident – Whether duty of care owed to plaintiff by driver causing accident.

Damages – Personal injury – Nervous shock – Plaintiff's family killed or badly injured in road accident caused by defendant's negligence – Plaintiff at home at time of accident – Plaintiff informed of accident and going to hospital – Plaintiff suffering nervous shock as a result – Whether defendant owing duty of care to plaintiff – Whether plaintiff's injury reasonably foreseeable – Whether as matter of policy court would not impose duty of care on defendant to plaintiff.

Damages – Personal injury – Nervous shock – Public policy – Whether public policy requiring legal limitations on recovery of damages for nervous shock.

The plaintiff's husband and three children were involved in a road accident caused by the negligence of the defendants. One of the plaintiff's children was killed and her husband and other two children were severely injured. At the time of the accident the plaintiff was at home two miles away. She was told of the accident by a motorist who had been at the scene of the accident and was taken to hospital where she saw the injured members of her family and the extent of their injuries and shock and heard that her daughter had been killed. As a results of hearing, and seeing the results of, the accident the plaintiff suffered severe and persisting nervous shock. The plaintiff claimed damages against the defendants for the nervous shock, distress and injury to her health caused by the defendants' negligence. The judge dismissed her claim on the ground that her injury was not reasonably foreseeable. On appeal, the Court of Appeal held that the plaintiff was not entitled to claim against the defendants either because as a matter of policy a duty of care was not to be imposed on a negligent defendant beyond that owed to persons in close proximity, both in time and place, to an accident, even though the injuries received by the plaintiff might be reasonably foreseeable as being a consequence of the defendants' negligence, or because the duty of care owed by a driver of a motor vehicle was limited to persons on or near the road. The plaintiff appealed to the House of Lords.

Held – The test of liability for damages for nervous shock was reasonable foreseeability of the plaintiff being injured by nervous shock as a result of the defendant's negligence. Applying that test, the plaintiff was entitled to recover damages from the defendants because even though the plaintiff was not at or near the scene of the accident at the time or shortly afterwards the nervous shock suffered by her was a reasonably foreseeable consequence of the defendant's negligence. The appeal would accordingly be allowed (see p 301 *j*, p 302 *a b* and *h* to p 303 *a*, p 305 *e* to *g*, p 306 *f g*, p 309 *g*, p 310 *a d e*, p 311 *f g*, p 313 *b c* and p 320 *h j*, post).

Dictum of Denning LJ in *King v Phillips* [1953] 1 All ER at 623 approved.

Dictum of Bankes LJ in *Hambrook v Stokes Bros* [1924] All ER Rep at 113 and of Lord Wright in *Hay (or Bourhill) v Young* [1942] 2 All ER at 405–406 applied.

Dillon v Legg (1968) 68 C 2d 728 considered.

Chester v Waverley Municipal Council (1939) 62 CLR 1 not followed.

Per Lord Russell, Lord Scarman and Lord Bridge (Lord Edmund-Davies not con-

curring). In the area of nervous shock caused by negligence on the highway, the sole test
a of liability is reasonable foreseeability without any legal limitation in terms of space,
time, distance, the nature of the injuries sustained or the relationship of the plaintiff to
the victim (although those are factors to be considered), since (per Lord Bridge) there are
no policy considerations sufficient to justify limiting the liability of negligent tortfeasors
by some narrower criterion than that of reasonable foreseeability. If (per Lord Scarman)
public policy requires such a limitation, the policy issue where to draw the line is not
b justiciable but a matter for legislation (see p 310 *b* to *h*, p 311 *c* to *g*, p 317 *h j*, p 319 *f* to
j and p 320 *e* to *g*, post).

Per Lord Wilberforce. The application of the reasonable foreseeability test in nervous
shock claims ought to be limited, in terms of proximity, so that what is foreseeable is
circumscribed by the proximity of the tie or relationship between the plaintiff and the
injured person, the proximity of the plaintiff to the accident both in time and place, and
c the proximity of communication of the accident to the plaintiff through sight or hearing
of the event or its immediate aftermath (see p 303 *d* to *f* and p 304 *f* to p 305 *e*, post).

Decision of the Court of Appeal [1981] 1 All ER 809 reversed.

Notes
For liability for nervous shock, see 34 Halsbury's Laws (4th edn) para 8, and for cases on
d the subject, see 17 Digest (Reissue) 145–147, 377–391.

For remoteness of damage, see 12 Halsbury's Laws (4th edn) para 1127, and for cases
on the subject, see 36(1) Digest (Reissue) 63–65, 306–307, 227–236, 1232–1236.

Cases referred to in opinions
Abramzik v Brenner (1967) 65 DLR (2d) 651, 17 Digest (Reissue) 152, *283.
e *Anns v Merton London Borough* [1977] 2 All ER 492, [1978] AC 728, [1977] 2 WLR 1024,
    HL, 1(1) Digest (Reissue) 128, 721.
Bell v Great Northern Rly Co of Ireland (1890) 26 LR Ir 428, 36(1) Digest (Reissue) 310,
    *2558.
Benson v Lee [1972] VR 879, 17 Digest (Reissue) 151, *277.
Boardman v Sanderson [1964] 1 WLR 1317, CA, 17 Digest (Reissue) 145, 378.
f *British Rlys Board v Herrington* [1972] 1 All ER 749, [1972] AC 877, [1972] 2 WLR 537,
    HL, 36(1) Digest (Reissue) 121, 466.
Byrne v Great Southern and Western Rly Co of Ireland (1884) unreported, cited in 26 LR Ir
    at 428, 36(1) Digest (Reissue) 310, *2557.
Chadwick v British Transport Commission [1967] 2 All ER 945, [1967] 1 WLR 912, 17
    Digest (Reissue) 147, 390.
g *Chester v Waverley Municipal Council* (1939) 62 CLR 1, 36(1) Digest (Reissue) 33, *103.
Dillon v Legg (1968) 68 C 2d 728, Cal SC.
Donoghue (or M'Alister) v Stevenson [1932] AC 562, [1932] All ER Rep 1, HL, 36(1) Digest
    (Reissue) 144, 562.
Dulieu v White & Sons [1901] 2 KB 669, [1900–3] All ER Rep 353, DC, 17 Digest (Reissue)
    146, 385.
h *Fender v Mildmay* [1937] 3 All ER 402, [1938] AC 1, HL, 12 Digest (Reissue) 325, 2352.
Hambrook v Stokes Bros [1925] 1 KB 141, [1924] All ER Rep 110, CA, 17 Digest (Reissue)
    145, 377.
Hay (or Bourhill) v Young [1942] 2 All ER 396, [1943] AC 92, HL; *affg* 1941 SC 395, 17
    Digest (Reissue) 146, 388.
Haynes v Harwood [1935] 1 KB 146, [1934] All ER Rep 103, CA, 36(1) Digest (Reissue)
j   245, 953.
Hedley Byrne & Co Ltd v Heller & Partners Ltd [1963] 2 All ER 575, [1964] AC 465, [1963]
    3 WLR 101, HL, 36(1) Digest (Reissue) 24, 84.
Hinz v Berry [1970] 1 All ER 1074, [1970] 2 QB 40, [1970] 2 WLR 684, CA, 17 Digest
    (Reissue) 147, 391.
Home Office v Dorset Yacht Co Ltd [1970] 2 All ER 294, [1970] AC 1004, [1970] 2 WLR
    1140, HL, 36(1) Digest (Reissue) 27, 93.

Donoghue (or McAlister) v Stevenson

[1932] All ER Rep 1

E [House of Lords (Lord Buckmaster, Lord Atkin, Lord Tomlin, Lord Thankerton
and Lord Macmillan), December 10, 11, 1931, May 26, 1932]

[Reported [1932] A.C. 562; 101 L.J.P.C. 119; 147 L.T. 281;
48 T.L.R. 494; 76 Sol. Jo. 396; 37 Com. Cas. 350]

Negligence—Duty of manufacturer to consumer—No contractual relation—No possibility
F *of examination of product before use—Knowledge that absence of reasonable care in*
preparation of product will result in injury to consumer—Bottle of ginger-beer
purchased from retailer—Dead snail in bottle—Purchaser poisoned by drinking
contents—Liability of manufacturer.

A manufacturer of products which he sells in such a form as to show that he
intends them to reach the ultimate consumer in the form in which they left him,
G with no reasonable possibility of intermediate examination, and with the knowledge that the absence of reasonable care in the preparation or putting up of the
products will result in injury to the consumer, owes a duty to the consumer to take
reasonable care, although the manufacturer does not know the product to be
dangerous and no contractual relation exists between him and the consumer.

Per Lord Atkin: The rule that you are to love your neighbour becomes in law:
H You must not injure your neighbour; and the lawyer's question: Who is my neighbour? receives a restricted reply. You must take reasonable care to avoid acts or
omissions which you can reasonably foresee would be likely to injure your neighbour. Who, then, in law is my neighbour? The answer seems to be persons who
are so closely and directly affected by my act that I ought reasonably to have them
in contemplation as being so affected when I am directing my mind to the acts or
I omissions which are called in question.

Per Lord Macmillan: A person who for gain engages in the business of manu-
facturing articles of food and drink intended for consumption by members of the
public in the form in which he issues them is under a duty to take care in the manufacture of those articles. That duty he owes to those whom he intends to consume
his products. He manufactures his commodities for human consumption; he
intends and contemplates that they shall be consumed. By reason of that very
fact he places himself in a relationship with all the potential consumers of his

commodities, and that relationship, which he assumes and desires for his own ends,   A
imposes on him a duty to take care to avoid injuring them.   He owes them a duty
not to convert by his own carelessness an article which he issues to them as whole-
some and innocent into an article which is dangerous to life and health.

The appellant and a friend visited a café where the friend ordered for her a bottle
of ginger-beer.   The proprietor of the café opened the ginger-beer bottle, which was
of opaque glass so that it was impossible to see the contents, and poured some of   B
the ginger-beer into a tumbler.   The appellant drank some of the ginger-beer.   Then
her friend poured the remaining contents of the bottle into the tumbler and with it
a decomposed snail came from the bottle.   As a result of her having drunk part of
the impure ginger-beer the appellant suffered from shock and gastric illness.   In
an action by her for negligence against the manufacturer of the ginger-beer,

Held by LORD ATKIN, LORD THANKERTON, and LORD MACMILLAN (LORD BUCK-   C
MASTER and LORD TOMLIN dissenting), on proof of these facts the appellant would
be entitled to recover.

Notes. Distinguished: *Farr* v. *Butters Bros. & Co.*, p. 339, post. Considered:
Pattendon v. *Beney* (1933), 50 T.L.R. 10. Applied: *Brown* v. *Cotterill* (1934),
51 T.L.R. 21; *Malfroot* v. *Noxal, Ltd.* (1935), 51 T.L.R. 551; *Grant* v. *Australian*   D
Knitting Mills, Ltd., [1935] All E.R.Rep. 209. Distinguished: *Evans* v. *Triplex Safety*
Glass Co., [1936] 1 All E.R. 283. Considered: *Otto* v. *Bolton and Norris*, [1936]
1 All E.R. 960: *Kubach* v. *Hollands*, [1937] 3 All E.R. 907; *Dransfield* v. *British Insulated*
Cables, Ltd., [1937] 4 All E.R. 382; *Barnes* v. *Irwell Valley Water Board*, [1938] 2
All E.R. 650; *Sharp* v. *Avery and Kerwood*, [1938] 4 All E.R. 85; *Square* v. *Model Farm*
Dairies (Bournemouth), Ltd., [1938] 2 All E.R. 740; *Daniels and Daniels* v. *White & Sons,*   E
Ltd. and Tarbard, [1938] 4 All E.R. 258. Distinguished: *Paine and Colne Valley*
Electricity Supply Co., [1938] 4 All E.R. 803. Explained and distinguished: *Old Gate*
Estates, Ltd. v. *Toplis and Harding and Russell*, [1939] 3 All E.R. 209. Applied:
Slennett v. *Hancock and Peters*, [1939] 2 All E.R. 578; *Barnes* v. *Irwell Valley Water*
Board, [1939] 1 K.B. 21. Considered: *Burfitt* v. *A. & E. Kille*, [1939] 2 All E.R. 372;
Hanson v. *Wearmouth Coal Co.*, [1939] 3 All E.R. 47. Distinguished: *Davis* v. *Foots,*   F
[1939] 4 All E.R. 4. Applied: *Herschthal* v. *Stewart and Ardern, Ltd.*, [1939] 4 All E.R.
123; *Barnett* v. *Packer & Co.*, [1940] 3 All E.R. 575; *Watson* v. *Buckley Osborne, Garrett*
& Co. and Wyrovoys Products, Ltd., [1940] 1 All E.R. 174; *Buckner* v. *Ashby and Horner,*
Ltd., [1941] 1 K.B. 321. Distinguished: *Travers* v. *Gloucester Corpn.*, [1946] 2 All E.R.
506; *Jerred* v. *Roddam Dent & Son*, [1948] 2 All E.R. 104. Considered: *Candler* v.
Crane Christmas & Co., [1951] 1 All E.R. 426; *Merrington* v. *Ironbridge Metal Works,*   G
Ltd. and Others, [1952] 2 All E.R. 1101. Applied: *White* v. *John Warwick & Co., Ltd.*,
[1953] 2 All E.R. 1021; *Hartley* v. *Mayoh & Co. and another*, [1953] 2 All E.R. 525;
Davis v. *St. Mary's Demolition, etc., Ltd.*, [1954] 1 All E.R. 578. Not applied: *Sellars*
v. *Best*, [1954] 2 All E.R. 389. Referred to: *Cunard* v. *Antifyre, Ltd.*, p. 558, post;
Bishop v. *Consolidated London Properties, Ltd.*, [1933] All E.R.Rep. 963; *Brown* v.
Cotterill (1934), 51 T.L.R. 21; *Haynes* v. *Harwood*, [1934] All E.R.Rep. 103; *Howard* v.   H
Furness Houlder Argentine Lines, Ltd. and Brown, Ltd., [1936] 2 All E.R. 781; *London,*
Midland and Scottish Rail. Co. v. *Ribble Hat Works, Ltd.* (1936), 80 Sol. Jo. 1038; *Read*
v. *Croydon Corpn.*, [1938] 4 All E.R. 631; *Kerry* v. *Keighley Electrical Engineering Co.*,
[1940] 3 All E.R. 399; *East Suffolk Rivers Catchment Board* v. *Kent*, [1940] 4 All E.R.
527; *Thomas and Evans, Ltd.* v. *Mid-Rhondda Co-operative Society, Ltd.*, [1940] 4
All E.R. 357; *Haseldine* v. *Daw & Son, Ltd.*, [1941] 3 All E.R. 156; *Bourhill* v. *Young*,   I
[1942] 2 All E.R. 396; *Glasgow Corpn.* v. *Muir*, [1943] 2 All E.R. 44; *Read* v. *J. Lyons &*
Co., [1944] 2 All E.R. 98; *Deyong* v. *Shenburn*, [1946] 1 All E.R. 226; *Woods* v. *Duncan,*
Duncan v. *Hambrook, Duncan* v. *Cammell Laird & Co.*, [1946] A.C. 401; *Read* v. *J. Lyons*
& Co., [1946] 2 All E.R. 471; *Dodd and Dodd* v. *Wilson and McWilliam*, [1946] 2 All E.R.
691; *Anglo-Saxon Petroleum Co.* v. *Damant, Anglo-Saxon Petroleum Co.* v. *R.*, [1947]
2 All E.R. 465; *Marshall* v. *Cellactite and British Uralite, Ltd.* (1947), 63 T.L.R. 456;
Stansbie v. *Troman*, [1948] 1 All E.R. 599; *Grant* v. *Sun Shipping Co.*, [1948] 2 All E.R.
238; *Buckland* v. *Guildford Gas, Light and Coke Co.*, [1948] 2 All E.R. 1086; *Davies* v.

Unfair Contract Terms Act 1977

PART I

1. Scope of Part I
(1) For the purposes of this Part of this Act, 'negligence' means the breach-
(a) of any obligation, arising from the express or implied terms of a contract, to take reasonable care or exercise reasonable skill in the performance of the contract;
(b) of any common law duty to take reasonable care or exercise reasonable skill (but not any stricter duty);
(c) of the common duty of care imposed by the Occupiers' Liability Act 1957 or the Occupier's Liability Act (Northern Ireland) 1957.
(2) This Part of the Act is subject to Part III; and in relation to contracts, the operation of sections 2 to 4 and 7 is subject to the exceptions made by Schedule I.
(3) In the case of both contract and tort, sections 2 to 7 apply (except where the contrary is stated in section 6(4)) only to business liability, that is liability to breach of obligations or duties arising-
(a) from things done or to be done by a person in the course of a business (whether his own business or another's); or
(b) from the occupation of premises used for business purposes of the occupier; and references to liability are to be read accordingly but liability of an occupier of premises for breach of an obligation or duty towards a person obtaining access to the premises for recreational or educational purposes, being liability for loss or damage suffered by reason of the dangerous state of the premises, is not a business liability of the occupier unless granting that person such access for the purposes concerned falls within the business purposes of the occupier.
(4) In relation to any breach of duty or obligation, it is immaterial for any purpose of this Part of this Act whether the breach was inadvertent or intentional, or whether liability for it arises directly or vicariously.

2. Negligence liability
(1) A person cannot by reference to any contract term or to a notice given to persons generally or to particular persons exclude or restrict his liability for death or personal injury resulting from negligence.
(2) In the case of other loss or damage, a person cannot so exclude or restrict his liability for negligence except in so far as the term or notice satisfies the requirement of reasonableness.

(3) Where a contract term or notice purports to exclude or restrict liability for negligence a person's agreement to or awareness of it is not of itself to be taken as indicating his voluntary acceptance of any risk.

3. Liability arising in contract
(1) This section applies as between contracting parties where one of them deals as consumer or on the other's written standard terms of business.
(2) As against that party, the other cannot by reference to any contract term-
(a) when himself in breach of contract, exclude or restrict any liability of his in respect of the breach; or
(b) claim to be entitled-
(i) to render a contractual performance substantially different from that which was reasonably expected of him, or
(ii) in respect of the whole of any part of his contractual obligation, to render no performance at all,
except in so far as (in any of the cases mentioned above in this subsection) the contract term satisfies the requirement of reasonableness.

6. Sale and hire-purchase
(1) Liability for breach of the obligations arising from-
(a) section 12 of the Sale of Goods Act 1979 (seller's implied undertakings as to title, etc.);
(b) section 8 of the Supply of Goods (Implied Terms) Act 1973 (the corresponding thing in relation to hire-purchase),
cannot be excluded or restricted by reference to any contract term.
(2) As against a person dealing as consumer, liability for breach of the obligations arising from-
(a) section 13, 14 or 15 of the 1979 Act (seller's implied undertakings as to conformity of goods with description or sample, or as to their quality of fitness for a particular purpose);
(b) section 9, 10 or 11 of the 1973 Act (the corresponding things in relation to hire-purchase),
cannot be excluded or restricted by reference to any contract term.
(3) As against a person dealing otherwise than as consumer, the liability specified in subsection (2) above can be excluded or restricted by reference to a contract term, but only in so far as the term satisfies the requirement of reasonableness.
(4) The liabilities referred to in this section are not only the business liabilities defined by section 1(3), but include those arising under any contract of sale of goods or hire-purchase agreement.

11. The 'reasonableness' test
(1) In relation to a contract term, the requirement of reasonableness for the purposes of this Part of this Act, section 3 of the Misrepresentation Act 1967 and section 3 of the Misrepresentation Act (Northern Ireland) 1967 is that the term shall have been a

fair and reasonable one to be included having regard to the circumstances which were, or ought reasonably to have been, known to or in the contemplation of the parties when the contract was made.

(2) In determining for the purposes of section 6 or 7 above whether a contract term satisfies the requirement of reasonableness, regard shall be had in particular to the matters specified in Schedule 2 to this Act; but this subsection does not prevent the court or arbitrator from holding, in accordance with any rule of law, that a term which purports to exclude or restrict any relevant liability is not a term of the contract.

(3) In relation to a notice (not being a notice having contractual effect), the requirement of reasonableness under this Act is that it should be fair and reasonable to allow reliance on it, having regard to all the circumstances obtaining when the liability arose or (but for the notice) would have arisen.

(4) Where by reference to a contract term or notice a person seeks to restrict liability to a specified sum of money, and the question arises (under this or any other Act) whether the term or notice satisfies the requirement of reasonableness, regard shall be had in particular (but without prejudice to subsection (2) above in the case of contract terms) to-

(a) the resources which he could expect to be available to him for the purpose of meeting the liability should it arise; and

(b) how far it was open to him to cover himself by insurance.

(5) It is for those claiming that a contract term or notice satisfies the requirement of reasonableness to show that it does.

12. 'Dealing as consumer'

(1) A party to contract 'deals as consumer' in relation to another party if-

(a) he neither makes the contract in the course of a business nor holds himself out as doing so; and

(b) the other party does make the contract in the course of a business; and

(c) in the case of a contract governed by the law of sale of goods or hire-purchase, or by section 7 of this Act, the goods passing under or in pursuance of the contract are of a type ordinarily supplied for private use or consumption.

(2) But on a sale by auction or by competitive tender the buyer is not in any circumstances to be regarded as dealing as consumer.

(3) Subject to this, it is for those claiming that a party does not deal as consumer to show that he does not.

13. Varieties of exemption clause

(1) To the extent that this Part of this Act prevents the exclusion or restriction of any liability it also prevents-

(a) making the liability or its enforcement subject to restrictive or onerous conditions;

(b) excluding or restricting any right or remedy in respect of the liability, or subjecting a person to any prejudice in consequence of his pursuing any such right or remedy;

(c) excluding or restricting rules of evidence or procedure;

and (to that extent) sections 2 and 5 to 7 also prevent excluding or restricting liability by reference to terms and notices which exclude or restrict the relevant obligation or duty.

(2) But an agreement in writing to submit present or future differences to arbitration is not to be treated under this Part of this Act as excluding or restricting any liability.

14. Interpretation of Part I

In this Part of the Act-

'business' includes a profession and the activities of any government department or local or public authority;

'goods' has the same meaning as in the Sale of Goods Act 1979;

'hire-purchase agreement' has the same meaning as in the Consumer Credit Act 1974;

'negligence' has the meaning given by section 1(1);

'notice' includes an announcement, whether or not in writing, and any other communication or pretended communication; and

'personal injury' includes any disease and any impairment of physical or mental condition.

Section 1(2)

SCHEDULE 1 SCOPE OF SECTIONS 2 TO 4 AND 7

1. Sections 2 to 4 of this Act do not extend to-

(a) any contract of insurance (including a contract to pay an annuity on human life);

(b) any contract so far as it relates to the creation or transfer of an interest in land, or to the termination of such an interest, whether by extinction, merger, surrender, forfeiture or otherwise;

(c) any contract so far as it relates to the creation or transfer of a right or interest in any patent, trade mark, copyright, registered design, technical or commercial information or other intellectual property, or relates to the termination of any such right or interest;

(d) any contract so far as it relates-

(i) to the formation or dissolution of a company (which means any body corporate or unincorporated association and includes a partnership), or

(ii) to its constitution or the rights or obligations of its corporators or members;

(e) any contract so far as it relates to the creation or transfer of securities or of any right or interest in securities.

2. Section 2(1) extends to-

(a) any contract of marine salvage or towage;

(b) any charterparty of a ship or hovercraft; and

(c) any contract for the carriage of goods by ship or hovercraft;

but subject to this sections 2 to 4 and 7 do not extend to any such contract except in favour of a person dealing as a consumer.

3. Where goods are carried by ship or hovercraft in pursuance of a contract which either-
(a) specifies that as the means of carriage over part of the journey to be covered, or
(b) makes no provision as to the means of carriage and does not exclude that means, then sections 2(2), 3 and 4 do not, except in favour of a person dealing as consumer, extend to the contract as it operates for and in relation to the carriage of the goods by that means.

4. Section 2(1) and (2) do not extend to a contract of employment, except in favour of the employee.

5. Section 2(1) does not affect the validity of any discharge and indemnity given by a person, on or in connection with an award to him of compensation for pneumoconiosis attributable to employment in the coal industry, in respect of any further claim arising from his contracting the disease.

Sections 11(2) and 24(2)

SCHEDULE 2 'GUIDELINES' FOR APPLICATION OF REASONABLENESS TEST

The matters to which regard is to be had in particular for the purposes of sections 6(3), 7(3) and (4), 20 and 21 are any of the following which appear to be relevant-
(a) the strength of the bargaining positions of the parties relative to each other, taking into account (among other things) alternative means by which the customer's requirements could have been met;
(b) whether the customer received an inducement to agree to the term, or in accepting it had an opportunity of entering into a similar contract with other persons, but without having to accept a similar term;
(c) whether the customer knew or ought reasonably to have known of the existence and extent of the term (having regard, among other things, to any custom of the trade and any previous course of dealing between the parties);
(d) where the term excludes or restricts any relevant liability if some condition is not complied with, whether it was reasonable at the time of the contract to expect that compliance with that condition would be practicable;
(e) whether the goods were manufactured, processed or adapted to the special order of the customer.

Index

Bold page numbers indicate where the term can be found in the vocabularies.